Performing the Apocalypse

Performing the Apocalypse

Analyzing the Public Recitation Event for the Delivery and Reception of the Book of Revelation

Garland Autry

WIPF & STOCK • Eugene, Oregon

PERFORMING THE APOCALYPSE
Analyzing the Public Recitation Event for the Delivery and Reception of the Book of Revelation

Copyright © 2025 Garland Autry. All rights reserved. Except for brief quotations in critical publications or reviews, no part of this book may be reproduced in any manner without prior written permission from the publisher. Write: Permissions, Wipf and Stock Publishers, 199 W. 8th Ave., Suite 3, Eugene, OR 97401.

Wipf & Stock
An Imprint of Wipf and Stock Publishers
199 W. 8th Ave., Suite 3
Eugene, OR 97401

www.wipfandstock.com

PAPERBACK ISBN: 979-8-3852-6177-2
HARDCOVER ISBN: 979-8-3852-6178-9
EBOOK ISBN: 979-8-3852-6179-6

VERSION NUMBER 10/23/25

Dedicated to my wife, Sarah,
who puts up with me in more ways than I deserve

and Fellowship Bible Church of Northwest Arkansas
for quite similar reasons

μακάριος ὁ ἀναγινώσκων καὶ οἱ ἀκούοντες τοὺς λόγους τῆς προφητείας καὶ τηροῦντες τὰ ἐν αὐτῇ γεγραμμένα, ὁ γὰρ καιρὸς ἐγγύς.
—John (Rev 1:3)

Contents

1 Hearing Revelation: Introduction and Methodology | 1
2 Review of Literature | 38
3 Performance Analysis of a Theophany Scene | 75
4 Performance Analysis of a Numbered Sequence Scene | 132
5 Performance Analysis of the Epilogue | 181
6 Summary and Conclusion | 219

Bibliography | 229

1

Hearing Revelation

Introduction and Methodology

FRAMING THE PROBLEM: REVELATION MUST BE STUDIED WITH AURAL PERFORMANCE IN MIND

HUMANS LOVE TO TELL and hear stories. This statement rings true across human culture both today and throughout human history. Just as today's film cinematographers and directors carefully and skillfully move the camera frame by frame, scene by scene to accomplish the aesthetic goals for which they set out as well as the broader intention of telling a compelling story, so too do all good storytellers. The perceptive audience notices such choices in direction in both the minute details as well as the obvious ones. In film, these features are employed by the use of the camera, the actors, the script, and the score, all imposed onto the screen. In a written text, these features are highlighted as well, marked by chapter break, paragraph break, word spacing, and punctuation. Such features are easily perceptible for the silent reader of written texts, as the medium creates such ease.

However, countless stories are told across the globe every day without the use of a screen or the page. They are simply heard. These unwritten stories are easily perceptible for the listening audience. While much of the modern world interacts with stories in a variety of mediums—screen, printed text, oral telling—the ancient world was different.[1] In this predominantly oral culture,[2] unfamiliar as it is to the modern literary

---

1. Ong, *Orality and Literacy*, i–ii.
2. More will be discussed on this in the Review of Literature below.

one, rightly appreciating how stories were told and heard rises to significant importance.³ What features would be employed to tell a tale for the listening audience? How do sounds and syllables work together to guide the hearer? How are discourses organized so that they can be cogently followed in aural-reception? Walter Ong rightly notes that "thought and expression in oral cultures is often highly organized." This organization is not the same as that of a text-based culture, however, as it "calls for organization of a sort unfamiliar to and often uncongenial to the literate mind."⁴ In short, there are significant differences between the choices made by the authors in an oral culture as opposed to a literate culture adapted to the silent reading of texts on the written page. These differences in thought and expression require careful attention.

The Roman world of the first century AD was largely an oral culture,⁵ with the majority of people interacting with discourses orally, often communally.⁶ Therefore, analysts of discourse composed in such a culture must not only appreciate this concept (doing the hard task of moving from the modern literate world and its expectations and placing themselves willingly into the oral world) but also develop methodology for analysis of texts composed for performance.⁷ Oral culture necessitated that the choices an author makes would be sensitive to the medium of communication. The features at the author's disposal to signal such choices were constrained by the culture in which he inhabits. These features, then, were designed for the ear, sensitive to the breath and cadence of the performer, and useful for memorization and repetition of the story in front of the gathered

---

3. This is not only true of the ancient world, but also of the oral cultures of the modern world, as well as the study of oral narration in general. Many scholars following the work of Milman Parry on Homeric verse, Albert Bates Lord, and Richard Bauman study the way in which stories are told and performed. See Parry, *Making of Homeric Verse*; Lord, *Singer of Tales*; Bauman, *Verbal Art as Performance*; Foley, *Singer of Tales*; Vansina, *Oral Tradition as History*, 34–37.

4. Ong, *Orality and Literacy*, i.

5. This statement will be defended and developed in chapters 2–3 below. For a brief introduction here, see Harris, *Ancient Literacy*, 1–42; Gamble, *Books and Readers*, 1–4; Botha, *Orality and Literacy*, 52–125; Horsley, *Text and Tradition*, 1–30.

6. Iverson, *From Text to Performance*, 19. See also Vansina, *Oral Tradition as History*, 34–41.

7. More to be explored in the pages that follow, but to understand the way in which the written text encodes a performance event, see Maxwell, "From Performance to Text"; Horsley, *Text and Tradition*, 223. See also Kelber, *Oral and Written Gospel*, xxii; and Vansina, *Oral Tradition as History*, 3–91.

community.⁸ To properly analyze the choices made by the story's composer, it is necessary to interact with and appreciate these features.

The opening benediction of Revelation acknowledges the public reader as well as the gathered hearers: Μακάριος ὁ ἀναγινώσκων καὶ οἱ ἀκούοντες τοὺς λόγους τῆς προφητείας καὶ τηροῦντες τὰ ἐν αὐτῇ γεγραμμένα (Blessed is the one reading aloud and the ones hearing the words of this prophecy and keeping what is written in it [Rev 1:3]).⁹ This leads most scholars to affirm that Revelation was intended to be heard out loud.¹⁰ When studying the text, however, most scholars not only fail to validate such a claim, but they also disregard the oral performance features entirely.¹¹ It is this claim, and a stubborn insistence on appreciating this claim, that produces the driving aim for this book: to examine how the book of Revelation was heard by its ancient (and modern) audience. What type of methodology would enable the modern reader to validate such a claim? How might the features of orality be analyzed, and what type of interpretive insight might they provide for the student of the book of Revelation? These are the questions that this monograph seeks to answer.

The thesis of this book is that the verbal and audible characteristics present in the text of Revelation reveal a work that was originally composed for a listening audience. While the book of Revelation is indeed a prophetic apocalypse,¹² it is also a story meant to be told out loud to assembled communities,¹³ and as such the text is skillfully crafted in order for the listening audience to follow and the speaker to artfully perform.¹⁴ These elements of the Apocalypse have been essentially ignored in the scholarship of Revelation, and the time has come for their voice—like the narrative itself—to be heard.

---

8. Ong, *Orality and Literacy*, 57–68. See also Vansina, *Oral Tradition as History*, 39–47; Harvey, *Listening to the Text*, 35–59.

9. All translations will be provided by the author.

10. For a representative of this position, see Bauckham, *Climax of Prophecy*, 1–2. More will be said concerning this axiom in the Review of Literature in chapter 2.

11. As an exception, and to be reviewed below in the Review of Literature in chapter 2, see de Waal, *Aural-Performance Analysis*, 1–132.

12. While certainly important, issues related to genre are beyond the scope of this book. Most scholars agree that the book of Revelation contains features of an epistle, a prophecy, and apocalyptic literature. The way in which the book of Revelation functions as a prophecy is not explored further in the paper. For a thorough review of these issues, see Beale, *Book of Revelation*, 37–43.

13. See part two of the literature review below.

14. Bauckham, *Climax of Prophecy*, 7.

THE PROPOSED THESIS: QUANTIFYING THE DATA TO INVESTIGATE THE AURAL PERFORMANCE CONTEXT OF REVELATION

The overall aim of this book is to analyze the book of Revelation with the listening audience in mind, in order to validate that indeed the text was composed as a text for performance. The first purpose, then, for this inquiry is to provide an adequate methodology for the task at hand. As such, subsequent researchers may appropriate the approach offered, reject it, or amend it. The review of literature below will demonstrate that too often scholars make assertions about the public situational context for the reception of the book of Revelation in the first century AD but do so without further examination. The methodology proposed below, while indeed eclectic in nature, provides the necessary tools to validate the thesis of this paper. Therefore, techniques from the fields of oral-biblical criticism, discourse analysis, and biblical performance criticism will be combined in order to analyze the text of Revelation as a text intended for performance.

The second purpose is to highlight the way in which the book of Revelation would have been heard. Simply amassing data from the proposed methodology is not enough. This second aim is to re-hear John's Apocalypse, for indeed the sound of the message was part of the message.[15] Thus, features that would be particularly relevant for oral performance will be noted and explored, with special emphasis on the cues for prosody that remain within the text itself. Manuscripts of written texts from primarily oral cultures were often written "from dictation, recited orally, and heard aurally."[16] Most manuscripts, therefore, contain written texts meant to be heard and processed out loud and from memory.[17] Whether read publicly or privately, proficiency in reading aloud was prized.[18] As such, texts were not read in a monotone flat style,[19] but

---

15. Caragounis, *Development of Greek*, 401.

16. Horsley, *Text and Tradition*, 223. For an objection to this, see Hurtado, "Oral Fixation," 321–40. Hurtado suggests that this is an oversimplification. In the Scope and Limitations section of the present chapter, defense will be provided, with a mediating position offered.

17. Kelber, *Oral and Written Gospel*, xxii. See also Bauckham, *Jesus and the Eyewitnesses*, 249, 280–89; Ong, *Orality and Literacy*, 57–68.

18. Shiner, "Oral Performance," 53.

19. Vansina, *Oral Tradition as History*, 34–35. See also Rhoads, "Performance Criticism, Pt. II," 173–80; de Waal, *Aural-Performance Analysis*, 9–10; Shiner, "Oral Performance," 54–59.

skilled readers would animate their telling of the story through pace of voice, pitch of voice, dramatic pause, gesturing, and the movement of the body.[20] While the performance of any ancient text, including the book of Revelation, cannot be experienced (as we do not in fact live in the ancient Roman Empire), the residual cues for the performance remain in the text itself and these will be explored.[21] Each section analyzed will include a visual representation of potential suggestions for the performer's variation in tone, pace, pitch, and bodily gesture. The reason for this purpose is simple: scholars and students of Revelation alike have not appreciated how the book would have been heard aloud, and this section of the paper aims to restore such an appreciation.

The final purpose of this investigation aims to validate what many scholars have noted in passing but fail to rigorously verify: that the data accumulated in accomplishing the first two purposes indicate choices made by the author. These choices suggest that the book of Revelation was composed as a text for performance.[22] This, then, corroborates the thesis of this book. Therefore, purposes one and two will aim to analyze the book of Revelation from the perspective of its aural performance in order to produce the third purpose, which is to validate the thesis that the text was composed with the performance in mind.

THE SCOPE AND LIMITATIONS OF THE INVESTIGATION

The investigation must begin with the text, for the text is all we have.[23] While this book will approach the book of Revelation as a piece of literature designed for oral performance, it is still a text. Thus, the text must be front and center. For the purposes of this study, the *Nestle-Aland Greek New Testament*, 28th edition, will be utilized throughout, and it is beyond the scope of this book to address text critical issues unless it is significant to the passage at hand. Additionally, the scope will be limited to the text

---

20. Rhoads, "Performance Criticism, Pt. I," 124. This contention is debated and will receive defense in upcoming sections.

21. Rhoads, "Performance Criticism, Pt. I," 124.

22. As noted, many scholars acknowledge this but fail to provide any methodology for validating such a claim or analyzing the oral features themselves. Again, see Horsley, *Text and Tradition*, 223; Rhoads, "Performance Criticism, Pt. I," 121–26.

23. For the way in which written texts were utilized for oral performance, see Horsley, *Text and Tradition*, 223; Rhoads, "Performance Criticism, Pt. I," 121–26; Ong, *Orality and Literacy*, 47–56; Harvey, *Listening to the Text*, 35–59.

of the book of Revelation and not other Johannine literature or New Testament writings. Issues such as the authorship and extent of the Johannine corpus will not be addressed. It would make a fine study indeed to compare and contrast aural performance features of John's Apocalypse with other apocalyptic literature, but such a study is also beyond the scope of the current inquiry.

Moreover, modern scholarship of John's Apocalypse is dominated by material concerning four significant and difficult issues, which are summarized by Grant Osborne in his comprehensive commentary and include: the symbolism and the meaning of symbols, the structure of the book, theories for interpretation, and the author's use of the Old Testament.[24] What is more, issues of authorship, sources, dating of composition, text-criticism, and genre are also weighty. It is necessary for any student of the book of Revelation to understand the complexity of these issues, and thus many scholars writing on the book devote a significant amount of time to these issues.[25] While certainly each of these retain their vital importance to understanding the book of Revelation, it is beyond the scope of the present book to provide detailed exploration of these issues. Where the present study interacts with any of them will be articulated in the analysis that follows.

As pertains to the scope of this investigation, it must be stated that pursuit of the purposes of this book for all of the book of Revelation would spill the banks of the page limitations for this study; therefore, sections of the text will be analyzed in a representative manner. These sections were chosen intentionally. Each section will be long enough to get a sense of John's storytelling techniques in action with the hopes that these representative sections are illustrative of other material in the book.[26] The first section, Rev 4–5, is part of a theophany-experience; the second section, Rev 6–8, comprises one of the three numbered sequences of events, including an interlude, which are utilized elsewhere in the book; and the third section, Rev 22:6–21, explores the epilogue of the narrative with the parallel prologue (Rev 1:1–8) in mind.[27] This third section contains some

---

24. Osborne, *Revelation*, 30–58.

25. For a representative example, G. K. Beale's commentary has an introduction that stretches nearly two hundred pages, looking in detail at every one of these issues. See Beale, *Book of Revelation*, 1–178.

26. Where features noted in the chapters below surface in sections outside the scope of this paper, they will be noted in footnotes throughout each chapter.

27. This book agrees with Bauckham, Beale, and Fanning in recognizing that the repetition of ἐν πνεύματι signifies "major transitions within the whole vision," and that

of the most structurally difficult verses in the whole of John's Apocalypse, thus it was chosen for its importance for continuing scholarship. It is hoped that this investigation into these representative sections will provide guidance for future study on the rest of the text in like manner.

One crucial limitation to this book is the inability to reconstruct the actual performance of the text. There were no audio recording devices in the ancient Roman world and there are no native Koine Greek speakers, as the language is no longer extant in any living community. Great strides have been made, however, in recreating the way in which Koine Greek was spoken,[28] but the written text is all that remains of the ancient performance-event. This may even suggest that the entire investigation is erroneous: Why, after all, analyze aural performance features of a written text? Does not the fact that John did in fact write his story down mean that aural features are irrelevant?[29]

This sharp dichotomy is unwarranted, however. Chrys Caragounis applies the teachings of ancient literary critics in order to demonstrate that the arrangement of words in ancient writings contributed to a pleasant or enjoyable discourse, which was essential for effective communication. In short, the acoustics of the message were part of the message itself.[30] Additionally, Harry Gamble suggests that the distinction between a text written and a text read out loud is not a binary one.[31] For Gamble, the emergence of written literature in the early Christian community demonstrates the importance of the stories for the church,[32] yet affirms that even written texts were drafted with the listener in mind.[33] Thus, to read an ancient manuscript requires both a careful analysis of the text as it was written, for the written manuscript contains the imprint of the

---

when coupled with the changes of setting that follow form the macro-structure of the Apocalypse. See Bauckham, *Climax of Prophecy*, 3–4; Beale, *Book of Revelation*, 110–12; and Fanning, *Revelation*, 63–64. It is beyond the scope of this study to adjudicate the seemingly endless theories of structure; thus, this note is sufficient for the present purposes.

28. See Kantor, *Short Guide to Pronunciation*; Caragounis, *Development of Greek*, 339–565. For a summary, see Campbell, *Advances*, 192–208.

29. Again, for the way in which written texts were utilized for oral performance, see Horsley, *Text and Tradition*, 223; Rhoads, "Performance Criticism, Pt. I," 121–26; Ong, *Orality and Literacy*, 47–56; Harvey, *Listening to the Text*, 35–59.

30. Caragounis, *Development of Greek*, 401–4.

31. Gamble, *Books and Readers*, 30. See also Niditch, *Oral World*, 1–7.

32. Gamble, *Books and Readers*, 8–10.

33. Gamble, *Books and Readers*, 30.

oral culture in which it was birthed.[34] Richard Horsley notes that texts were often written "from dictation, recited orally, and heard aurally,"[35] therefore they are embedded in the dominant medium for communication (oral recitation) and serve both the reader and the community alike.

Following Susan Niditch, Horsley goes a step further, offering the ancient Jewish scribal community as a point of comparison with the prophetic leaders of the early church.[36] Scribes exhibited a practice that is best described as "oral-written,"[37] with the written manuscript serving both to authorize the message, preserve its contents,[38] and aid in its proliferation through memorization.[39] Given the price of acquiring a manuscript and the broad inability to read and write, written manuscripts were monumental and testimonial, extraordinary and sacred.[40] Even among the literate minority, manuscripts were expensive and learning was primarily done through oral recitation and memorization.[41] It is critical to recognize that in ancient scholarly debate, the written page was rarely consulted. Rather memorized words spoken out loud were the marks of a well-argued case.[42] As such, these texts contain residual clues that demonstrate the oral medium of the ancient world.[43] Holly Hearon's words serve a mediating role:

> There is, indeed, an expectation that oral traditions will appear in written texts and written traditions will be heard in oral texts. The distinction between the two in terms of content and structure, therefore, is blurred, and no clear sequence of, for example, first oral, then written can be discerned. In "rhetorical culture" the oral and the written text are bound together in a dynamic relationship.[44]

---

34. Niditch, *Oral World*, 3.
35. Horsley, *Text and Tradition*, 224.
36. Horsley, *Text and Tradition*, 53–72; Niditch, *Oral World*.
37. Horsley, *Text and Tradition*, 59.
38. Niditch, *Oral World*, 106–7.
39. Horsley, *Text and Tradition*, 57–60.
40. Niditch, *Oral World*, 107.
41. Gerhardsson, *Memory and Manuscript*, 79–181.
42. Gerhardsson, *Memory and Manuscript*, 85–121. See also Horsley, *Text and Tradition*, 58.
43. Rhoads, "Performance Criticism, Pt. I," 124.
44. Hearon, *Performing the Gospel*, 8–9.

Within the present study, it may be stated that emphasis will be placed on the features of orality within the book of Revelation. Part two of the review of literature below will demonstrate that this emphasis is warranted, as much of the scholarship concerning the book of Revelation has focused too narrowly on the written text only, without proper appreciation for the oral culture in which it was composed and received.

A second limitation to this investigation is the value of sound mapping as an analytical tool. While this book will analyze the text from colon to colon, working with the tool of a sound map of the text, this technique's value may be difficult to quantify. For example, a writer may employ an *ου* sound at the end of a word not because he is repeating a sound to please his audience, but simply because, say, he is representing nouns in interaction with one another and is limited by the rules of grammar. If, for instance, the genitive case was his only option to express the relationship between these two nouns appropriately, his only choice would then be to end this noun with an *ου* sound. To claim that an author is intentionally repeating a syllable or sound for performance may be missing a simpler explanation: the author's only choice grammatically was the genitive case, thus the *ου* sound that accompanies that case. While certainly a limitation for this study, recognition of the way in which oral recitation both contributed to the composition of a text as well as its reception remains necessary.[45] Moreover, since the sounds of the syllables used in texts was so significant, authors routinely sought to harmonize words with others within the collocation, often "transposing words within a sentence in order to find a more appropriate place for them."[46] An author's choice to employ euphonic sounds as opposed to cacophonous sounds and vice versa warrants the production and analysis provided by a sound map.

Yet one more limitation to this investigation is the complexity of the field of narrative or discourse analysis. This book is not a comprehensive application of any particular school or method of discourse analysis. Rather, this study will analyze the language as it is used and the methodology of the work of linguists like Robert E. Longacre, Stephen Levinsohn, and David Mathewson will be employed, but no broader commitment to a methodological school of discourse analysis will be defended. Discourse analysis is a multifaceted field with varying

---

45. Horsley, *Text and Tradition*, 224.
46. Caragounis, *Development of Greek*, 423.

terminology and techniques. Picking and choosing from such a complex assortment without a rigorous commitment to any one school or method creates a limitation for the present study.[47] In response, it may be stated that one of the main goals of discourse analysis is to analyze the way that a literary unit functions above the sentence level,[48] and this commitment drives the present investigation, however eclectic it may be.

THE STRUCTURE OF THIS INVESTIGATION

This investigation is organized into six chapters. The present chapter aims to introduce the topic and thesis of this study, with the following section articulating the proposed methodology employed to validate this thesis. Chapter 2 is a review of relevant literature related to the application of these tools to the book of Revelation. The literature review will be divided into subsections, the first of which is an introductory survey of the scholarship pertaining to orality and literacy in the Greco-Roman world. This section will be representative in its selection, building on the work of three pillars in recent scholarship: William V. Harris, Walter J. Ong, and Werner H. Kelber. Building on the work of these scholars, the way in which later scholars have approached the New Testament as a collection of texts written in a predominantly oral culture will be reviewed, settling on the contributions from the field of biblical performance criticism.

The second subsection of the review of literature reconstructs a hypothetical conversation between leading Revelation scholars, noting specifically how these scholars interact with the text for oral performance. Here, it will be seen that many scholars do, in fact, recognize that the text of Revelation was most likely meant to be read out loud to a gathered listening audience. Yet, as stated above, many of these scholars fail to say much more concerning the Apocalypse's oral features. This section of the review summarizes this conversation, beginning with a clear statement of the question at hand: was Revelation meant for performance and how would this be analyzed? The scholars' various responses to this question will be summarized, starting with those who ignore the question altogether and ending with more recent scholars who have begun to explore

---

47. See below for methodology used in this book. For a review of the variety of "schools" of discourse analysis, see Campbell, *Advances*, 148–91; as well as Porter, *Linguistic Analysis*, 133–44; and for discourse analysis in application to the New Testament writings, see Scacewater, *Discourse Analysis*.

48. Levinsohn, *Discourse Features*, vii–viii.

the orality of the Apocalypse with more earnestness.[49] Many of the scholars chosen were selected because of their influence in the field of Revelation study, as well as their careful examination of the question at hand.

Chapters 3 through 5 apply the proposed methodology above to three representative sections of the book of Revelation. These sections were chosen intentionally, as one explores a detailed theophany experience (Rev 4–5), one a complete series of seven elements of judgment (Rev 6:1—8:1), and one the epilogue of the book itself (Rev 22:6–21). Thus, chapters 3 through 5 will analyze the above sections in turn. It is hoped that investigating the epilogue in chapter 5 will illuminate elements within the prologue (Rev 1:1–8) as well.

It may be argued that such a sample size is too small to properly validate the proposed thesis of this inquiry. While such a concern is understandable, the representative sections were chosen intentionally. Chapter 3 addresses several of the structuring features, stylistic features, and thematic features that occur regularly elsewhere in the book. Chapter 4 explores a numbered sequence episode in its entirety. This style, structure, and repetition found in this episode repeats two additional times in the book. In fact, roughly one-third of the book of Revelation is contained in the three numbered judgment sequences (Rev 6–11; 16). Thus, analyzing one episode may guide study on the other two. Finally, chapter 5 investigates features employed in the epilogue—discourse framing, audience address, and the interaction between the taleworld and storyrealm[50]—which occur throughout the book of Revelation. It is hoped that the contributions found in chapter 5 provide insight into the rest of the book, not just the prologue. While not exhaustive, parallel features employed within the Revelation outside the representative sections explored below will be noted in footnotes throughout each chapter.

Chapter 6 aims to verify the thesis of the book. Given the proposed methodology (chapter 1), the survey of scholarship regarding orality in

---

49. It would be helpful to also review the scholars who have contributed to the proposed methodology for this book, selected from the fields of oral-biblical criticism, discourse analysis, and biblical performance criticism. Such an undertaking would be simply too lengthy and beyond the scope of the present inquiry. At best, any such review would be highly selective. While this qualifies as a limitation of sorts to this review of literature, this book is not a book *about* discourse analysis per se. Rather it is an application of tools *from* discourse analysis to the text of Revelation. Therefore, the methodology section below provides an adequate overview of the scholars and their methods as they pertain to this book, but no further review is undertaken.

50. To be defined and explored in chapter 5.

the ancient world (chapter 2), and the detailed examination of representative sections of Revelation (chapters 3 through 5), the final chapter provides a clear articulation and defense of the proposed thesis of this book. Here, a summary of the findings is given, as well as some brief comments regarding the implications for future scholarship and recommendations for further research.

THE PROPOSED METHODOLOGY: ORAL CRITICISM, DISCOURSE ANALYSIS, AND PERFORMANCE CRITICISM WORK TOGETHER

Four Founding Assumptions

A foundational assumption undergirding the methodology of this book is profound yet simple: choice implies meaning.[51] For the analyst of any communication among human beings, this maxim should form the drumbeat of his work. Authors, performers, speakers, and storytellers, in arranging and shaping their communication, are in a constant state of making choices. These choices guide both the small details of an utterance (the choice of connectives, the words chosen, the register, the ending of a phrase) to the most obvious and salient aspects of an utterance (the kind of story; the beginning, middle, and end; the peak and climax).[52] Anyone seeking to understand an utterance, then, must appreciate this basic assumption. In the following study, this assumption is followed rigorously in hopes to defend and advance the working thesis that the choices made by the author of Revelation betray an oral performance intention behind the words of the text itself.[53]

A second founding assumption is the growing recognition of the misstep of the Erasmian pronunciation of Greek developed in the sixteenth century.[54] If the acoustic dimension of the text is important for understanding its meaning, then it is imperative to understand the way in

---

51. Runge, *Discourse Grammar*, 5–7.
52. Vansina, *Oral Tradition as History*, 68–91.
53. Maxwell, "From Performance to Text."
54. It is impossible to provide a detailed analysis of either the history of the pronunciation of Greek as well as the methodology used to defend either the Erasmian or the historical Greek pronunciation. For a detailed analysis, see Kantor, *Guide to the Pronunciation*; Caragounis, *Development of Greek*, 339–96. See also Gignac, *Grammar of the Greek*, 189–277.

which letters were spoken aloud. This monograph will follow Benjamin Kantor, Constantine Campbell, and Chrys Caragounis's lead in using the historical Greek pronunciation system, thus bypassing the Erasmian.[55] The difference between the two will not be addressed in the chapters that follow, and the application of the historical Greek pronunciation will be used throughout.

Another founding assumption is that authors are constrained by the medium in which they communicate their message.[56] To put it simply, there are differences between stories told in a predominantly oral culture as opposed to a literate one.[57] Thus, the way in which a text's grammatical and syntactical features effect the ear as opposed to the eye must be rightly understood.[58] While much more will be said in part one of the review of literature below, the second assumption working behind-the-scenes of this book is that "Greek grammar has aural patterns at the syllable level that would have assisted ancient hearers to follow the message."[59] Printed texts enjoy the benefit of visual aids encoded in the medium itself, such as spacing, punctuation, paragraph breaks, chapter breaks, and the enclosure of the text itself into a book held in the hand. When listening to an oral recitation, however, other aids are required. The listener must follow the reading syllable by syllable, with structural and narrative cues embedded through a variety of means,[60] such as repetition, rounding, elongation, introductory formula, and reported speech. These aid both the reader and the hearer to follow the text accordingly.[61]

The fourth founding assumption is that ancient aural performances took on many different styles, from the dramatic and the theatrical to the simple oral recitation of a written text.[62] Here, it is critical to define what is meant by the term aural performance. For the present study, aural performance simply implies the public reading of a text out loud before a listening audience. The reader orally communicates the message, and

---

55. Caragounis, *Development of Greek*, 339–96; Campbell, *Advances*, 192–208.

56. Marshall McLuhan, *Understanding Media*, 7.

57. Ong, *Orality and Literacy*, i, 34–43, 117–51; Harvey, *Listening to the Text*, 35–60; Horsley, *Text and Tradition*, 1–30.

58. Harvey, *Listening to the Text*, 41; de Waal, *Aural-Performance Analysis*, 6–9.

59. de Waal, *Aural-Performance Analysis*, 18.

60. Ong, *Orality and Literacy*, i.

61. Dean, "Grammar of Sound," 53–60; Harvey, *Listening to the Text*, 301.

62. Johnson and Parker, *Ancient Literacies*, 187–88; see also Hurtado, "Oral Fixation," 334.

the hearers aurally receive it.[63] Reading the book of Revelation out loud would take about one hour, which is not unreasonable in the ancient world.[64] This communication could be delivered in a variety of ways, and on this point scholars disagree strongly.

Holt Parker suggests restraint in assuming too theatrical a delivery. Here, Gamble's recognition of the interplay between the written word and the spoken word is again helpful.[65] In Parker's estimation, there was a sharp dichotomy between the kind of performance that took place in a theater, whereby actors physically embodied characters and performed from memory, and the out loud reading of a written text in a home. In the case of the latter, Parker posits that it would have been unusual in the ancient world for the reciter to add dramatic emphasis through bodily movement and facial expression.[66] Additionally, Parker rejects the notion that texts were memorized and recited without the aid of the written manuscript. Rather, readers held the text in their hands and read from a seated position and without theatrical aid.[67] Larry Hurtado commends Parker's work, further adding that written texts were not dictated from aural performance but were the result of a lengthy process, normally done with a secretary at hand.[68]

Kelly Iverson argues the opposite contention, suggesting instead that there is ample evidence in the ancient world to affirm that texts were meant to be read well, often employing prosody, gestures, bodily movements, and dramatic effect. To Iverson, even performance events in which the reader recited aloud from a written manuscript involved these kinds of techniques. Citing both literary evidence as well as inscriptional evidence, Iverson recognizes that the delivery style of ancient texts was multifaceted. In the painting *Admetus and Alcestis* found in a home in Pompeii, a performance event is depicted with the reader explicitly portrayed using his right hand to gesture while also looking intently at one of the audience members.[69]

---

63. In the analysis to follow, the terms performance, recitation, and oral storytelling may be considered synonymous, given the definition provided here.

64. Barr, *Tales of the End*, 291.

65. Gamble, *Books and Readers*, 8–10. See also Elder, "Between Reading and Performance," 1–13.

66. Parker, "Books and Reading Latin," 203.

67. Parker, "Books and Reading Latin," 203.

68. Hurtado, "Oral Fixation," 335; Hurtado, *Destroyer of the Gods*, 105–42. See also Richards, *Paul and Letter Writing*, 47–121.

69. Iverson, "Oral Fixation," 193.

Admetus and Alcestis painting, Pompeii[70]

Iverson further reveals that many ancient orators studied the theatrical arts in order to gain advice and techniques to enhance their delivery style.[71] He concludes that while the written text may have been a regular and necessary part of the performance event, that does not necessitate that the text was read in a monotone and flat style. Additionally, texts were frequently composed through a combination of both oral dictation and writing processes performed by ancient secretaries,[72] thus the oral register remained imprinted on the written page.[73] This does not mean that they were composed during or in performance, but rather through a process of oral dictation and writing.

---

70. Yair-haklai, "Alcestis and Admetus Ancient Roman fresco (45–79 AD) from the Augusteum-Basilica, Herculaneum.jpg," https://commons.wikimedia.org/wiki/File:Alcestis_and_Admetus_Ancient_Roman_fresco_%2845[...]80%9379_AD%29_from_the_Augusteum-Basilica,_Herculaneum.jpg.

71. Iverson, "Oral Fixation," 194–95.

72. Richards, *Paul and Letter Writing*, 47–121. See also Stein, "Is Our Reading," 69.

73. Maxwell, "From Performance to Text"; Horsley, *Text and Tradition*, 223.

Both Parker and Iverson agree, however, that for the vast majority of people in the ancient world, texts were received and experienced in an oral context.[74] Thus, for the purposes of the present investigation, it is a foundational assumption that these oral contexts necessitated an aural performance of some kind. Ancient readers, including the readers of John's Apocalypse, may have utilized manuscripts in their recitation, they may not have.[75] They may have mostly memorized the manuscript or read from the written page directly. They may have used theatrical gestures to a great degree or a minimal degree. These issues, while certainly important, cannot minimize the salient point: the ancient audience would have encountered the book of Revelation through public oral recitation.[76] Again, the opening benediction of Rev 1:3 provides evidence within the text that the original hearers would have been just that: hearers.

The methodology proposed for this book, therefore, builds upon these four foundational assumptions and suggests that any analysis of ancient texts must interact with them. Furthermore, working with these assumptions in mind provides valuable interpretive insight. To the present writer, then, it is imperative for the student of a text written in a primarily oral culture, such as John's Apocalypse, to analyze the text with these assumptions in mind, working from syllables to stories, noting the author's choices for public reading.[77] How do authors use sounds and repetition of sounds to highlight certain phrases or words? How does an author's style change in the telling of the narrative and what effect would this have on the audience? How does an author aid both the performer's memory in recitation as well as the audience's ability to follow the storyline? How do grammatical features signal prominence for the performer to highlight? How is structure determined by the constraints of the listening ear as opposed to the written page?[78] How does the pace of the narrative ebb and flow in order to build tension and suspense as well as signal peak and prominence? Finally, what stylistic features signal the performer's prosody, enabling the performance to both inspire, challenge, and encourage the audience?[79] These questions flow from the four foundational assumptions and are often underdeveloped in the scholarship regarding

---

74. Iverson, "Oral Fixation," 198.
75. Iverson, "Oral Fixation," 198.
76. Iverson, "Oral Fixation," 198.
77. Lee, *Sound Mapping*, 168.
78. Ong, *Orality and Literacy*, 34–43; Harvey, *Listening to the Text*, 301.
79. Vansina, *Oral Tradition as History*, 34–35.

the book of Revelation. Finding answers to these questions requires a working methodology that is eclectic in nature.

Controlling Principles

In order to properly defend the thesis and answer the questions driving this inquiry, the methodological approach for this book aims to bring together several components from different linguistic frameworks: namely oral-biblical criticism, discourse analysis, and biblical performance criticism. Thus, building on the foundation of the above assumptions, the components from these linguistic frameworks work like methodological building blocks, stacked side by side in order to construct a validation of the thesis. The components include sound mapping, sound patterning, style analysis, identification of markers of orality in composition, narrative discourse features, and cues for oral performance, including mnemonic cues as well as cues for prosody in performance. When brought together in unison, these tools from multiple disciplines will enable the student of John's Apocalypse to better understand the choices made in crafting the narrative itself.

Two controlling principles ground the combination of these particular tools. The first is an emphasis to examine the text for its oral features, in order to balance much of the scholarship that has neglected doing so. Perhaps this swings the pendulum in the other direction, but the emphasis remains warranted. The second principle follows the functional approach offered by Stephen Levinsohn, recognizing that the insights from different fields offer value in analyzing a text in use.[80] While seemingly eccentric, bringing together potentially varying instruments from different scholarly ensembles, this paper will instead employ an eclectic methodology in order for these components to work together to create a pleasing harmony. Since these instruments must work together, it is important to first understand each individually and then their significance for the purposes of this book.

---

80. Levinsohn, *Discourse Features*, vii.

Oral-Biblical Criticism

Sound Mapping and Sound Patterning

The first building block of the proposed methodology for this inquiry is the development of a working sound map of the book of Revelation, beginning with the grammar of sound. Scholars of ancient rhetorical training have noted that for the Greek-speaking culture, "grammar [was] typically defined as a science of sound,"[81] as the study of grammar "began by identifying the elements of sound and all their possible combinations then spoken sounds with written symbols."[82] Margaret Ellen Lee and Bernard Brandon Scott, taking elements from other practitioners who went before them, developed a comprehensive methodological approach to mapping a text according to the science of sound. This technique analyzes a composition a syllable at a time, which "makes it possible to discover how sound builds a composition's structure and guides the meaning-making process."[83] As such, the sound map is a visual representation of a text, beginning with each syllable and expanding to the level of the colon.[84]

Sounds were organized into comprehensible patterns by the use of repetition and proximity.[85] Around a century before the writing of the book of Revelation, the famed Greek literary critic Dionysus provided an analytical methodology for studying a text. In his *On the Composition of Words,* he shows how to apply this methodology in order to decipher the "mental processes of an author in the arrangement of his words, in order to achieve a pleasant or enjoyable, beautiful, and successful discourse."[86] Just as lyrics in modern music frequently employs the use of rhythm and rhyme to make the tune more memorable, ancient writers had several prerequisites that made for a delightful and beautiful composition, which in turn made the communication effective.[87] These prerequisites included melody, rhythm, variety, and appropriateness.[88] Since choice implies meaning, these choices must be properly identified in examining ancient texts, including the book of Revelation.

81. Dean, "Grammar of Sound," 58.
82. Dean, "Grammar of Sound," 58.
83. Lee, *Sound Mapping*, 167.
84. de Waal, *Aural-Performance Analysis*, 14–15.
85. Harvey, *Listening to the Text*, 42.
86. Caragounis, *Development of Greek*, 404.
87. Lee, *Sound Mapping*, 145.
88. Caragounis, *Development of Greek*, 408.

Margaret Dean suggests an interpretive method that works from sound to sense. "Such a method should track repeated sounds, especially repeated syllables and phrases, and analyze their aural interplay. Sound-based interpretation should look for a text's primary clues to meaning in its repeated aural patterns and especially in their variations and transformations."[89] Additionally, analysts speak of "style" in reference to a discourse's sound quality. David Aune notes that this insight has "important interpretive significance, for ancient authors not only chose words to convey the meanings they intended but also chose words whose *sounds* effectively communicated those meanings."[90] A period may be marked by an austere style, which has harsh sounds and multi-syllabic words; a polished style, marked by the avoidance of harsh sounds and hiatus and frequently have balanced cola; and finally, a blended style in which the two are combined.[91] An author, in effect, has a choice of which style to appropriate and can vary the style from period to period depending on the content of the message.[92] An author may choose an austere style for certain units of the text, but a polished for others.

According to the ancient literary critic Dionysus, euphony was created by combining liquid (λ, ρ) and nasal (μ, ν) consonants with open vowel sounds (α/αι, η).[93] The long back ω vowel was considered grand full and grand, while the ε was considered sharp and thin and the least euphonic, according to Dionysus. The epsilon was suited for quick and energetic speech, but not lofty prose.[94] Stops were created through the use of dental and labial consonants, with β, δ, and γ creating round voiced stops and π, κ, and τ creating more firm, voiceless stops. Aspirate consonants (ζ, θ, χ, φ) were considered less pleasant and serve to create a more windy sound as air moves through the mouth.[95] The sibilant consonant (σ) was to be limited or softened if possible, with Dionysus calling this consonant "charmless and nauseating when used overmuch excruciating."[96] Finally, double consonants (ψ, ξ) were to be avoided, particularly in clusters. As scholars gain a greater clarity on the way in which

---

89. Dean, "Grammar of Sound," 62.
90. Aune, *Revelation*, 21 (emphasis original).
91. Lee, *Sound Mapping*, 114. See also Caragounis, *Development of Greek*, 414–19.
92. Harvey, *Listening to the Text*, 41.
93. Lee, *Sound Mapping*, 176–79.
94. Dionysus, *Composition*, 14–19.
95. Kantor, *Short Guide to Pronunciation*, 34–77.
96. Dionysus, *Composition*, 14.

Koine Greek was pronounced, the sound created by diphthongs becomes increasingly important. It is beyond the scope to provide a thorough analysis of the development of the Greek diphthong here, but scholars largely agree that each of the following vowels and diphthongs generated roughly the same sound as the "i" in the English word "sit": ι, υ, ει, οι, υι.[97] The ου diphthong was hollow and dark and often avoided in high-styled writing.[98] Dionysus acknowledges an element of subjectivity, but many scholars see Dionysus not so much as *creating* a tradition but *codifying* a tradition already well-established.[99]

Each period within the sound map provided below will be analyzed with these stylistic features in mind. In so doing, the style of John's work and the manner in which he varies that style come into play and must be rightly understood in order to fully appreciate the choices made in the composition of the text. Thus, the first step in methodology for this book is to provide a sound map of representative sections of Revelation, broken down into cola. The second is to analyze the way in which sounds are arranged and grouped, giving special attention to the patterns of sound, both in their repetition and variation.

In unvarnished language, Lee and Scott suggest that "it is not possible reliably to identify an author's rhetorical style before analyzing a composition's component cola."[100] The colon, according to Lee and Scott, is "the building block of analysis because it represents a breath unit, a unit of speech."[101] The first order of business then for this book will be to divide the text of representative sections of the book of Revelation according to colas. These colas typically contain a finite verb or a verbal element of some kind.[102] Ancient hearers of text read orally followed along not sentence by sentence, but colon by colon. Through the artful manipulation of sound and syllables, cola were designed with the hearer in mind.

Cola combine to form periods, which can be combined "paratactically or by means of grammatical subordination."[103] In short, a period is a group of cola that combine together to form a complete discourse

---

97. Caragounis, *Development of Greek*, 352; Kantor, *Short Guide to Pronunciation*, 79–102.

98. Dionysus, *Composition*, 14–19.

99. Caragounis, *Development of Greek*, 397–422.

100. Dean, "Grammar of Sound," 140.

101. Dean, "Grammar of Sound," 140.

102. Dean, "Grammar of Sound," 170.

103. Lee, *Sound Mapping*, 171.

thought. While this is certainly still true with modern writing—modern sentences employ the period marker to signify the end of a thought or sentence—in oral cultures, void of the presence of such visual markers, sound structured the beginning and the end of these thoughts. Ancient authors writing with the aural performance in mind combine sounds at the colon and period level to form the "style" of their composition. Since the word "style" smacks of subjectivity, what precisely is the reader looking for? For the purposes of this section of the investigation, the word "style" is defined as the way in which the cola and periods interact with one another. Thus, style can be either continuous—the cola advance with "no end in itself and only stops when the sense is complete,"[104] or periodic—the cola are balanced and grammatical subordination connects lines together.

This point cannot be easily brushed over, as readers adjusted to modern printed texts experience difficulty empathizing with a culture in which people engaged with texts largely through the ears and not the eyes. If one were to pick up a printed text in the modern world, each of the following would be assumed: page numbers, table of contents, punctuation—including punctuation that marks heightened emotion or actions(!), paragraph breaks, chapter breaks, numbered chapters, not to mention the ability at any time to return to previously read material by simply flipping the page. In an oral culture, however, each of these assumptions vanishes, and a whole separate host of tools must be adopted.

Thus, period boundaries were often marked by certain features such as rounding, balance, and elongation.[105] Rounding occurs when similar sounds begin and end a period creating a balance to the utterance that is pleasing to the ear.[106] Elongation is another technique that lengthens the final colon in a period in order to signify its end. Period boundaries were also marked by literary features, such as a change in referent or change in topic. Therefore, the third step in methodology is to arrange the cola into periods. Finally, the fourth step aims to articulate the period boundary forming technique, whether that be rounding or elongation or sound patterning. Within the sound map to be developed below, these periods will be marked and numbered, with their structuring device articulated in the prose to follow. These four steps provide a working methodology

---

104. Aristotle, *Art of Rhetoric*, 1409a.
105. Lee, *Sound Mapping*, 171.
106. Lee, *Sound Mapping*, 110.

for the production of a detailed sound map of the representative sections of Revelation, which forms the foundation on which the rest of the analysis will build.

Narrative Discourse Analysis

Markers of Orality

STRUCTURAL MARKERS

Since this book has as its aim the verification and the analysis of the book of Revelation as a text designed for aural performance, the proposed methodology must strive to serve those ends. Scholars of oral literature have noted several features in ancient texts that demonstrate that those texts were most likely composed in performance and with performance in mind. With the methodological foundation laid with the sound mapping above, the next methodological building block will be to note these features and analyze them accordingly. Bauckham posits that, because the Apocalypse was composed with the listening audience in mind, structural markers must be obvious and emphatic.[107] Modern print readers of discourses have the ability to move forward and backward in the text, enabling them to recover information that may have been forgotten and thus enabling modern authors to craft more intricate stories with more complicated structures. Audiences of discourse in performance, however, have no such luxury.[108] As a result, structural features must be recognized in real time and performers must cue the audience to hear them.[109] As a famous example, in Dr. Martin Luther King Jr.'s "I Have a Dream" speech, Dr. King's repetition of the phrase "I have a dream" marks units of thought. These structural markers include introductory formula, numbering sequence, repetition of phrases or words, chiasmus or inclusio, and transposition. In exploring the book of Revelation, it is assumed that the "surviving transcripts bear the imprint of these oral performances,"[110] and these structural markers guide the analyst in recognition of these imprints.

---

107. Bauckham, *Climax of Prophecy*, 7.
108. Ong, *Orality and Literacy*, 139–55.
109. Harvey, *Listening to the Text*, 301.
110. Rhoads, "Performance Criticism, Pt. I," 124.

Style Markers

Other markers of orality in composition are suggested by Walter Ong in *Orality and Literacy* and his fellow-scholar Albert Lord in *The Singers of Tales*. Here, Ong builds on the work of linguists and students of oral culture and posits that, in an oral culture, certain features persist in greater degree than in written culture.[111] These features are normative among cultures steeped in orality and include: additive prose, not subordinate; aggregative style, not analytic; redundant and "copious,"[112] not economical; an agonistic tone; empathetic and participatory, not objective.[113] Yet another feature of orality, contributed by Albert B. Lord, is the recognition that texts composed from a primarily oral culture are acoustically, rather than visually, oriented.[114] It is important to recognize Walter Ong's admonition that simply because these characteristics appear does not indicate that the text must derive from an oral culture. Rather, it is the preponderance of these features in oral cultures, combined with the frequency with which authors in a literate culture limit this preponderance, that leads analysts to conclude that the text emerged from an oral culture.[115] Chapters 3 through 5 will identify these stylistic elements revealed in each section, noting that the text of Revelation demonstrates these characteristics.

An additional marker of aural performance, again following Ong's salient work, is the lack of "sequential parallelism."[116] By this, Ong means that the linear order of events in the discourse parallel the chronological order in the world to which the discourse refers.[117] Ong further suggests that this sort of strict linear presentation, following a neat temporal sequence, is a hallmark of typographic and electronic literary culture. In an oral culture, however, the teller of tales in performance is "not greatly concerned with exact sequential parallelism between the sequence in the narrative and the sequence in extra-narrative referents."[118] Frequently, the

---

111. John Miles Foley provides crucial insight in stating that it is the communicative medium that is salient to understanding the way that verbal art was employed. See Foley, *Singer of Tales*, 7.

112. Dooley, *Analyzing Discourse*, 16.

113. Ong, *Orality and Literacy*, 37–57.

114. Lord, *Singer of Tales*, 33.

115. Ong, *Orality and Literacy*, 37–50, 117–35.

116. Ong, *Orality and Literacy*, 147.

117. Ong, *Orality and Literacy*, 147.

118. Ong, *Orality and Literacy*, 147.

narratives designed for performance will demonstrate features that occur in performance from memory and include failing to follow a linear sequence, as well as what can only be termed as simple distraction. Distraction is not meant to sound pejorative, rather it simply means recognizing that, in oral performance, the speaker may get caught up in vivid descriptions of seemingly unimportant objects or persons and completely lose track of the narrative.[119] As will be demonstrated under the third tool below, for ancient composers of oral narratives, a place, image, or person recalled in the mind may trigger a lengthy aside regarding said person or image,[120] following easy-to-memorize patterns like working from the foot to the head or top of the setting to the bottom. Lord disagrees slightly with Ong, suggesting that this sort of lengthy description serves a ritualistic function for the listening community.[121] As such, these asides are not for mere fulsomeness or memory aids but rather evidence what Lord calls a ritual elaboration, which the community would recognize.

Narrative Discourse Features

Discourse Type

A next and most crucial step to remember is that John does not merely string sounds and syllables together in order to merely make pleasing sounds; he is telling a story. Thus, it is important to apply an eclectic set of tools from the field of discourse analysis to the sections under review. This part of the methodology serves as something of a bridge between oral-biblical criticism and biblical performance criticism, signaling to the performer markers of structure, suspense, and prominence. While a comprehensive articulation of the various methods of discourse analysis is beyond the scope of this book,[122] the methodology employed here requires explanation. Richard Longacre suggests that before any analysis of a discourse can be undertaken, the student must first ascertain the type of discourse he is reading.[123] Since the book of Revelation contains agent orientation and contingent temporal succession (albeit not always in a strict linear progression), the discourse is at its most basic level a

---

119. Ong, *Orality and Literacy*, 147.
120. Barr, "Apocalypse as Oral Enactment," 245–46.
121. Lord, "Characteristics of Orality," 58–64.
122. See above under "Limitations of the Investigation."
123. Longacre, *Holistic Discourse Analysis*, 35.

narrative.[124] While scholars agree that the book of Revelation enjoys a multifaceted genre—it is rightly at home as both a piece of Apocalyptic literature, prophetic literature, and epistolary literature—its narrative features must be appreciated; and since discourse analysis explores language as it is used[125] above the sentence level,[126] the tools for describing narrative discourse will be utilized.

Verbal Aspect and Storyline

The storyline of any narrative is carried along by participants and events. Thus, attention to both is crucial to rightly understanding the meaning of a narrative discourse.[127] Since all narratives, even complex ones, are "a linguistic production undertaking to tell of one or several events, it is perhaps legitimate to treat it as the development—monstrous, if you will—given to a *verbal* form, in the grammatical sense: the expansion of a verb."[128] While certainly coherent stories could be told by a simple listing of participants and events, stories are more than simply participant lists (what a bland story indeed!).[129] Support and background material, dialogue, peak and prominence, and evaluation all contribute to making a good story. It behooves the student of any narrative discourse, then, to recognize the important distinction between the event-line (or storyline) of the discourse and the supporting material and nonevents,[130] recognizing which participants and events are marked for prominence.

Linguists have noted that "past tense characterizes the mainline of narrative discourse,"[131] which is not surprising given the reality that events narrated necessarily must follow the events themselves. The book of Revelation narrates a series of events that John reports in the first

---

124. Barr, *Tales of the End*, 1–5.

125. Campbell, *Advances*, 164.

126. Campbell, *Advances*, 163–65; Porter, *Linguistic Analysis*, 138–42; and Porter, *Idioms*, 298–307.

127. It is beyond the scope of this study to delve into the various definitions proposed by linguists regarding particular definitions of what constitutes a narrative, story, or narrative discourse. For a brief introduction, see Genette, *Narrative Discourse*, 25–32.

128. Genette, *Narrative Discourse*, 30.

129. Runge, *Discourse Grammar*, 14.

130. Longacre, *Grammar of Discourse*, 21. See also Dooley, *Analyzing Discourse*, 79–85; Campbell, *Advances*, 124–26.

131. Genette, *Narrative Discourse*, 30.

person as events that in fact happened to him. The expected tense for such stories would be the past, while the expected aspect would be the perfective.[132] The aorist is suited for such reporting,[133] and John moves his story forward largely through the use of the aorist tense.[134] In Revelation, the aorist frequently follows καί, creating the rhythmic drumbeat by which the story's events are told. In fact, the καί + aorist construction dominates the book of John,[135] and this formulaic redundancy is yet another characteristic of orality.[136]

Yet John is not universal in his use of verbs within the book of Revelation. There are significant instances where variation occurs, sometimes in important moments within the story. Since choice implies meaning, this variation away from the καί + aorist must be analyzed. It is beyond the scope of this investigation to contribute to the ongoing debate among Koine Greek scholars regarding the nature of verbs and how they are used.[137]

In a masterful monograph, David Mathewson explored the functional use of verbs in the book of Revelation and posited significant results.[138] Mathewson suggests that John's use of verb signals prominence within the narrative. This assertion follows Steven Runge's theory of markedness,[139] whereby the literary analyst may presuppose that one member of a set of linguistic options available to an author is the most basic or default member of the set.[140] Thus, all the other members "signal or 'mark' the presence of some unique quality, one that would not have been marked if the default option were used. The marked options are described based on how they uniquely differ both from the default and from

---

132. Runge, *Discourse Grammar*, 11. See also Campbell, *Advances*, 125.

133. Runge, *Discourse Grammar*, 11.

134. In the pages that follow, a brief interaction with the ongoing debate between the nature of Greek verbs will be undertaken.

135. This construction carries the narrative along. Mathewson, "Verbal Aspect in the Apocalypse," 65.

136. See Foley, *Singer of Tales*, 4; Ong, *Orality and Literacy*, 37–40.

137. For a survey of recent scholarship, see Campbell, *Advances*, 105–33; Porter, *Idioms*, 302.

138. Mathewson, *Verbal Aspect in Revelation*. This was first developed and applied to chapter 5 in Mathewson, "Verbal Aspect in the Apocalypse," 58–77. These findings regarding the "strange" use of the verb in relationship to tense and time are noted as well by Porter, "Language," 589–90.

139. Runge, *Discourse Grammar*, 10–16.

140. Runge, *Discourse Grammar*, 11.

one another."¹⁴¹ This functional definition leads to the conclusion that the aorist verb serves as the default member within John's Apocalypse, with the present and perfect verbs marked as unique.¹⁴² Rather than "default," Mathewson refers to the use of the aorist as "background," which carries the story along and forms the backbone of the narrative.¹⁴³

Mathewson also differentiates between the "marked" members that, in this case, include the present and the perfect verbs. Again, following Runge, he posits that since the expected tense in storytelling is the past tense and the expected aspect is the perfective,¹⁴⁴ deviation indicates prominence. Other verb options require explanation for their selection, both from the default member but also from each other.¹⁴⁵ Thus, Mathewson notes that the present tense and the imperfective aspect serve to highlight *foregrounded* events, while the perfect tense highlights *frontgrounded* ones. *Foreground* refers to "events or characters which are of major importance and which stand out against background material, signifying the information central to the author's purpose,"¹⁴⁶ drawing attention to certain elements or themes within the narrative. Moreover, *frontgrounded* material refers to "those linguistic elements that stand out unexpectedly in the discourse, and upon which the readers are called to focus special attention."¹⁴⁷ Given that the perfect is the most rarely used verbal aspect in the book of Revelation, this proposal seems warranted. It must be stated that Mathewson's functional approach is not meant to solve the scholarly conundrum concerning the Greek verb,¹⁴⁸ but rather highlights the way in which certain elements were semantically marked.

Mathewson's application of markedness theory to the choices of verb tense within Revelation functions to reveal prominence in the narrative. Some scholars are skeptical of such a pragmatical approach to the verb, suggesting that any functional marker for prominence accomplished by a particular verb choice is at best a secondary role.¹⁴⁹ Silva goes a step further, rejecting the notion that a writer would leave major points of

---

141. Runge, *Discourse Grammar*, 11.
142. Mathewson, "Verbal Aspect," 65.
143. Mathewson, "Verbal Aspect," 65.
144. Runge, *Discourse Grammar*, 128–29.
145. Runge, *Discourse Grammar*, 11.
146. Runge, *Discourse Grammar*, 11.
147. Runge, *Discourse Grammar*, 11.
148. Again, see Campbell, *Advances*, 105–33.
149. Reed, "Verbal Aspect, Discourse Prominence," 190.

emphasis to such subtle grammatical distinctions.[150] In response, it may be stated that the position of the present author is not that the grammatical differences between the verb tenses evolved as markers for prominence or planes of discourse.[151] Rather, that authors do indeed possess the ability to choose which verbal tense they like when forming their stories, and that these choices reflect a discourse function.[152] The debate concerning the semantics of the Greek verb may continue to rage on for the foreseeable future, but the pragmatic effects of the author's choices within any particular work may still be explored.

A small pericope in Mark's Gospel serves as a helpful conversation partner. In Mark 5:21–43, the verb tenses shift dramatically and often. The heart of the story moves back and forth between the aorist and the present repeatedly. Some have explained this as a use of the historical present; others have suggested examples of solecisms in the text. Three perfect indicative verbs in the passage stand out as most rare (Mark 5:29, 33, 34), and, in each case, it is the choice on the part of the author that warrants investigation. In each case, the aorist or the perfect would suit. Why the change to the perfect? Again, this is not to reject the idea that the grammatical rules of Greek do in fact encode a particular viewpoint regarding the action. However, at a discourse level, the choice of the perfect seemingly provides greater prominence for these dramatic moments in the text. While Silva may reject this as a happy coincidence or secondary in nature,[153] the choice of the perfect does indeed functionally mark these events as more prominent than the surrounding material.[154]

Prominent elements would be significant for oral performance, both for the reader as well as the hearer. Since skillful recitation was prized among oral cultures, these markers of prominence may serve as cues for prosody, variation in tone of voice, and bodily expression. Put simply, if the text itself encodes elements marked for prominence, speakers would be attuned to such cues, and the audience would be expected to understand them.[155]

---

150. Silva, *God, Language, and Scripture*, 115.

151. Porter, *Idioms*, 22–23.

152. Porter, *Idioms*, 22.

153. Silva, *God, Language, and Scripture*, 115.

154. Runge, *Discourse Grammar*, 14–17.

155. Vansina, *Oral Tradition as History*, 3–54. See also Rhoads, "Performance Criticism, Pt. I," 121–26.

Participants and Rank

Next, another tool of discourse analysis is to analyze how participants are introduced and rank within the narrative. As Runge rightfully notes,

> A story in which every character was equally important and every event equally significant can hardly be imagined. Even the simplest story has at least a central character and a plot, and this means one character is more important than the others, and certain events likewise. Human beings cannot observe events simply as happenings; they observe them as related and significant happenings, and they report them as such.[156]

The first requirement in examination of characters in a narrative is to ascertain the point of view through which the story progresses.[157] Point of view is simply the way the story is told, the "actions of the characters, their speech, their rhetoric, and the setting are presented through the narrator's perspective."[158]

Here, it is important to distinguish properly "between *mood* and *voice*, that is to say, between the question *who is the character whose point of view orients the narrator's perspective?* And the very different question *who is the narrator?*"[159] The narrator's point of view may be presented internally, from one of the characters themselves, or externally. These are significant choices—not between grammatical forms, but narrative postures[160]—which every storyteller makes in composing a story, and these choices are often overlooked (particularly in the case of the book of Revelation); thus, they will be explored in this section of the investigation. Once the narrator's point of view has been established, it is then crucial to determine the narrator's temporal position relative to the story.[161] How does the narrator choose to present the verbal elements (actions) of the story and what effect does that have in the story's presentation? These questions will take priority in examining the participants provided by the Apocalypse's author.

Next, what other participants "take the stage" within the narrative as it unfolds? Longacre and Hwang suggest ten types of "discourse

---

156. Runge, *Discourse Grammar*, 14.
157. Genette, *Narrative Discourse*, 10.
158. Resseguie, *Revelation of John*, 42.
159. Genette, *Narrative Discourse*, 10 (emphasis original).
160. Genette, *Narrative Discourse*, 244.
161. Genette, *Narrative Discourse*, 216.

operations" that signify prominence among participants of a discourse. These ten components include noting: a participants first mention within a story, how the participant is integrated into the story as central, how the participant is tracked (rarely or routinely), whether or not the participant is restaged, whether or not the participant's presence marks boundaries between scenes or episodes, how the participant is confronted or changes, how the participant contrasts with others, how the participant is evaluated by narrator, how the participant is addressed in dialogue, and how the participant's exit is expressed.[162] These features functionally indicate prominent characters within the narrative and will be analyzed in chapters 3 through 5 below.

The way in which John marks certain characters for prominence is important for the performer and the audience. Characters that serve in the background cluster together, often within a numbered sequence, thus enabling their contribution to the story to be recalled in the mind of the performer. However, more prominent characters are both restaged throughout, indicating their importance. Put simply, John spends significant time describing prominent characters rather than advancing the storyline, which, according to Ong, is prevalent in oral as opposed to scribal or written culture.[163] These markers of prominence will be noted and analyzed, as well as the way in which John restages prominent participants throughout.

Pace, Event, and Nonevent

What is striking to the careful reader of the text of Revelation is how much of the material recorded is simply non-action. Much work across many languages around the world "has underscored the value of distinguishing the event-line, or *storyline* from other narrative material."[164] Foregrounded material in narrative usually follows the events of the story. An event is an action or happening that "extend the basic structure of the mental representation. It is presented as happening at a particular time and place and is generally told in temporal sequence with other events."[165] These form the basic framework for the story and comprise

---

162. Longacre, *Holistic Discourse Analysis*, 84.
163. Ong, *Orality and Literacy*, 147.
164. Longacre, *Grammar of Discourse*, 21.
165. Dooley, *Analyzing Discourse*, 81.

the foreground of the narrative. Nonevents, however, are of various types. Following Grimes,[166] this investigation will analyze the following: participant orientation, setting, explanation, evaluation, performative information, and reported conversation.

In the book of Revelation, a narrative with so many characters and so much tension, these nonevents are employed extensively and serve to vary the pace of the narrative.[167] While certain sections of the book of Revelation contain a rapid-fire succession of events (normally in carefully constructed, easy-to-memorize scenes, employing numbering devices and repetition), others contain elaborate descriptions, monologue, dialogue, and lengthy lists. It is, in fact, curious how often the narrative's event-line is interrupted by these devices. This support material is carefully placed and sometimes even laborious in reading (see Rev 7:4–8; 18:11–13).[168] Often, these nonevents form mini-scenes in themselves (Rev 1:12–16), which Ong suggests is precisely what one would expect in discourse composed in a largely oral culture as opposed to a written one.[169]

The narrative pacing of the discourse, thus, must be explored and analyzed. When reading Revelation in its original language, this rhythm is easily detectable: καί + aorist construction carries much of the storyline forward. As will be seen in the analysis to follow, this construction groups periods together, creating an additive narrative style consistent with oral storytelling.[170] While Mathewson has correctly demonstrated that John's use of verbs provides insight into the elements marked as prominent, it is also important to analyze John's use of verbs, not for aspect but rather for their significance in pacing the narrative. Put simply, John's variation of the καί + aorist construction alters the pace of the discourse—at times slowing it to a virtual crawl and, at other times, moving it forward at a blistering pace. In the prosody in performance section below, it will be suggested that these features cue the performer for dramatic pause and elevation of tone of voice in speaking. All of these features will be marked in chapters 3 to 5 below, with special attention given to the way in which

---

166. Grimes, quoted from Dooley, *Analyzing Discourse*, 82.

167. Dooley, *Analyzing Discourse*, 79–85.

168. In the many times I have listened to the book of Revelation read aloud, in English as well as Greek, each time I find myself desiring to hit the fast-forward button in these sections. The choice to provide such an extensive and detailed set of background material displays intentionality on the part of the author.

169. Ong, *Orality and Literacy*, 147.

170. Ong, *Orality and Literacy*, 34–36.

these features create an episodic structure for the text of Revelation in performance.

Biblical Performance Criticism

The Oral Performance Event

The field of biblical performance criticism has been developed with the assumption that ancient cultures were largely illiterate and, therefore, most discourses were not read silently on a page but were read out loud for public consumption.[171] With this most scholars agree, and this study shares this assumption. Given this assumption, then skill was required to read texts appropriately in the ancient world.[172] While flat, monotone recitation of written texts certainly did occur,[173] additional dramatization was also frequently employed in order to enhance the experience of the audience.[174] Jan Vansina's contribution lends crucial support for the argument that the performer's verbal prosody, gestures, and expressions are important. In examining modern oral cultures, Vansina proposes a typical storytelling event in which the audience gathers to hear the speaker, and the speaker enacts the story with various theatrical techniques.[175] This could be the case with or without the presence of a written manuscript.[176] This could be the case if the story was performed from memory or not. Given the vividness, noise, speech-acts, and agonistic tone represented in the book of Revelation, as well as the acknowledgment of the special place of the reader at the book's beginning (Rev 1:3), this study assumes that the book of Revelation was indeed read out loud, and that various techniques enhanced such an aural-experience.

---

171. Starting with the groundbreaking work of Kelber, *Oral and Written Gospel*. See also Vansina, *Oral Tradition as History*; Gamble, *Books and Readers*. The field of biblical performance criticism has developed and now includes its own monograph series published by Cascade Books. Many of these will be cited in the book to follow, but for an overview of the development of the scholarly field, see Hearon, *Bible in Media*; Botha, *Orality and Literacy*, 52–125; Horsley, *Text and Tradition*, 1–30; and Iverson, *From Text to Performance*.

172. Vansina, *Oral Tradition as History*, 3–54; Dunn, *Jesus Remembered*, 192–209.

173. Parker, "Books and Reading Latin," 187–88. See also Hurtado, "Oral Fixation," 334.

174. Iverson, "Oral Fixation or Oral Corrective," 193. See also Rhoads, "Performance Criticism, Pt. I," 121–24.

175. Vansina, *Oral Tradition as History*, 34–55.

176. Iverson, "Oral Fixation," 193.

While the words "performance," "performer," and "audience" will be used throughout this study, they are meant to be synonymous with the terms "recitation," "reader," and "hearers." That the book was received as an aural performance event is beyond dispute (see the Review of Literature below). That certain skills and expectations were brought to bear in the aural performance event is also most probable. Certainty as to the extent of the dramatic flair expected in the original performance event is impossible. However, it is possible to analyze the text for elements that may have signaled such techniques, as well as devices that indicate that the text was meant to be put to memory. These work together to signal probability that the book of Revelation was composed to be circulated and read from memory in public performance.

Episodic and Redundant Storytelling

Walter J. Ong challenges modern scholars steeped in the literate world to recognize that thought and expression expressed in an oral culture was highly organized but organized in a way that is highly unfamiliar to the literate mind.[177] Moreover, stories were often recited from memory, and compositions were put together with this in mind.[178] Thus, features that enhance memory and enable the public performer to structure the text were utilized by ancient authors.[179] These structural and organization cues remain in the printed text.[180]

Since oral performance was often done from memory,[181] triggers for the recall of subsequent material were crucial.[182] Ancient rhetors taught their students a trick, one that aided ancient performers. Recall of a particular place guided the host of images and description that follow.[183] The function of place in memory, then, unlocked an entire sequence of images and events with accompanying description. It also served to call to mind the participants associated with that place. For example, David Barr, in working with the book of Revelation, suggests that each of the

177. Ong, *Orality and Literacy*, i.
178. Maxwell, "From Performance to Text."
179. Rhoads, "Performance Criticism, Pt. I," 124.
180. Rhoads, "Performance Criticism, Pt. I," 124.
181. Shiner, "Oral Performance," 54–59.
182. Harvey, *Listening to the Text*, 40–42; Hearon, *Bible in Media*, 53.
183. Barr, "Apocalypse as Oral Enactment," 245–46; Vansina, *Oral Tradition as History*, 44–47.

seven letters in Rev 2–3 bring to mind seven places, and these seven places have imagery associated with them that the ancient performer and audience would recognize.[184]

With such triggers understood, the lengthy description of the scenery and participants in the theophany scene that follows in Rev 4–5 are "loaded" in the performer's recall by the simple mention of the heavenly throne room. In short, a host of material follows naturally after remembering this specific location, thus enabling the scene that follows to be presented in turn. That this technique evidences an ancient mnemonic device would be difficult to prove in and of itself. When combined, however, with the additional characteristic of orality described above, the proof may be easier to demonstrate. This provides a good example of how the various tools from multiple fields work together to create the harmony that this methodology pursues.

These units of material form scenes, which join together to create the many episodes that make up the Apocalypse. Episodic storytelling differs from a more linear plot development that emerged with the rise in literacy and the proliferation of the printed text.[185] A modern novel that includes similar bizarre and fantastical images as found in Revelation, such as J. R. R. Tolkien's *The Lord of the Rings*, involves a lengthy linear plot that moves forward over the course of three separate volumes. While there are participants and elements that each of the volumes include, the overall storyline of the book moves ever forward.

This is significantly different from episodic storytelling, in which the episodes follow a similar pattern and structure.[186] Ong maintains that "an oral culture has no experience of a lengthy, epic-size or novel-size climactic linear plot,"[187] since both the performer and the audience would struggle to organize the material in such a studious and relentless manner. Thus, stories embraced a more episodic and redundant pattern, as this facilitated familiarity and recall. As noted above, scenes work together to form these episodes in the book of Revelation.[188] These episodes repeat thematic elements,[189] introduce the same characters but in completely dif-

---

184. Barr, "Apocalypse as Oral Enactment" 246.

185. Ong, *Orality and Literacy*, 144.

186. Ong, *Orality and Literacy*, 147.

187. Ong, *Orality and Literacy*, 143.

188. Beale, *Book of Revelation*, 108–16; Smalley, *Revelation to John*, 19–20; Fiorenza, *Book of Revelation*, 163; Aune, *Revelation*, xci–ci.

189. These themes surface throughout each episode: judgment, perseverance,

ferent ways,[190] and enjoy a fitting conclusion in which the evil powers are seemingly vanquished and the powers of good prevail.[191] Again and again, however, the ending is a false ending, and a subsequent episode begins anew.[192] For example, the three numbered series of seven progress rather similarly.[193] Additionally, the episodes that form Rev 17:1—19:10 and Rev 21:9—22:9 share almost the exact same introductory formula, participants, and concepts.[194] It must be stated here in the methodology section that, while it is certainly beyond the scope of this book to wade into the complexities and sheer volume of theories concerning the macro-structure of the book of Revelation,[195] any system of structuring the book that fails to appreciate the episodic nature of the discourse may be starting off on the wrong foot indeed. Thus, in the analysis to follow, attention to these features will be noted, with the recognition that these may signal that the episodes were composed to be easily recalled for public performance from memory.

Moreover, as has been suggested above, oral composers often experience difficulty getting the story moving. Again, it must be stated that the process of producing a written manuscript often involved a back-and-forth between dictating the spoken word and the secretary's subsequent production of the written text. If the book of Revelation is the product of a skilled pastoral leader of the early church, recording potentially years-worth of compelling episodic stories told again and again in local church communities, what sort of features would be left imprinted on the written text? In addition to the characteristics of orality suggested by Ong above, he further proposes that oral storytellers are often distracted by lengthy descriptions of characters or objects; they often plunge the reader into the middle of the drama without what appears to be a strict chronological order;[196] they use clear structuring devices that are easily recalled by the speaker and recognized by the audience; they often rely on formulaic

---

reward for faithfulness, victory, defeat, worship of God as opposed to worship of the powers of the world.

190. Jesus appears as one like a son of man (Rev 1:13), a lamb (Rev 5:5-6), a child (Rev 12:4-5), and a rider on a white horse (Rev 19:11-16).

191. Barr, *Tales of the End*, 18-25.

192. Barr, *Tales of the End*, 256-59.

193. Aune, *Revelation*, cxii-cxv.

194. Beale, *Book of Revelation*, 109-10. See also Aune's lengthy comparison: *Revelation*, 1144-1146.

195. For a summary, see Bandy, "Layers of the Apocalypse," 469-99.

196. Ong, *Orality and Literacy*, 143.

phraseology; and they often repeat similar themes and elements.[197] All of these features will be identified and analyzed in chapters 3 to 5 below, with the aim that the weight of the evidence produced lends verification to the probability that the book of Revelation was composed from oral recitation and for oral recitation.[198]

Prosody Features

What remains to be explored is the way in which the text would have been cued for performance. Scholars working in the field of biblical performance criticism posit that the surviving transcript of the written text contains components that demonstrate the careful placement of cues for the performer of the discourse. They suggest that in an oral culture, even written texts were "embodied, public, and communal"[199] in their composition and thus in their intended delivery. The performer embodied the story through prosody, gesturing, and emphasis, reciting largely from memory.[200] Texts written for such a receptivity were crafted with this in mind, yielding "clues and suggestions for performance."[201] David Rhoads rightly notes that because the composer of a discourse in a primarily oral culture expects his work to be read orally and communally,[202] the text itself includes what might be akin to "stage directions" for the public reading.[203] Some scholars, however, have rebuked this assertion as both subjective and overstated,[204] which necessitates the formulation of a methodology to validate Rhoads's claims.

What kinds of cues would one be searching for when examining a written text for prosody features meant for oral recitation? Functionally, within the book of Revelation, the following serve as potential markers: cues for vocalization, such as the use of verbs that describe participants crying out or screaming or singing; cues of emotion, such as descriptions when participants are amazed, confused, or frightened; cues for prosody,

---

197. Foley, *Singer of Tales*, 4.
198. Horsley, *Text and Tradition*, 223.
199. Iverson, *From Text to Performance*, 19.
200. See Hearon, *Bible in Media*, 51–59. Also see Janse van Rensburg, "All the Apocalypse," 4–5.
201. Rhoads, "Performance Criticism, Pt. II," 167.
202. Barr, *Tales of the End*, 291.
203. Rhoads, "Performance Criticism, Pt. II," 167.
204. See pages 7–9 above.

such as added vividness that accompany verbs of speaking that indicate elevation or the lowering of vocal pitch (i.e., "the angel cried out in a loud voice"); cues for audience participation, such as hymns, songs, or other liturgical devices; cues of audience address, such as the author speaking through the performer directly to the audience; cues for nuance of speech, such as sarcasm, command, rhetorical questions; and cues for framing the Taleworld[205] and the movement between the Taleworld and the audience's "real world."[206] Again, it is worth stating that this study presupposes an emphasis on the spoken word as opposed to the written word in an effort to overcorrect the lack of appreciation in the scholarship of Revelation.

When examined in isolation, any of the above features may not be significant in itself, but when all these elements are combined, they make it probable *that* the text was composed for oral performance. Moreover, they may also provide insight into *how* the text might have been heard in performance.[207] It has been said that Revelation "is the noisiest book in the New Testament ... a spirited and seemingly endless performance of Tchaikovsky's *1812 Overture*."[208] Therefore, Revelation contains a myriad of examples of the cues listed above. "Momentous events seem to require a loud, mighty, or great voice,"[209] trumpets announce angelic messages, thunder booms, eagles scream the triplet of woes, the saints cry "how long?" and the merchants of the earth wail. Thus, the scholar or student who sits down to enjoy the book of Revelation must rightly understand the noise within.

Here, it is hoped that a return to hearing the book of Revelation enables modern scholars to appreciate how this story would have been heard by its original audience, and thus how the hearing would have affected the listener. After all, stories were not merely told to be told, they also were meant to make an impact on the audience.[210] In synthesizing all of the above data, the proposal made by numerous scholars *that* the book of Revelation was received in an oral performance event will be satisfactorily validated. Subsequent scholarship concerning the book must begin with this in mind and appreciate this concept as they analyze the text.

205. Young, *Taleworlds and Storyrealms*, 1–68.
206. Rhoads, "Performance Criticism, Pt. II," 126–31.
207. Bauckham, *Climax of Prophecy*, 1–3, 7.
208. Resseguie, *Revelation of John*, 21.
209. Resseguie, *Revelation of John*, 21.
210. Hearon, *Bible in Media*, 91.

2

Review of Literature

INTRODUCTION

Given the purposes of this book, it is first necessary to provide an overview of scholarship regarding the oral culture of the first century Roman world. This is a crucial section of the present investigation though, because an oral culture is vastly different from a culture capable of widespread literacy.[1] This simple fact is loaded with profundity, and scholars investigating ancient texts, including the sacred Scriptures, often fail to appreciate it. Thus, the first part of this review of literature aims to situate the modern reader within this ancient culture. While work had been ongoing concerning the literacy of the ancient Roman world, William V. Harris's comprehensive 1989 monograph *Ancient Literacy* emerged as a valuable resource in understanding that world. Building upon this important text, this review of literature interacts with scholars and seeks to establish the largely oral culture of ancient Rome and the early church in her midst, and to insist that this must be rightly appropriated in scholarship of ancient texts. In short, the medium has a great effect on the message,[2] and while this review of literature will be selective and not exhaustive, it is critical in providing the right "backdrop" for the rest of the investigation to play out before.[3]

1. Ong, *Orality and Literacy*, i.
2. McLuhan, *Understanding Media*, 7.
3. This study, however, is not an inquiry into ancient Roman literacy rates, but

Next, a survey of the scholarly literature regarding the oral performance of the book of Revelation is provided. Commentary regarding the structure, symbolism, interpretive schemas, solecisms, and theological importance of the book of Revelation are countless, and while a survey of scholarship concerning these issues would be important, it is not relevant to the task at hand unless it interacts directly with the issue of aural performance. For example, scholars note that theories pertaining to the structure of the book are legion,[4] and while this study does not propose a novel structural proposal, the episodic nature of the book's content does have import to issues of structure.[5] Thus, some interaction here would be necessary on this particular issue. It is important in the first section, then, to acknowledge that this review of literature aims to focus the scholarly conversation around the topic at hand: Does the text of Revelation suggest a composition intended for aural performance? Do scholars interact with the proposed thesis suggested by this investigation or not? If so, how? Thus, this portion of the review of literature will examine selected scholars who have written on the book of Revelation and provide a brief summary of the literature. These will be developed not chronologically but according to the scholars interaction with the performance features of the text.

PART ONE: ENTERING AN ORAL CULTURE

Ancient Literacy

William V. Harris

The most salient work in which every scholar who has followed is required to interact is the comprehensive and impressive monograph published in 1989 by William V. Harris. *Ancient Literacy*, published by Harvard University Press, guides the modern reader through the ancient Greco-Roman world in a systematic and linear fashion. Beginning with the importance of defining "literacy" and establishing the levels of literacy in the ancient world, Harris then leads his students through a diachronic exploration of the way in which literacy both spread and rose

---

rather an investigation concerning the way in which the orality of the ancient world affects the biblical text.

4. See Bandy, "Layers of the Apocalypse," 469–99.
5. Ong, *Orality and Literacy*, 143–47.

in the Hellenistic and then late Roman worlds. This book is detailed yet big-picture, selective yet comprehensive, informative yet illuminating. As such, almost every scholar who has investigated questions concerning literacy in the Greco-Roman world interacts with Harris's text.

What, then, does Harris suggest? First, he posits that in defining literacy, one must appreciate that the category is not binary but nuanced, with some in the ancient world capable of fluent reading and writing, to those who could read slowly but could not write, to those who could read simple texts but not complex or lengthy ones, to those who could not read or write anything at all.[6] Harris refers to these in the middle as "semi-literates," and suggests that this provides difficulty for any historian seeking to establish a precise percentage for any ancient culture.[7] Harris makes a rather bold statement in the early pages of his monograph: "It may seem obvious that nothing in the nature of mass literacy can *ever have existed* in the ancient world."[8] He continues by stating that the "vital preconditions for wide diffusion of literacy were always absent in the Graeco-Roman world, and that no positive force ever existed to bring about mass literacy."[9] For those seeking at least an educated estimate for the percentage of those in the first-century AD Roman world who were literate, Harris suggests that, although there were certainly differences among different populations and regions of the Roman Empire, "the overall level of literacy is likely to have been below 15%."[10] While numbers such as this are certainly helpful in imagining the lived experience within the ancient world, other forms of functional literacy are difficult to measure and quantify.[11] Thus, while Harris's estimates are likely accurate, precision in recognizing functional literacy among the population of the Roman world remains difficult.

In light of this finding, Harris demonstrates the importance of orality during the same period. He states that it is a "commonplace in some scholarly circles that the Greek and Roman worlds always remained highly dependent on oral communication"[12] and that this was true throughout each period of the Hellenistic and Roman eras. The need

---

6. Harris, *Ancient Literacy*, 5.
7. Harris, *Ancient Literacy*, 8.
8. Harris, *Ancient Literacy*, 8 (emphasis mine).
9. Harris, *Ancient Literacy*, 12.
10. Harris, *Ancient Literacy*, 267.
11. Hurtado, "Oral Fixation," 330–34.
12. Harris, *Ancient Literacy*, 29.

for personal writing was mitigated, he suggests, by the ancient world's prevalent and impressive use of memory. "There is reason to believe that non-literate cultures are characterized by people with remarkable capacious and tenacious memories for continued texts."[13] Harris details how ancient orators were expected to commit extended texts to memory, and "specialized techniques were devised"[14] that enabled people to do this. These techniques were placed within the written text, enabling the performer to retell the story or the announcement or the poem freely from memory.

Texts, even the ones designed for performance, were not accessible to everyone. Given the proposed level of literacy among the ancient Romans given above, most people were unable to memorize from a written text. Access to information, therefore, was mediated through others. Harris shows that "speeches and recitations, like performances of plays, transferred thoughts from the written page to the listener"[15] through the performance of the text from memory. Additionally, most people, simply unable to read, were reliant upon the aid of an intermediary to gain access to written information. It was "utterly commonplace" for written texts to be read by a trained reader, as well as in the public sphere for persons to simply ask a bystander to read or explain a written inscription.[16]

What, then, is the purpose of writing in such a culture? Harris suggests dozens of examples, such as indicating ownership, labeling commodities or products, recording edicts, casting votes, writing letters, declaring birth or death, practicing magic, announcing invitations, and writing literature, among others.[17] He states that writing served the Empire as it enabled the rise of the more advanced cities, which are often exploitive of the countryside. Moreover, writing provides a cultural hegemony in that a collection of texts read and heard by all creates unity.[18] This unifying power of the written word can both be benevolent and abusive. A strange development in the importance of the written word occurred with the rise of the Christian community. Indeed, it is the unique flavor of the early Christian community, according to Harris, which suggest a

13. Harris, *Ancient Literacy*, 31.
14. Harris, *Ancient Literacy*, 33.
15. Harris, *Ancient Literacy*, 35.
16. Harris, *Ancient Literacy*, 34.
17. Harris, *Ancient Literacy*, 26–27.
18. Harris, *Ancient Literacy*, 39–40.

"coming change in the religious importance of the written word"[19] in the ancient Roman world. Harris notes that it is possibly the forcefulness with which the letters of Paul were written that may have enabled their survival and contributed to this new development in the significance of written texts.

Yet through it all, the oral transmission of literary works remained supreme. Harris quotes Suetonius in revealing that even Augustus himself, when struggling to sleep, summoned readers or storytellers to his bedside instead of reaching for the written page.[20] Orality and not literacy characterized the world of first-century Rome. This initial survey of this most salient monograph is lengthy indeed but critical, for it sheds valuable light on the way in which ancient cultures, including the one in which the early church grew, interacted with texts. In summary, texts were written in a culture where the majority could never read them, and most people's interaction with said text would be through the text in performance, often by a trained orator or reader speaking from memory.

William A. Johnson and Holt N. Parker's Ancient Literacies

Johnson and Parker's *Ancient Literacies: The Culture of Reading in Greece and Rome* finds points of agreement with Harris's work while also challenging several conclusions. In the introduction, Johnson acknowledges Harris's monograph as a "thoughtful, immensely learned, and important book,"[21] but also critiques the work as too narrowly focused, dealing with percentages of reading and writing as opposed to more functional literacy, rooted in "text-oriented events embedded in particular sociocultural contexts."[22] What follows in this book is a comprehensive and well-developed exploration of the way texts were composed and used in various communities and social settings in the Roman world.

Holt Parker's essay "Books and Reading Latin Poetry" explores the way in which ancient performances were given. Parker suggests that there was a sharp distinction between the dramatic performance done from memory in the theater and the more subdued oral recitation from

---

19. Harris, *Ancient Literacy*, 220.
20. Harris, *Ancient Literacy*, 226.
21. Johnson and Parker, *Ancient Literacies*, 3.
22. Johnson and Parker, *Ancient Literacies*, 3.

a written manuscript that occurred in a home.²³ The performance events required two different styles, and the student of the orality of ancient Rome must recognize these differences. As noted in the methodology section in chapter 1, Kelly Iverson disagrees with Parker's overgeneralization, noting that there were a variety of styles employed in a variety of settings in the ancient world. Skillful recitation of texts involved prosody on the part of the reader, thus the modern student may explore the written text with these oral features in mind.²⁴

Walter J. Ong

In a series of lectures given at Yale University in 1964, Walter J. Ong revealed the way in which language and communication are drastically affected by the culture and the medium in which they are employed. Ong posits that "our entire understanding of classical culture has to be revised—and with it our understanding of later cultures up to our own time—in terms of our new awareness of the role of the media in structuring the human psyche and civilization itself."²⁵ In the modern literate world steeped in written texts, it is nearly impossible to appreciate the way in which language (indeed everyday life itself) was experienced in a primarily oral-aural culture. In his 1982 monograph *Orality and Literacy*, Ong again warns that "thought and expression in oral cultures is often highly organized by calls for organization of a sort unfamiliar to and often uncongenial to the literate mind."²⁶ It follows, then, that any student of an ancient text like the book of Revelation must appreciate this simple fact.

In reviewing linguistic theory, Ong notes that much of the scholarship concerning ancient narratives, tales, poetry, and the like have struggled to break free of the presuppositions of scholars looking in from the present literate world, and then provides a series of suggestions for those looking to immerse themselves in the oral world. He reveals that, whereas written words have "residue," "oral tradition has no such residue or deposit,"²⁷ and therefore, the student in an oral culture does not "study"

---

23. Parker, "Books and Reading Latin," 203.
24. Iverson, "Oral Fixation or Oral Corrective," 183–200.
25. Ong, *Presence of the Word*, 18.
26. Ong, *Orality and Literacy*, i.
27. Ong, *Orality and Literacy*, 12.

at all in the manner in which the modern student might understand the term. Whereas writing encodes words into a visual representation, in an oral culture, the word has a different sense, made up of sounds and syllables. Whereas modern scholars may refer to texts with the term "literature," such a term betrays the bias of the literate culture, for the term itself derives etymologically from the *letters* of the alphabet, whereas the term "text" is much more appropriate, for the term "text" derives etymologically from the concept of *weaving* things together. Following the work done by Milman Parry from 1928, Ong suggests that many features of ancient Homeric poetry are due to the "economy enforced by oral methods of compositions,"[28] and that this discovery marked a revolution in literary circles.

Ong then gives helpful guidance for the student of oral culture. He notes that even the way that thought is sustained in an oral culture differs from the literate one. Thus, "protracted orally based thought, even when not in formal verse, tends to be highly rhythmic, for rhythm aids recall, even physiologically."[29] These rhythms are implemented through repetition of sounds and repetition of formulas, which act as memory aids for ancient orally-based thought. What is more, Ong provides a summary of what the analyst would expect in a text composed in an oral-based culture.[30] Oral communication is additive rather than subordinate in nature, aggregative not analytic, redundant, agonistic, empathetic and participatory rather than objective.[31] Ong further notes that in oral cultures, memory works best with what he refers to as "heavy" characters ("persons whose deeds are monumental, memorable, and commonly public"), colorful or bizarre characters or figures, as well as "formulary number groupings."[32] Lastly, Ong suggests that storyline and narrative flow differ greatly from an oral to a literate culture. Here, Ong is masterful, detailing that the notion of a detailed and complex linear plot, following Freytag's pyramid, betrays a world of written texts where the reader is able to hold together layers of material by the simple ability to turn the page backward

---

28. Ong, *Orality and Literacy*, 21.

29. Ong, *Orality and Literacy*, 34.

30. This is picked up by other scholars, notably Albert B. Lord, who regularly refers to Walter Ong as Father Ong. See Lord, *Singer of Tales*. See also Lord, "Characteristics of Orality," 54–72. Lord disagrees with Ong as to the function of some of these characteristics, but both of them agree that they evidence the residue of an oral culture.

31. Ong, *Orality and Literacy*, 36–57.

32. Ong, *Orality and Literacy*, 70.

and review previous content. This limitation alters the way oral cultures develop the storyline of narratives, as "an oral culture has no experience of a lengthy, epic-size or novel-size climactic linear plot."[33] In examining ancient poetry told in a primarily oral culture, Ong teaches that the "episodic structure was the only way and the totally natural way of imagining and handling lengthy narrative."[34] These methodological suggestions were articulated in the proposed methodology above, as Ong indeed is a useful guide.

Ong's contribution continues as he details the way in which oral memorization and oral composition fit hand in glove. Again following the work of Parry, Ong suggests that ancient texts were indeed oral compositions—the bard or storyteller weaving together the story from a collection of fixed materials or episodes stored in the memory.[35] For the ancient "author," therefore, "originality consists not in the introduction of new materials but in fitting the traditional materials effectively into each individual, unique situation and/or audience."[36] Such compositions were not repeated verbatim, according to Ong, but were faithful both to the received material and the situational context.[37]

Oral Tradition

Werner H. Kelber

Published in 1983, the starting axiom of Kelber's *The Oral and Written Gospel* is rather simple: "The oral medium, in which words are managed from mouth to ear, handles information differently from the written medium, which links the eye to visible but silent letters on the page."[38] From this axiom, Kelber laments that biblical scholars have failed to appropriately appreciate and apply this assumption, instead consistently returning to a "chirographic bias."[39] Working primarily with the Gospel of Mark,

33. Ong, *Orality and Literacy*, 143.
34. Ong, *Orality and Literacy*, 144.
35. Ong, *Orality and Literacy*, 60.
36. Ong, *Orality and Literacy*, 60.
37. For additional support for the way in which oral cultures preserve traditional materials, see Bauckham, *Jesus and the Eyewitnesses*, 240–63. Also, see Dunn, *Jesus Remembered*, 202–3.
38. Kelber, *Oral and Written Gospel*, xv.
39. Kelber, *Oral and Written Gospel*, xv.

Kelber notes that it is vital for the student of biblical texts to remember that the composition of most ancient manuscripts were "dictated to a scribe and read aloud to audiences," and that these manuscripts then "were meant to be heard and processed in memory."[40] A Gospel narrative, like Mark's, therefore was written by a man who had a vast reservoir of stories, parables, sayings, episodes, and testimony concerning the person of Jesus, and these existed in a kind of cultural memory retained among the early church by memory and repeated oral narration.[41] Additionally, Kelber, like Ong before him, insists that "texts were likely to be composed in conformity with a phenomenology of sound more than sight,"[42] as ancient texts lacked punctuation signs that are utilized for the silent reader of texts.

Kelber applies the axiom thoroughly in his analysis of the Gospel of Mark, and a brief set of comments require attention here. Kelber notes several features that a written text composed for performance present, noting with clarity that the "oral profile [of Mark's Gospel] is far from being erased."[43] These features include first and foremost the episodic nature of the composition. According to Kelber, texts composed orally from memory to a scribe consist of short stories, or episodes, brought together to form the larger whole.[44] These stories are strung together by obvious "stereotypical" connective devices, including the abundant use of paratactic καί. These "line up episodes paratactically like beads on a string, producing a narrative that is jolting more than smoothly flowing,"[45] and these features—oral connectives, episodic syntax, and breathlessness of prose—demonstrate an effective story designed for hearing. Additionally, the repetition of ideas and themes and the consistency with which Mark's Gospel duplicates material, but not verbatim, suggests a progressive duplication that "serves both speaker and hearers narrative and mnemonic needs."[46] Kelber goes on to analyze the text of Mark's Gospel with these oral features in mind, as well as other New Testament texts.[47] Kelber's

---

40. Kelber, *Oral and Written Gospel*, xxii.
41. Kelber, *Oral and Written Gospel*, xxiii.
42. Kelber, *Oral and Written Gospel*, xxiv.
43. Kelber, *Oral and Written Gospel*, 64.
44. Kelber, *Oral and Written Gospel*, 64.
45. Kelber, *Oral and Written Gospel*, 65.
46. Kelber, *Oral and Written Gospel*, 68.
47. Much of the material in these chapters of Kelber's book are not directly applicable to the present study, yet still influential and important in their own right.

analysis has faced some criticism, particularly his suggestion that the writing of the text alienates it from the original oral form.[48]

Chrys Caragounis

In a masterful tour de force published in 2004, Chrys Caragounis supplied fresh insight into the development of the Greek language and its effects for New Testament scholarship. His book *The Development of Greek and the New Testament* has much to commend, and its sheer breadth of analysis is remarkable. Much of the second half of the book addresses the acoustic dimension of communication, from the pronunciation of the letters themselves to the melody and rhythm of a composition meant for aural reception. Caragounis notes that the verb "to hear" occurs in the New Testament no less than 410 times, stating that the contents of the text were not written "to be read silently by each individual in turn, but in order *to be read aloud* and *to be listened to* in the various congregations."[49] He laments that this is rarely appreciated and even more rarely analyzed. To combat this, Caragounis provides a working methodology, based on the recommendations of ancient literary critics, primarily Dionysus, to study the acoustic dimension of the New Testament texts. He then applies much of this to selected passages from the writings of the apostle Paul.

These four scholars briefly outlined thus far depict an ancient world that is difficult for the modern person to understand; a world largely void of interaction with lengthy written texts; a world in which even the literate man rarely read to himself but out loud; a world where the majority of people required assistance to read even basic texts or inscriptions; yet a world steeped in stories nonetheless. In short, the Greco-Roman (and Jewish) world in which the New Testament was birthed out of was primarily an oral culture, not a literate one. Scholars of this ancient culture must rightly appropriate this axiom when exploring ancient texts, for as Kelber notes, it is likely that these texts were composed orally with the aural performance of the text understood as the means of the texts reception. The medium in this case is the spoken word. William V. Harris provides the modern student of the ancient world with a window into the literacy and illiteracy of that ancient world; Walter J. Ong opens up the modern mind to the way in which the oral mind processes information

---

48. See this critique from Dunn, *Jesus Remembered*, 202–3.
49. Caragounis, *Development of Greek*, 401.

and dispenses it; Werner H. Kelber demonstrates how a New Testament text may evidence clues of its oral composition and reception; and Chrys Caragounis supplies the modern student with a methodology for recognizing the acoustics of the New Testament.

Jan Vansina

Jan Vansina spent decades studying oral cultures primarily in Africa, and using the expertise gained from this experience, Vansina's book *Oral Tradition as History* shed valuable light on features of oral storytelling. Vansina's exhaustive study begins with the very nature of messages, depicting the way that performers worked with memorized tradition,[50] and explores the social function of oral storytelling. Significant for the present investigation, Vansina proposes that oral storytelling was never a mere recitation. Rather, the performer would dramatize the story through bodily movements and gestures, as well as the raising and lowering of the voice.[51] Scholars after Vansina, including those working with the oral tradition behind the New Testament itself, regularly reference Vansina and his contribution.[52]

Harry Y. Gamble

A decade after Kelber's publication of *The Oral and Written Gospel*, Harry Y. Gamble explored the way in which the early church interacted with and utilized texts in his *Books and Readers in the Early Church: A History of Early Christian Texts*. Gamble follows Harris in presenting an early church that was largely illiterate, where the "ability to read, criticize, and interpret [Christian literature] belonged to a small number of Christians in the first centuries, ordinarily not more than about 10 percent in any given setting, and perhaps fewer in the many small and provincial

---

50. It would be too comprehensive to explore the many other scholars who contributed to the developing understanding of the way in which oral tradition is passed and shared. Of note: Bultmann, *Jesus and the Word*; Lord, *Singer of Tales*. See also Gerhardsson, *Memory and Manuscript*; Horsley and Draper, *Whoever Hears You Hears Me*; Foley, *Singer of Tales*; Bauckham, *Jesus and the Eyewitnesses*.

51. Vansina, *Oral Tradition as History*, 34.

52. Bauckham, *Jesus and the Eyewitnesses*, 240–63. Also, see Dunn, *Jesus Remembered*, 174–239. For a differing view to Bauckham, see Ehrman, *Jesus Before the Gospels*, 17–86.

congregations that were characteristic of early Christianity."[53] In his opening chapter, Gamble interacts with scholars Franz Overbeck and Adolf Deissmann, who both proclaimed that the early Christian movement was not a literary one in the proper sense, and that the literature born out of this movement was largely "occasional and intramural," not destined for a wide public and void of literary artistry.[54] Gamble then develops the thinking of form critics and folklorists who maintain that the Gospel texts betray the oral culture in which they were composed, and that the oral tradition reflected in these texts demonstrate a "conversion to the written medium" but not necessarily a "change in the nature of the material," still bearing the "marks of oral formation."[55]

For Gamble, however, the emergence of the written Christian literature and the importance of the text itself demand explanation. In opposition to Kelber, Gamble suggests that, with the rise of Christian literature, the mutual exclusion of the oral and written cultures is unwarranted. Rather, Gamble maintains that texts were composed for the reading but that most reading in antiquity, whether public or private, was done out loud, which in effect converts even the written page to the oral mode.[56] Ancient authors knew and appreciated this fact in composing literature, thus it is most probable that their written texts were written for the ear as much as for the eye.[57] For those persons who are the product of a primarily literature culture, where written texts are primarily read privately and silently, this concept is crucial to recognize. Gamble's contribution is helpful, both conceding that oral and written communications were indeed different modes of communication, but also insisting that these two modes were not mutually exclusive and interacted freely in antiquity.[58]

These texts were written, according to Gamble, mostly on scrolls in the broader Roman world. The standard scroll "comprised twenty [papyrus]

---

53. Gamble, *Books and Readers*, 5. Gamble also rightly notes that even in a Jewish community, the literacy rate would have been quite low. He suggests that, while it is true that Jewish communities had a strong interest in basic literacy, this education was aimed to enable participation in Jewish life, not necessarily literacy as such. See Gamble, *Books and Readers*, 7.

54. Gamble, *Books and Readers*, 13–14.

55. Gamble, *Books and Readers*, 15.

56. Gamble, *Books and Readers*, 30.

57. Gamble, *Books and Readers*, 30.

58. Gamble, *Books and Readers*, 8–10. See also Elder, "Between Reading and Performance," 1–13.

sheets and ran to about 3 ½ meters" in length.[59] These scrolls could be cumbersome to work with, requiring a particular skill set not familiar to all. Perhaps because of this, Gamble notes the peculiar exception to this general preference for the scroll within the Christian community of the first three centuries, as the early church had a strong favoritism and early adoption of the codex (first wooden, then papyrus).[60] This preference indicates the importance of the dissemination of these texts to the Christian community, reflecting both the "setting in which they were prepared and the purposes for which they were intended. They were neither private texts nor products of the trade, but books produced by and for the use of small Christian communities."[61] Overall, Gamble's corrective to Kelber's overemphasis of the binary nature of oral and written composition is helpful, and his contribution enables students of the New Testament to appreciate how early Christian texts were composed and received.

Biblical Performance Criticism

Holly E. Hearon and Philip Ruge-Jones

Holly E. Hearon and Philip Ruge-Jones, publishing in 2009, posited a fresh appreciation for the medium in which the Scriptures were composed. Building on much of the work of Werner Kelber, their edited monograph *The Bible in Ancient and Modern Media* opens the door to biblical performance criticism.[62] In citing primary sources such as Quintilian, Whitney Shiner notes that "reading, acting, and rhetorical delivery were considered related skills" in the ancient Roman world as public speaking was prized. Thus, to effectively communicate in a public setting with appropriate skill, "written material would be memorized if it was considered important and if the length of the writing allowed."[63] To Shiner, the New Testament texts were long, indeed, but short enough for memorization,[64] and that ancient rhetoricians "typically memorized

---

59. Gamble, *Books and Readers*, 45.
60. Gamble, *Books and Readers*, 49–56.
61. Gamble, *Books and Readers*, 78.
62. An equally important contributor to this "open door" to biblical performance criticism is David Rhoads's two-part series published in 2006: "Performance Criticism, Pt. I," and "Performance Criticism, Pt. II."
63. Shiner, "Oral Performance," 53.
64. See also the contribution by John D. Harvey, *Listening to the Text*, 40–42.

speeches even if they lasted several hours or more," and that flatly reading a speech or text was disrespectful, according to Quintilian.⁶⁵ Thus, narration was composed with the aural performance in mind, necessitating vividness, prosody, emotion, and audience reaction.⁶⁶

David Rhoads

David Rhoads, in a separate entry, further adds, since letters were written on scrolls one after another without punctuation or spacing between words, that "even when writing, writing was not done for its own sake. Rather, orality remained primary, and writing was secondary and served the needs of orality."⁶⁷ Gamble's caution again must be noted, and the oral and written must not be made mutually exclusive, but insistence on the appreciation of the aural performance reception of ancient communication is needed.⁶⁸ Ancient texts, including the New Testament writings, unveil the residue of this aural-nature.⁶⁹ Like fossils in the ground provide a "trace record of what was once a living creature, so the New Testament writings are trace records of live performances in the first century."⁷⁰ Methodology for recognition of these "fossils" was detailed in chapter 1 above and will be employed in chapter 3 below.

Peter J. J. Botha

Peter J. J. Botha, following the work (and title) of Ong and the scholarship of Kelber, further explores the nature of the oral culture of the first century Roman world in *Orality and Literacy in Early Christian Writings*, published in 2012. Botha posits that Mark's Gospel does not "merely contain oral-traditions, but *is* oral tradition."⁷¹ Like Ong, Botha agrees that "communication media not only *reflect* culture but also *influence*

---

65. Shiner, "Oral Performance," 52.
66. Shiner, "Oral Performance," 54–62.
67. Rhoads, "What Is Performance Criticism?," 85.
68. Rhoads, "Performance Criticism, Pt. II," 173–80.
69. Rhoads, "Performance Criticism, Pt. I," 124.
70. Rhoads, "Performance Criticism, Pt. I," 87.
71. Botha, *Orality and Literacy*, 11. Another companion of Botha's monograph is a series of articles published by Brill in the same year: see Minchin, *Orality, Literacy, and Performance*.

it fundamentally."[72] While much of Botha's contribution is summary in fashion, repeating much of the already articulated material suggested by the scholars surveyed above,[73] Botha's chapter detailing the way in which oral reading of texts was experienced is particularly relevant to the present task. In this chapter, Botha posits that "reading in antiquity was not experienced as a silent scanning, mainly mental activity," but rather "it was performative, vocal, oral-aural event."[74] The reader was not merely monotonously sounding syllables either, but instead "recited, with vocal and bodily gestures the text that one usually memorized beforehand."[75] Botha further develops Gamble's assessment of use of papyrus scrolls by further noting that scrolls were not easy to use. Scrolls were cumbersome, read aloud while unrolling and rerolling, and were "fairly readable while standing up and when the specific column of writing to be read does not matter, but physically demanding for reference and comparison."[76] Botha further notes that the lack of punctuation and the utilization of *scriptio continua* necessitated that texts were read syllable by syllable, with punctuation and markers governing movement from section to section enforced by the astute reader.[77] According to Botha, this thrust a responsibility upon the ancient reader: to rightly combine syllables into words and words into demarcated units. This trust in the reader to perform this task demonstrates, to Botha, that texts were written to be committed to memory. *Scriptio continua* "forced the reader to punctuate the text but also aided the reader in memorizing, in making the text truly one's own."[78] Thus, he argues, structure in ancient writings was oriented mnemotechnically, "based on the logic of recollection,"[79] and the composition of ancient texts was a memory-based activity.

72. Botha, *Orality and Literacy*, 11.
73. Much of the contribution from Botha echoes that of Vansina, Ong, and Kelber.
74. Botha, *Orality and Literacy*, 103.
75. Botha, *Orality and Literacy*, 104.
76. Botha, *Orality and Literacy*, 106.
77. Botha, *Orality and Literacy*, 109.
78. Botha, *Orality and Literacy*, 114.
79. Botha, *Orality and Literacy*, 116.

Ancient Literacy in General-Reference Works

The Eerdmans Dictionary of Early Judaism contains an article devoted to the literacy rates in Second-Temple Judaism. David M. Carr notes that literacy "is a highly variable competence."[80] Literacy, then, is not a binary set of abilities but exhibits a range of skills from the ability to simply scratch one's name, to the ability to keep rudimentary bookkeeping, to more complex competencies.[81] Such variation means that any understanding of the literacy of ancient Israel and the surrounding Roman world must be approximate at best, reflecting this variation.[82] This same variation was likely represented within the early community of Jesus followers in the first century AD. In the *Anchor Yale Bible Dictionary*, it is Werner Kelber himself who provides the article concerning orality in the early church, noting that "the oral tradition in the NT developed in a world which had set a high premium on both the written and the spoken word."[83] However, just as in the broader culture of the Roman Empire in which this community grew, oral speech remained the primary form of communication.[84]

In summary, the purpose of this first section of the review of literature is to bring to light the oral culture that was ancient Rome. Recent scholarship paints a picture of an ancient world in which communication occurred primarily through the spoken word. Texts had their place, and a significant one at that within the early church, but writing was supplemental and complementary of the oral medium, and this selective review is intended to reframe the study of the book of Revelation within the oral culture in which it was composed. While much recent work has been done in exploring the way in which New Testament texts, especially the Gospels and Pauline epistles, were composed with oral performance in mind, there is still much ground to tread. This is particularly so concerning the book of Revelation, and to the application of this axiom to the book of Revelation this investigation now turns.

---

80. Carr, "Literacy and Reading," 888.

81. Carr, "Literacy and Reading," 888.

82. A. R. Millard goes as far as to say that "measuring literacy is a subjective enterprise," suggesting a more significant amount of at least semi-literate people even among rural communities. See Millard, "Literacy (Ancient Israel)," 4:339.

83. Kelber, "Oral Tradition: New Testament," 5:30.

84. Kelber, "Oral Tradition: New Testament," 5:31.

PART TWO: ORALITY IN REVELATION SCHOLARSHIP

Introduction

Bauckham's Axiom

This portion of the review begins with a rather simple quote from a leading New Testament scholar, and what is more, it occurs on the first page of his commentary on the book of Revelation. Richard Bauckham, former professor of New Testament studies at St. Andrews University, suggests in the second paragraph of his masterful treatment, "Revelation was evidently designed to convey its message to some significant degree on first hearing."[85] In the next sentence he adds, "It is important to realise that the essential structure of the book, without recognition of which it would be incomprehensible, must have been intended to be perceptible in oral performance."[86] What is more, just a page later, Bauckham continues by stating that the meaning conveyed in the work is closely tied to the structuring of the book for oral performance, and that these features would certainly be signaled by linguistic markers. Bauckham pleads with his readers to recognize this axiom: "John, it is important to remember, was writing in the first place for *hearers* (Rev 1:3),"[87] and while Bauckham will suggest highly detailed and complex structuring devices later in his commentary, he begins with the acknowledgement that the text of Revelation "was intended for oral performance."[88] A review of literature recreates a supposed conversation between noted experts on the given topic. In this hypothetical reconstruction, Richard Bauckham has placed a rather significant concept onto the stage, and it becomes important to explore how scholars interact with Bauckham's claim. Thus, the second section of this chapter aims to demonstrate how various scholars, both before and after Bauckham, have involved their investigation into the Book of Revelation with his suggestion in mind, and the scholars will be presented in chronological order.

---

85. Bauckham, *Climax of Prophecy*, 1.
86. Bauckham, *Climax of Prophecy*, 1–2.
87. Bauckham, *Climax of Prophecy*, 1–2 (emphasis original).
88. Bauckham, *Climax of Prophecy*, 1–2.

Bauckham's Axiom in Revelation Studies

R. H. Charles

Seventy years before Bauckham's *Climax of Prophecy*, R. H. Charles wrote *A Critical and Exegetical Commentary on the Revelation of St. John*. The two-volume commentary numbers over one thousand pages, with the introduction alone nearly two hundred pages. In this thorough introduction, Charles explores seemingly every detail and facet of the book of Revelation, from its structure to its authorship to its sources to its grammatical features to its theological impact.[89] What is notably absent, however, is any suggestion that the text of Revelation was intended to be performed orally. The reception-situation is not explored in any significant way in this commentary. While Charles details every clause and phrase within the book, and at times even suggests clausal breaks that almost mirror the cola and period posited below,[90] the oral intention of John's composition is not appreciated. As a significant contribution to Revelation scholarship from the last century, this omission is glaring.

Have more recent scholars addressed this omission? A trend among recent analysts of Revelation has emerged: following Charles, many commentators, in crafting introductions to the book of Revelation (and sometimes rather lengthy introductions), largely ignore the oral performance features and their implications for understanding meaning, yet then offer a brief remark concerning the oral reception of the book of Revelation in the exegesis of Rev 1:3. Looking chronologically through several significant contributors to Revelation scholarship, this trend becomes clear.

Robert H. Mounce

Mounce's 1977 commentary gave Revelation scholarship a comprehensive and well-developed treatment of the book, with a careful exegesis of the text and a helpful introduction. In the over forty-page introduction to the commentary, however, Mounce makes no mention of the oral nature of the Roman culture of the first century. Yet, just like Fanning decades later, Mounce notes the Apocalypse's likely oral delivery in an ever-so-brief comment on Rev 1:3: "The public reading of Scripture was taken over from

---

89. Charles, *Critical and Exegetical Commentary*, xxix–clxxviii.

90. For a representative example, see Charles, *Critical and Exegetical Commentary*, 105–7.

Jewish practice. At first the reader was probably someone chosen from the congregation who had acquired some proficiency in the art. The ability to read well was not widespread in antiquity."[91] This passing comment receives no further attention and the effect that this public reading would have had on both the composition of the book of Revelation as well as the aural-reception of the book of Revelation is not explored.

Adela Yarbro Collins

Collins's work *Crisis and Catharsis* excellently examines the way in which the tension in the book of Revelation builds and releases through the symbolism and literary technique of the author. Scholars writing after the publication of this monograph consistently interact with her work, recognizing that Collins returned the social and communal elements of the early church to the fore, enabling readers to understand the way in which a narrative like Revelation would have affected its readers. This attention to the social-situational context breathed fresh life into subsequent studies of the book, and her insistence that "the primary purpose of the book is not to impart information . . . [but] rather to call for *commitment* to the actions, attitudes, and feelings uttered"[92] forces those interacting with her monograph to rightly appreciate the commissive nature of Revelation.

Collins is correct in stating that "as expressive language, the book of Revelation creates a visual experience for the hearer or reader."[93] She continues by noting, once again in line with this recent trend, that "it is likely that the Apocalypse was read aloud before the assembled Christians of a given locality, perhaps at regular intervals . . . For this reason it is better to speak of the first 'hearers' of Revelation, rather than the 'readers.'"[94] It will be defended in the chapters that follow that Collins assertion is accurate, but again, her scholarly contribution goes no further than simply to state this as an assumed fact and then move on. There is no concern to validate this claim or analyze the text *as* a text for performance. Collins advances toward the oral performance at least in small measure by stating that the

---

91. Mounce, *Book of Revelation*, 66.
92. Collins, *Crisis and Catharsis*, 144.
93. Collins, *Crisis and Catharsis*, 144.
94. Collins, *Crisis and Catharsis*, 144.

Apocalypse "is as evocative as it is expressive,"[95] inviting imaginative participation from the audience, but this is as far as she goes.

In *The Combat Myth in the Book of Revelation*, Collins posits that John's Apocalypse follows an episodic pattern modeled after ancient near eastern combat mythology.[96] The structure of the book, according to Collins, is cyclical, retelling the story from the shared mythological background. For Collins, then, the "combat myth is the conceptual framework which underlies the book as a whole."[97] While the present writer does not follow Collins at every turn, her suggestion that the book follows an episodic and cyclical pattern is instructive to the present book, as this sort of episodic storytelling betrays a culture experienced in hearing narratives read orally.

David E. Aune

The trend continues in the *Word Biblical Commentary*'s nearly 1,300 page multi-volume work published in 1997. Aune's introduction alone is over two hundred pages and examines seemingly every significant issue related to rightly understanding the book, yet again, there is no mention of the aural reception of the text. Aune's presentation of the apocalyptic features, grammatical features, structural features, and literary features is impressive and detailed, and many of these serve the student of the book of Revelation well, including the analyst looking for performance elements in the text. In fact, Aune's contributions here are excellent and will be utilized in the investigation below. What is significant for the present purpose, however, is the omission of the performance situational context of Revelation. Like many who came before and after him, Aune addresses the issue in passing while exegeting Rev 1:3. Aune's thorough comment, though, stands above the rest. He notes that terms for reading and hearing in antiquity were often synonymous, that reading silently was quite rare, and that texts were often read silently only to then be performed publicly by rhetoricians from memory.[98] He even suggests that this recognition has "important interpretive significance, for ancient authors not only chose words to convey the meanings they intended but also chose

---

95. Collins, *Crisis and Catharsis*, 145.
96. Collins, *Combat Myth*, 207–31.
97. Collins, *Combat Myth*, 231.
98. Aune, *Revelation*, 20–21.

words whose *sounds* effectively communicated those meanings."[99] Later, Aune goes even further, positing that the blessing of Rev 1:3 "makes it evident that the author intended, even designed, his composition to be read aloud before Christian congregations assembled for worship."[100] The present author would agree heartily, yet in the commentary that follows, Aune provides very little interaction with this rather significant claim. Indeed, the omission of such an assertion and development of a methodology for analyzing this assertion in the general introduction to the commentary is remarkable.

G. K. Beale

Beale's impressive commentary is thought of by many as the gold-standard in scholarship on the book of Revelation.[101] This work stretches nearly 1,200 pages, with the introduction alone numbering over 170 pages.[102] Beale's analysis is thoughtful, detailed, exegetical, and comprehensive. Yet even in this massive work, the oral features receive only passing remarks. In detailing the literary outline of the book as a whole, Beale suggests that the broad structural markers of the book are determined by the text's literary design, noting that the repetition of the phrase ἐγενόμην ἐν πνεύματι ("I was in the Spirit," NASB) or ἀπήνεγκέν με ἐν πνεύματι ("he carried me away in the Spirit," NASB) in 1:10; 4:2; 17:3; and 21:10 form the basic literary structure of the book, dividing it into four broad movements.[103]

This broad structural layout aligns with Bauckham's and follows the narrative staging that Bauckham suggests would be easily discernible to the listening audience. In this, Beale's contribution is to be commended. Pertinent to the present inquiry, though, it is in this presentation regarding the structural layout of the book that Beale notes, "John used verbal repetition to indicate these broad divisions of the book because

---

99. Aune, *Revelation*, 21.

100. Aune, *Revelation*, 23.

101. Among many blogposts by pastors and scholars recommending Revelation commentaries, this one is almost always in the top three and often the highest rated. It is also the highest rated on the commentary review website, bestcommentaries.com.

102. The book is so influential, a shorter volume was published sixteen years later: Beale, *Revelation: A Shorter Commentary*.

103. Beale, *Book of Revelation*, 11. This is in line with Bauckham's macro-structural divisions as well.

oral recitation would require such structural markers, so that the hearers would be enabled better to perceive these divisions."[104] This follows the trend among many of the most reputable scholars of John's Apocalypse in that Beale makes a passing comment regarding the oral delivery and reception of the text, and yet goes no further in analyzing the text for its oral performance features.

Grant R. Osborne

Following Aune, Osborne's commentary published in 2002 is readable and thorough. Like many who came before him, Osborne notes the four primary problems scholars face when reading Revelation: the symbolism, the structure, the strategy for interpretation, and the author's use of the Old Testament. Osborne's review of these problems and proposals for solutions provides great benefit for any student of the book of Revelation, and indeed most of his fifty-page introduction is dedicated to this end. What is noteworthy, however, is Osborne's brief interaction with David L. Barr's[105] suggestion that the book is "not just literary but oral."[106] Osborne summarizes Barr's proposal with approval, then quickly brushes it aside to attend to matters of genre. In fact, Osborne's development of this crucial element garners only three sentences in the introduction. Again, following the established trend, in the exegesis of Rev 1:3, Osborne notes that "John intended the book for oral reading in a ritual setting,"[107] even detailing the likely number of readers in the early church adopted from Jewish practice. Still, no methodology for validating this claim is provided, nor a methodology for analyzing the text's oral performance features.

Stephen S. Smalley

Collins's proposal is followed by Stephen S. Smalley, who does not affirm that the combat myth lies as the conceptual framework for the whole book but does affirm the episodic nature of the book of Revelation's narrative framework. For Smalley, the book of Revelation is not ordered according to temporal chronology, rather it is "theologically and thematically

---

104. Beale, *Book of Revelation*, 11.
105. Barr will be presented below in the review of literature.
106. Osborne, *Revelation*, 12.
107. Osborne, *Revelation*, 57.

conceived."[108] Smalley notes how the drama of the Apocalypse builds again and again to a hoped-for resolution, only to withhold such resolution repeatedly.[109] For Smalley, this creates a dramatic suspense that cycles throughout the book of Revelation, reflecting elements popular in Greek drama.[110] For the purposes of the present book, this contention requires further exploration, to which Smalley heartily agrees:

> Scholars have seemed reluctant to explore the idea that the Apocalypse *in toto* has been arranged as a sustained and carefully constructed dramatic presentation. It appears to me that Revelation lends itself naturally to such an interpretation, and that to approach the work in terms of its dramatic structure throws floods of light on John's central testimony.[111]

Smalley's proposal forms part of the motivation for the present investigation.

Craig R. Koester

Koester provides a brilliant overview of the way in which Revelation has been interacted with by scholars through the two-thousand-year history of the church. Additionally, much of his introduction provides the reader with literary features that will be considered in this book below. These narrative literary devices, such as the way characters are portrayed and grouped, the development of plot and pace, and the frequent use of hymns or songs that serve to unify the audience in a liturgical setting, receive analysis and attention from Koester, and here his work must be commended. However, in his nearly 150-page introduction, he makes no mention of the nature of oral culture in the Roman world, nor does he explore the way in which Revelation would have been performed or heard. This omission would be easily overlooked if not for the translator's note he provides for Rev 1:3. Here, Koester, following the same trend, posits that the book of Revelation would have been presented "orally in a group setting."[112] He then goes on to provide three precedents for why

---

108. Smalley, *Revelation to John*, 19. Smalley here cites Fiorenza, *Book of Revelation*, 163.
109. Smalley, *Revelation to John*, 20.
110. Smalley, *Revelation to John*, 20.
111. Smalley, *Revelation to John*, 20.
112. Koester, *Revelation*, 213.

this sort of expectation would have been normal in the early church. Yet, Koester does not analyze the text of Revelation for features of oral performance and this lack of attention to these features forms the purpose for this present book.

Buist A. Fanning

Fanning's contribution in his commentary published in the *Exegetical Commentary on the New Testament* in 2020 is comprehensive and skillful in articulating and explaining the significant factors that make interpretation and understanding of the book of Revelation difficult. His introduction spans over fifty pages, exploring issues of authorship, structure, symbolism, use of the Old Testament, and interpretive strategy, yet nowhere in this detailed introduction does Fanning provide analysis of the oral culture of the first century or offer methodology for analyzing features of orality. What is more, this introduction nowhere articulates that the book of Revelation was originally designed for oral performance. In a commentary written nearly thirty years after Bauckham that interacts with Bauckham extensively, this is at least a curious omission.

Strikingly, however, as Fanning moves to the exegesis section of the commentary and in the comments concerning Rev 1:3, he acknowledges that the blessing Μακάριος ὁ ἀναγινώσκων καὶ οἱ ἀκούοντες (Blessed is the one reading aloud and the ones hearing) "comes from the common practice in the ancient world of a lector reading a text out loud in the hearing of others—something required by the lower levels of literacy and publication prevalent in those days."[113] He goes on to recognize that even "private reading was typically done audibly to oneself rather than silently as we are accustomed to do" and that "reading Scripture in the worship service was the expected practice, and communicated addressed to the churches in general would be read aloud to the whole community when they gathered."[114] While Fanning's commentary interacts with literary features that require attention in the present study, such as verbal aspect, structural markers, and repetition, the commentary does not develop a methodology for either validating the situational context of the aural performance of Revelation or the implications for composition and meaning of a text created for such a performance. Here, the trend is clear: briefly

---

113. Fanning, *Revelation*, 78.
114. Fanning, *Revelation*, 78.

acknowledge that the book of Revelation was almost certainly read aloud to its original hearers in passing on verse 3 while largely ignoring this axiom in analyzing the text itself.

The Orality of Revelation in General-Reference Works

Douglas J. Moo and D. A. Carson's *An Introduction to the New Testament* exposes students to the multifaceted and complex world of New Testament studies with a succinct general overview of the world of the New Testament as well as the individual texts within the New Testament corpus. In their treatment on Revelation, however, no mention is made concerning either the oral reception of Revelation or the situational context of its reading to the early churches. There is a brief examination of the proposed occasion for the book,[115] but the features of oral performance are not articulated in any way, not even in a footnote. This pattern is continued in N. T. Wright and Michael F. Bird's New Testament introduction, *The New Testament in Its World*. Here, the various issues and points of contention concerning the book are explored, as well as a brief commentary, but only in passing in the form of a parenthesis do the authors acknowledge the corporate and aural performance of the book of Revelation.[116]

In *Discourse Analysis of the New Testament Writings*, a collection of scholars contributed their methodology and application of discourse analysis to each of the New Testament texts. Each scholar proposed a methodology appropriate for the text assigned to them, making each chapter unified in that each chapter applied tools from the field of discourse analysis, but also different in that each scholars' methods were varied slightly. Stephen Pattemore wrote the chapter exploring the book of Revelation, imposing Relevance Theory adopted largely from Regina Blass's *Relevance Relations in Discourse: A Study with Special Reference to Sissala*. For Pattemore, a central dictum appropriated from Blass is this: "Every part of a narrative must be there for a reason," and is either relevant in its own right or in the way it contributes to the relevance of later material.[117] Another primary axiom suggested from Blass and employed by Pattemore is that "a unit of text is a unit of relevance if relevance is

---

115. Carson, *Introduction*, 697–725.
116. Wright, *New Testament*, 830.
117. Pattemore, "Revelation," 717.

REVIEW OF LITERATURE 63

optimized over it."[118] While Pattemore provides some important insights to the macro-structure of the book of Revelation, he fails to articulate the way in which the orality of the ancient Roman world effects the composition of the book of Revelation. In fact, the oral performance of the book is never addressed in any meaningful way in Pattemore's essay. All of these general-reference works provide helpful introductory material, survey the significant points of contention among scholars, and seek to aid the student of the Scriptures in understanding the New Testament text, and yet none of them offer a robust awareness of the lack of literacy and the prevalence of orality in the ancient world.

This sampling of noteworthy scholars is representative of many in the academic field.[119] It is the assumption of the present author that because the book of Revelation has so much material that is debated, difficult, and significant for interpretation, commentators and experts simply do not have adequate space to explore the oral performance features in great detail. Others simply may have failed to truly appreciate the oral nature of the first century Roman world, unable to see beyond the fog of the modern literate world and into the ancient one. Even Bauckham, whose provocative statement begins his commentary and this section of the review of literature, only briefly returns to articulate the "relatively obvious" structural features of the book, but then explores at great length the "fuller meaning" that progressively reading the written text yields through "closer acquaintance and assiduous study."[120] To be sure, Bauckham notes how the structural clues both guide the listening audience as well as build suspense and anticipation (and these will be utilized in the analysis below), but his main emphasis turns quickly from the obvious markers of oral performance to the more intricate features only accessible from reading and re-reading the text in written form.[121]

118. Pattemore, "Revelation," 710.

119. This survey has interacted so far with many of the most comprehensive commentaries analyzing Revelation. Other scholars, however, likewise follow the approach of these commentaries and, for the sake of space, must be simply acknowledged here. The following scholars both articulate a possible oral or liturgical reception of the Apocalypse yet provide no further analysis or methodology for approaching the text as such. Fiorenza, "Composition and Structure," 344–66; Bandy, "Layers of the Apocalypse," 469–99; Jang, "Narrative Plot," 381–90.

120. Bauckham, *Climax of Prophecy*, 1.

121. It is a bit subjective to say this, and the evidence is simply on the weighting of material covering these more obvious aspects and the more intricate details of structure only available to the more discerning and literate mind. The subjectivity involves articulating which features would be "obvious" as opposed to opaque. Bauckham gives

Most of these scholars have articulated *that* the book of Revelation was most likely experienced as an oral performance heard out loud as opposed to silent reading of a written text. Bauckham and Aune have even suggested that the book of Revelation was *designed* with this oral performance in mind. Many of these scholars have carefully articulated literary features, grammatical features, and structural features important for interpreting the text, and much of that work is commendable. However, most of these scholars provide almost no analysis of the way in which sounds were employed by the author to develop the story, the way in which the oral culture of the first century constrained lengthy linear plot development, the episodic nature of the book of Revelation,[122] or markers for memory in performance. Methodology for exploring such features is also lacking. Following Bauckham's proposal, however, there are scholars who emphasize these features more readily.

Scholarship Exploring Oral Features of Revelation

James L. Resseguie

In his 2009 narrative commentary, James Resseguie explores the book of Revelation as a narrative first and foremost. The first sentence of the introduction invites the reader to interact with his thesis that careful attention to how the narrative is constructed is central to understanding the meaning. According to Resseguie, the analyst must first enter John's apocalyptic world in order "to see what John sees and to hear what he hears."[123] This commentary provides something of a breath of fresh air to the ongoing scholarly conversation regarding the book of Revelation, as Resseguie insists that the book of Revelation is intended to be understood as a narrative and that the drama and development of the plot, setting, character development, as well as the way in which John's rhetorical style accomplishes the aims of his composition. Resseguie does not view the grammatical infelicities as a sign of an unintentional mistake by an incompetent author, but rather as form part of his "overall strategy to

---

no criteria for such an investigation, and it is the purpose of this book to provide a more workable methodology for determining features that would be easily ascertainable to the listening audience.

122. For an exception here, see Aune's comment on the episodic nature of apocalyptic literature in *Revelation*, lxxxii.

123. Resseguie, *Revelation of John*, 17.

force the reader and listener to pay attention."[124] Resseguie's work is to be commended for its ability to sharpen the focus of scholarship of Revelation in order to clearly see the way in which a narrative such as this was crafted and what effect it may have on the reader.

For the purposes of this investigation, however, Resseguie's work, while rightly employing narrative discourse features[125] (some of which will be utilized in the analysis below), his work does not go far enough in establishing how both the performer and listener would have interacted with a text read out loud. For example, in noting John's use of numbering throughout the book of Revelation, Resseguie does what most scholars do, which is provide a detailed analysis of the way in which numbers symbolize certain thematic elements within the book. This analysis in his commentary persists for nearly five pages. At the beginning of this section, he suggests that "numbers place boundaries on activities and happenings; accent a character's traits; or reinforce an ideological point of view."[126]

The present author agrees, but Resseguie provides no further analysis of the use of numbering for aid in memory or listener reception. Yet all the while, Resseguie at least acknowledges that the book of Revelation was likely orally received:

> The double blessing [of Rev 1:3] suggests a liturgical setting for the book in which a lector reads the book while an audience listens to the words. Hearing, however, involves more than listening to a lector; it requires attentive listening that internalizes and obeys the words that are read.[127]

Resseguie has furthered the scholarly discussion for the purposes of this investigation, however, in that he consistently approaches his analysis of the book from a narrative literary perspective. This contribution enables the student of Revelation to move beyond the prevalent issues important

---

124. Resseguie, *Revelation of John*, 48.

125. Resseguie served as an external reader for a book presented to Southeastern Baptist Theological Seminary published in 2019 by David Blaine Wagner Phillips. Here, Phillips follows Barr and Resseguie in examining the book of Revelation from a narrative perspective, suggesting the way in which 19:11–16 serves as the narrative climax. Phillips notes the way in which suspense and tension build in the narrative, eventually giving way to the resolution that climaxes in chapter 19, but he does not in any way interact with the narrative as one written for oral performance.

126. Resseguie, *Revelation of John*, 28.

127. Resseguie, *Revelation of John*, 64.

for scholarly inquiry into the book (the four listed by Osborne and detailed above) and instead approach the book of Revelation with a fresh awareness of its literary devices.

David L. Mathewson

While not a commentary on the book of Revelation, per se, Mathewson's important monograph (and shorter essay released two years prior)[128] interacts with the way in which the Greek verb is employed in John's Apocalypse. Again, it is beyond the scope of this book to wade into the deep waters of the current debate among scholars regarding the use of the Greek verb in the New Testament and elsewhere, but sufficient for the present purposes, Mathewson's contribution cannot be overlooked. Following Runge[129] and Porter,[130] in systematic and exhaustive fashion, Mathewson's *Verbal Aspect in the Book of Revelation: The Function of Greek Verb Tenses in John's Apocalypse*, published in 2010, explores how John functionally highlights or backgrounds characters and events within his narrative. Assuming various options for Greek verbs at his disposal, why did John choose the verb tenses he did in the places in which he did within his narrative? This question requires elucidation. Mathewson's proposal provides explanatory power for these choices, assuming the default option to be the aorist, and provides a potential tool to explore prominent events marked within the text.

Although Mathewson does not further develop the way in which John's use of verbal aspect indicates prominence *for* oral performance, his work serves as something of a guide for the present investigation. It will be posited in the analysis below that Mathewson's work not only sheds valuable light on characters and actions that John intends to highlight but also enables the skillful reader and hearer to "pick up" on these highlighted features in oral performance. Put simply, if Mathewson's proposal is valid, then the action marked for prominence by the choice of verbal aspect would be relevant for ancient performers of Revelation, as they would potentially signal prosody in public recitation.[131]

128. Mathewson, "Verbal Aspect," 58–77.
129. Runge, *Discourse Grammar*, 3–365.
130. See Porter's discussion of verbal opposition and planes of discourse sections in *Idioms*, 22–27.
131. Vansina, *Oral Tradition as History*, 3–54. See also Rhoads, "Performance Criticism, Pt. I," 121–26.

David L. Barr

Barr's contribution to the field of Revelation scholarship cannot be overlooked. Many scholars have been forced to interact with his proposals. In 1981, Barr presented a paper to the Society of Biblical Literature entitled "The Apocalypse as Symbolic Transformation of the World: A Literary Analysis," which was later edited for publication in 1984. In this article, Barr precedes Bauckham's suggestion that the obvious narrative features must be perceptible to the oral audience by stating that the structure of the book of Revelation consists of three clearly discernible great acts: "the risen Christ dictates seven letters; the Lamb opens a sealed book in a heavenly throne scene; the dragon makes war on the elect but loses, resulting in the replacement of the whore by the bride."[132] Barr sees a continuity of meaning, but not continuity of sequencing, as each act stands on its own.[133] Where Barr's work is instrumental for performance analysis of the Apocalypse stems from his recognition of the many ways in which the author addresses the audience directly.[134] For Barr, this betrays a framing technique which bridges the imagination of the audience from the "real world" to the unveiled fictive world of the narrative itself.[135] Following other scholars, Barr further notes that this feature would be highly significant in oral recitation to both situate the author authoritatively but also to transform the hearer personally. Barr suggests that the composition of the book of Revelation had a liturgical recital in mind, and that this "liturgical recital of the Apocalypse becomes a real experience of the Kingdom of God."[136] Here, Barr takes seriously the oral performance context of the book; but in an article published two years later, Barr takes his analysis a step further.

In 1986, Barr published "The Apocalypse of John as Oral Enactment." In this essay, Barr's thesis is clear from the beginning as he comments on John's insistence that Ὁ ἔχων οὖς ἀκουσάτω τί τὸ πνεῦμα λέγει ταῖς ἐκκλησίαις (The one having ears, hear what the spirit says to the churches [Rev 2:7]). Barr's contention is simple:

---

132. Barr, "Apocalypse as Symbolic Transformation," 39–50.

133. A weakness to Barr's theory, here, is that there is continuity between referents or symbols between acts, which he acknowledges.

134. See Rev 1:4–5; 13:9–10; 22:21; with more to be articulated in the analysis below.

135. Barr, "Apocalypse as Symbolic Transformation," 46.

136. Barr, "Apocalypse as Symbolic Transformation," 46.

> We [modern scholars] have so truncated our experience of hearing that we usually understand this plea as simply, 'pay attention,' but it is the thesis of this essay that the orality of the Apocalypse is an essential element of its hermeneutic. The original audience encountered it as an aural experience (Rev 1:3), and that experience determined both the way the Apocalypse is structured and the meaning the auditors found in it.[137]

In this essay, Barr then goes on to provide the starting point of a methodology for right investigation of the oral features of the text. He first notes that while the book is lengthy, it's reading normally takes roughly one hour to complete.[138] Barr continues by stating "that the prophet meant for the auditor to retain the structure of the work in memory seems likely. In fact, he provides a great deal of assistance,"[139] providing techniques that aid both performer and audience alike. Barr lists three primary techniques: the use of numbering sequences, the use of place and imagery, and the use of the scrolls.[140] Much of this material was detailed in the methodology section above and will be employed in the analysis below, as Barr provides a helpful tool in analyzing the text for markers for verbalization and oral-patterning.[141] Barr's interests lie largely in reenacting an oral situational setting, and to this endeavor his article aims. What is at least noteworthy is that these three techniques, while certainly important, form the only articulated methodological approach to analyzing the oral features of the book. There is nothing said about oral patterning, sound repetition, the episodic nature of the book, etc.

Barr's work on the Apocalypse has continued for decades, culminating in a narrative commentary first published in 1998. In *Tales of the End: A Narrative Commentary on the Book of Revelation*, like Resseguie above, Barr analyzes the text of Revelation as a narrative first and foremost, even acknowledging the narrative as one likely performed for an audience.[142] Later, Barr quotes from Dio Chrysostom's lament at the sheer noisiness of the ancient world, then recognizes that the ancient world was "a noisy world, because everybody did things out loud. More basically, all reading

---

137. Barr, "Apocalypse as Oral Enactment," 243.
138. Barr, "Apocalypse as Oral Enactment," 244.
139. Barr, "Apocalypse as Oral Enactment," 244.
140. Barr, "Apocalypse as Oral Enactment," 244–45.
141. See Osborne, *Revelation*, 12.
142. Barr, *Tales of the End*, 3.

was done aloud, even private reading."[143] Applying this to his investigation of Revelation, Barr notes that "Revelation itself clearly shows itself to be an oral experience, mentioning the public reader (1:3) and repeatedly urging the audience to listen."[144] What is more, in summary of his introduction to the commentary, Barr again states that the Apocalypse "is a text meant to be read aloud. Such an aural appropriation of the story would not fixate on small details and would not demand exact consistency. The author of the Apocalypse narrated his vision so that the hearers of the story might share that experience.

For Barr, hearing Revelation was an experience meant to transform the listener."[145] Yet much of this commentary concerns itself with the way in which the narrative features of the text work together. Important as these features are to the understanding of the text, Barr provides little further methodology than has been articulated here. *That* Revelation was orally performed, Barr is clear. *That* Revelation is a narrative meant to invite the listening audience in, Barr is clear. *That* Revelation's structure and design must be rightly discernible to a listening audience, Barr is clear. *How* the book of Revelation's oral features were composed and cued for the reader and the performer, Barr is more opaque. Barr suggests three characteristics that signal orality, and these will be considered in the analysis below, yet a methodology for studying the text as a text composed for performance is not offered.

Raymond Brewer

Following the work of F. Palmer at the turn of the twentieth century, in 1936, Raymond Brewer published "The Influence of Greek Drama on the Apocalypse of John." In this fascinating article, Brewer explored the way in which the "dramatic power of the book presupposes some acquaintance with the choral music and the histrionic art of the only drama the people of the day knew."[146] Brewer's analysis of the repetition of the choral material enables the analyst of the oral performance of Revelation to appreciate that these repeated choruses form "the bond between the lyric and the dramatic elements in the plot . . . and are the bond of unity

---

143. Barr, *Tales of the End*, 10.
144. Barr, *Tales of the End*, 10.
145. Barr, *Tales of the End*, 39.
146. Brewer, "Influence of the Greek," 79.

running through the swiftly moving action and the ever shifting scenes of the book."[147] In a text designed for performance, such repetition must be considered, and Brewer's article enters the scholarly conversation with force. Brewer's theory was embraced by later scholars, notably Stephen S. Smalley, who lamented in his 2005 commentary that "scholars have seemed reluctant to explore the idea that the Apocalypse *in toto* has been arranged as a sustained and carefully constructed dramatic presentation . . . and that to approach the work in terms of its dramatic structure throws floods of light on John's central testimony."[148] Elizabeth Schüssler Fiorenza responds with something of a caution, however, noting a few of the differences between a true Greek drama and the book of Revelation.[149]

David Seal

More recently, in "The Reception and Delivery of the Oracle in Revelation 13:9–10," David Seal works from an assumption that the book of Revelation was likely heard orally, noting that "the oral cultural context from which [New Testament books] originated decisively shaped their form and contents and must, therefore, be considered for analysis."[150] In this, Seal accepts Bauckham's axiom. While Seal applies this to the direct address to the audience in Rev 13:9–10, the point for this review of literature remains simple: Revelation scholars are more widely exploring the text as a text for performance. Seal posits that as the poetic oracle contained in these two verses "was brought to life by the lector, the audience would have recognized its unique language, which perhaps would have alerted them to the importance of the communication, its divine origin, and the need for it to be considered dependable and binding."[151] Seal's insights are important but limited.

Hanre Janse van Rensburg

Hanre Janse van Rensburg's 2019 article published in *HTS Theological Studies* analyzes the book of Revelation as a performative text and does so

---

147. Brewer, "Influence of the Greek," 90–91.
148. Smalley, *Revelation to John*, 20.
149. Fiorenza, "Composition and Structure," 353–55.
150. Seal, "Reception and Delivery," 9–10.
151. Seal, "Reception and Delivery," 10.

with zeal. She states that most within the scholarly field "do not recognize the Apocalypse's power as performative text."[152] Additionally, she chides scholars for becoming so "engrossed with studying the different aspects of Revelation—whether it be textual, symbolic, historical, and so on—that [they] have lost sight of the [performance] stage."[153] She laments that "in most cases, even when we as biblical scholars and exegetes do acknowledge the key performative aspect of the Apocalypse, it is not necessarily explored in any further detail."[154] The present writer agrees heartily as this review of literature has hoped to demonstrate. Janse van Rensburg's critique, however, comes with a summons to again appreciate the performative aspects of Revelation that would have engaged the ancient (and modern) audience. She suggests a liturgical-functional methodology for analysis of the book, looking for the affect the reader would embody and signal to eager listeners.

While some of her methodology would take this present investigation outside its present scope, Janse van Rensburg's aim is to "identify and start exploring a method of exegesis of the text which allows [scholars] to, once again, physically participate in the Book of Revelation."[155] For Janse van Rensburg, this method of exegesis largely involves exploring the repeated words and formulas, particularly in prayers and songs. As articulated in the methodology section above, such repetition of sounds, words, and formulas create mnemonic aids for the performer and helpful guides for the audience, which Janse van Rensburg suggests "play an essential part in the narrative's emotive and evocative impact."[156] What makes Janse van Rensburg's article so significant for the present inquiry concerns her insistence on the performance of the text, noting how the text betrays cues for "gestures that can be used when partaking in performative actions,"[157] sensory pageantry, and sacral architecture. Bauckham's axiom is receiving its necessary attention.

---

152. Janse van Rensburg, "All the Apocalypse," 1.
153. Janse van Rensburg, "All the Apocalypse," 2.
154. Janse van Rensburg, "All the Apocalypse," 2.
155. Janse van Rensburg, "All the Apocalypse," 3.
156. Janse van Rensburg, "All the Apocalypse," 3.
157. Janse van Rensburg, "All the Apocalypse," 4–5.

Kayle B. de Waal

While many more scholars could be brought into the discussion, one remains whose voice requires an audience. Kayle B. de Waal serves as the Head of the Avondale Seminary and Senior Lecturer in New Testament at Avondale College in Australia and has published two significant monographs for Revelation studies. The first, *A Socio-Rhetorical Interpretation of the Seven Trumpets of Revelation* was published in 2012 and examines the trumpet scene beginning in Rev 8:2 from what de Waal calls a "Socio-Rhetorical Interpretation," which focuses on "values, convictions, and beliefs as discovered in the text as well as in the world in which we live,"[158] and is largely not pertinent to the present investigation. De Waal's 2015 monograph *An Aural-Performance Analysis of Revelation 1 and 11*, however, speaks loudly and with importance into the present scholarly conversation. Janse van Rensburg laments that many scholars have lost sight of the performance of the Apocalypse, but no such lament is necessary for de Waal. De Waal articulates that his study is "an investigation into the aural and performative elements of Revelation that focuses on ancient media culture as these features have been neglected in scholarship on Revelation,"[159] which aims to "demonstrate that the early Christians heard and experienced the message of Revelation through a dynamic reading and that this experiential communal approach to understanding has been overlooked by the scholarly community."[160]

This impressive monograph begins by providing a detailed and thorough methodology for approaching the study of Revelation as a text for performance. This methodology serves as the most formative guide for the present book, combining elements of oral-biblical criticism and biblical performance criticism. Although the methodology proposed for this investigation aims to employ narrative discourse analysis techniques more thoroughly, de Waal blazes the trail for analysts of the oral performance of Revelation to follow. In addition to providing a working methodology, de Waal also interacts with multiple scholars in a brief literature review before turning to application of his methodology on chapters 1 and 11 of Revelation. He first breaks the text into cola and periods, analyzes these for repetition and patterning, provides a social-rhetorical analysis in the form of a brief commentary, then makes suggestions for

---

158. de Waal, *Socio-Rhetorical Interpretation*, 4.
159. de Waal, *Aural-Performance Analysis*, 1.
160. de Waal, *Aural-Performance Analysis*, 3.

prosody and gesturing in the performance of the text. Much of this methodology will be mirrored in the analysis below. Suffice it to say, Kayle B. de Waal's contribution to the present conversation is significant, enabling the student to appreciate and analyze the oral performance features of the text with a rigorous and defensible approach.

Summary of Literature Review

While scholars of Revelation have tended to gravitate toward many significant and controversial issues regarding the text and its interpretation, many have simply brushed passed one of the most salient and foundational questions that must be answered in order to properly understand an utterance, namely: through what kind of medium was the message delivered and received?[161] If the culture of the Roman world was largely illiterate, interacting with text (even written texts) primarily through the oral reading of the text to the listening ear, then the way in which authors compose their texts with this occasion in mind must be considered in analyzing a text.

Most scholars undertaking the difficult task of writing a technical commentary on the book of Revelation either ignore this salient question or push it to a passing comment or footnote. As such, no methodology for exploring further the way in which the aural performance of the text is offered, and no analysis provided. Many, in fact, continue on as if these factors have no bearing on the meaning of the text at all. This consistent omission necessitates further development. Indeed, some recent contributors appreciate the need to allow Revelation to be studied with its narrative features in full view, still many fail to articulate the way in which narratives were publicly performed in antiquity. While Janse van Rensburg and de Waal come closest in that they both argue for a methodology with aural performance mind and then apply it to the text of Revelation, the narrative discourse features and episodic nature of the text remains undeveloped. De Waal certainly furthers the discussion, but more work is needed.

The first purpose of this book, then, is to further develop a working methodology for such analysis. Such methodology must be eclectic in nature, combining elements from many of the fields and many of the scholars surveyed in this literature review. This methodology enables both a bottom-up examination as well as a top-down episodic and

---

161. McLuhan, *Understanding Media*, 7.

narrative approach. Secondly, in step with Janse van Rensburg and de Waal, cues for prosody in the performance must be identified and reviewed. Finally, with these twin purposes accomplished, the thesis that the book of Revelation was indeed composed for aural performance may be verified. It is the humble objective of the present author to contribute this evaluation to the ongoing conversation regarding John's Apocalypse, and to that objective this study now turns.

3

Performance Analysis of a Theophany Scene

INTRODUCTION TO REV 4–5

As demonstrated in the literature review above, many scholars devoted to the book of Revelation acknowledge that the book was most likely intended for oral recitation. The audience of this oral performance, the listening community of Jesus-followers in the first century, heard the text; they did not read it. This is necessary given the relatively low literacy rates and the value placed on reading aloud. Thus, in agreement with Richard Bauckham, it is worth remembering that John was writing in the first place for hearers. In chapter 1, a methodology was proposed for this investigation combining elements from several different scholarly fields—oral-biblical criticism, discourse analysis, and biblical performance criticism—with the goal of analyzing the book of Revelation with the hearer in mind. Since choice implies meaning, it becomes important to examine the text of Revelation from syllables to story, keeping in mind that in the ancient Greco-Roman world, "grammar was typically defined as the science of sound."[1] In this particular chapter, points of comparison with the theophany scene in Rev 1 will be noted in the footnotes throughout, with the aim of corroborating the methodology as well as the selection of material analyzed in this book as representative of the whole.

---

1. Dean, "Grammar of Sound," 58.

THE SCIENCE OF SOUND IN REV 4–5

In application of the proposed methodology, the first step involves the development of a sound map of the representative portions of the book of Revelation under study.[2] This sound map was produced with the length of speaker's breath in mind[3] and shaped by the present author's repeated oral readings of the Greek text, as well as many aural hearings of the Greek text read aloud by modern Greek speakers.[4] Sound maps enable the student to visually see the text's sound patterns and repetition, proceeding colon by colon, breath by breath,[5] providing clarity for the analyst to see significant features within the text.[6]

In the sound map which follows, cola are visually represented and numbered in order to make reference easier. Colometric boundaries often circumscribe a sense unit and are often controlled by a finite verb or other verbal element.[7] The cola are combined into periods, grouped paratactically, or through grammatical or narrative subordination.[8] Periods combine cola functionally, not formally, and comprise individual units of the discourse.[9] These periods are also numbered in the sound map below. Periods combine to form narrative units, and in the book of Revelation, these are often marked structurally. These narrative units will be referred to in this paper as scenes, which will be examined much more thoroughly in the pages below; but for the purposes of the sound map, however, scenes are also labeled and numbered.[10] To make recognition of patterns and repetition clearer, visual aids were applied to this sound map: words or phrases used more than once in any period are underlined.[11]

---

2. Lee, *Sound Mapping*, 168.

3. Lee, *Sound Mapping*, 169.

4. This was accomplished by listening to the Greek text read by modern Greek speakers in audio form online.

5. Lee, *Sound Mapping*, 168.

6. Lee, *Sound Mapping*, 385.

7. Lee, *Sound Mapping*, 169.

8. Lee, *Sound Mapping*, 171.

9. Lee, *Sound Mapping*, 109.

10. Scenes then combine into scenes, which form the main acts that make up the book of Revelation. Granted, there is debate concerning the way these scenes and acts interact, but the language of scene and act will be utilized in later sections of the present analysis.

11. Articles and conjunctions were excluded, as well as καί.

Additionally, the quality of John's style must be appreciated. Indeed, to some in the ancient world, the quality of the sound was as important if not more important than the content.[12] Since texts were expected to be read aloud, ancient composers combined sounds and sound-groups, working with the audience's ears in mind, rather than their eyes.[13] Sound quality can be recognized as either austere or polished, creating dissonance or harmony in the ears of the listener.[14] Quintilian, the ancient rhetorician, noted sound quality's significance: "In the first place, nothing can penetrate to the emotions that stumbles at the portals of the ear, and secondly man is naturally attracted by harmonious sounds."[15] These features will be noted in the analysis that follows each period or group of periods.

Sound Map of Rev 4:1—5:14 with Analysis

Scene 1 (Rev 4:1-11)

Period 1 (4:1)

1. <u>Μετὰ ταῦτα</u> εἶδον,
2. καὶ ἰδοὺ
3. θύρα ἠνεῳγμένη ἐν τῷ οὐρανῷ,
4. καὶ ἡ φωνὴ ἡ πρώτη ἣν ἤκουσα
5. ὡς σάλπιγγος λαλούσης μετ' ἐμοῦ λέγων·
6. ἀνάβα ὧδε,
7. καὶ δείξω σοι ἃ δεῖ γενέσθαι <u>μετὰ ταῦτα</u>.

The dominant vowel sounds in the opening of this scene are the most pleasant α/αι and η sounds, and this period contains very few examples of the thin ε sound. Additionally, the vowels enjoy a flowing and open sound, with limited harsh consonants, employing a majority of liquid consonants throughout. The lack of sharp stops caused by repeated consonant sounds is avoided, creating a soft melody throughout.

---

12. From Quintilian, *Institutio Oratia*, 9.4.10. Sourced from Lee, *Sound Mapping*, 176–79.

13. Harvey, *Listening to the Text*, 42.

14. Lee, *Sound Mapping*, 176–79.

15. From Quintilian, *Institutio Oratia*, 9.4.10. Sourced from Lee, *Sound Mapping*, 176–79.

The repetition of the harsh σ consonant in the fifth colon, ὡς σάλπιγγος λαλούσης (as a trumpet speaking), may be intentional, as the comparison is made to the sound of a trumpet. John employed the technique of rounding in this opening period, repeating μετὰ ταῦτα (after this) in the first and last cola, in order to mark the structural change of the narrative. This repetition reenforces for the audience the change of scene to the heavenly throne room before continuing with the narrative.

Period 2 (4:2–3)

1. Εὐθέως ἐγενόμην ἐν πνεύματι,
2. καὶ ἰδοὺ <u>θρόνος</u> ἔκειτο ἐν τῷ οὐρανῷ,
3. καὶ ἐπὶ τὸν <u>θρόνον</u> καθήμενος,
4. καὶ ὁ καθήμενος
5. <u>ὅμοιος</u> <u>ὁράσει</u> λίθῳ ἰάσπιδι καὶ σαρδίῳ,
6. καὶ ἶρις κυκλόθεν τοῦ <u>θρόνου</u>
7. <u>ὅμοιος</u> <u>ὁράσει</u> σμαραγδίνῳ.

Both o/ω and ει/ι are the main vowel sounds in this period, and both were considered to be pleasant to the ear. Additionally, liquid consonants again occur throughout, keeping the melody easy to both speak aloud and enjoyable to the ear. The repetition of κ brings a repeated voiceless stop pattern to the sound of this period, but again the melody has a smooth and open quality. Repeating elements θρόνος, καθήμενος, ὅμοιος, and ὁράσει serve both to create symmetry as well as to emphasize the majesty of the one seated on the throne for the audience.

Period 3 (4:4)

1. Καὶ κυκλόθεν τοῦ <u>θρόνου</u>
2. <u>Θρόνους</u> <u>εἴκοσι</u> <u>τέσσαρες</u>,
3. καὶ ἐπὶ τοὺς <u>θρόνους</u>
4. <u>εἴκοσι</u> <u>τέσσαρας</u> πρεσβυτέρους καθημένους
5. περιβεβλημένους ἐν ἱματίοις λευκοῖς
6. καὶ ἐπὶ τὰς κεφαλὰς αὐτῶν στεφάνους χρυσοῦς.

The third period contains a nice balance of euphonic and cacophonous sounds, as long vowels o/ου/ω dominate the period. This is balanced, however, with the less pleasant repetition of the sibilate ς sound both at the end of many of the words as well as repeated phrase εἴκοσι τέσσαρες (twenty-four). The mix of soft consonants with voiceless stops and voiceless aspirates make the period much more irregular than the first two, but the repeated words and phrases creates an almost ceremonial feel, which is suited for the content of the period itself.

Period 4 (4:5–6a)

1. Καὶ ἐκ τοῦ <u>θρόνου</u>
2. ἐκπορεύονται ἀστραπαὶ καὶ φωναὶ καὶ βρονταί,
3. καὶ <u>ἑπτὰ</u> λαμπάδες πυρὸς καιόμεναι
4. <u>ἐνώπιον τοῦ θρόνου</u>,
5. ἅ εἰσιν τὰ <u>ἑπτὰ</u> πνεύματα τοῦ θεοῦ,
6. καὶ <u>ἐνώπιον τοῦ θρόνου</u> ὡς θάλασσα ὑαλίνη ὁμοία κρυστάλλῳ.

Things change with the movement to the fourth period, as multiple clusters of consonants (κλ, θρ, πρ) converge with multiple voiceless aspirates (θ, φ) and voiceless stops (κ, π, τ), adjusting the smooth rhythm created with the first two periods in this scene. This is highly appropriate given the mention of lightning and thunder and noise within the period itself. These sounds certainly alter the melody of the period, but this is balanced with the use of the most pleasant ἀ/αἰ sounds throughout. The elongation of the final colon, which closes the period, nicely serves to bring the period to a conclusion.

Period 5 (4:6b–7)

1. Καὶ ἐν μέσῳ τοῦ <u>θρόνου</u>
2. καὶ κύκλῳ τοῦ <u>θρόνου</u>
3. τέσσαρα <u>ζῷα</u> γέμοντα ὀφθαλμῶν ἔμπροσθεν καὶ ὄπισθεν.
4. καὶ τὸ <u>ζῷον</u> τὸ πρῶτον <u>ὅμοιον</u> λέοντι
5. καὶ τὸ δεύτερον <u>ζῷον</u> <u>ὅμοιον</u> μόσχῳ
6. καὶ τὸ τρίτον <u>ζῷον</u> ἔχων τὸ πρόσωπον ὡς ἀνθρώπου
7. καὶ τὸ τέταρτον <u>ζῷον</u> <u>ὅμοιον</u> ἀετῷ πετομένῳ.

The clear structuring technique to this period is the numbering of the living creatures, and the consistent use of long ῷ, ου, ὁ sounds provides a rhythmic and round meter. This is also achieved by introducing each of the creatures with identical language. Before the creatures are introduced, however, the third colon is both longer and more challenging to the speaker and hearer, combining voiceless aspirates, sibilants, and voiced aspirates. Given the consistency of the rest of the cola to follow, choosing to introduce the subsequent material this way may indicate intentionality.

Period 6 (4:7–8a)

1. καὶ τὰ τέσσαρα ζῷα,
2. ἓν καθ' ἓν αὐτῶν ἔχων ἀνὰ πτέρυγας ἕξ,
3. κυκλόθεν καὶ ἔσωθεν γέμουσιν ὀφθαλμῶν,
4. καὶ ἀνάπαυσιν οὐκ ἔχουσιν ἡμέρας καὶ νυκτὸς λέγοντες·

Period 7 (4:8b)

1. <u>ἅγιος ἅγιος ἅγιος</u>
2. κύριος ὁ θεὸς
3. ὁ παντοκράτωρ,
4. ὁ ἦν
5. καὶ ὁ ὢν
6. καὶ ὁ ἐρχόμενος.

These two periods work together, as Period 6 introduces the content of the recorded speech in Period 7. Both periods have a highly euphonic rhythm, mostly avoiding clustered consonants and unpleasant vowel sounds. The words flow nicely, one to another, and with a mix of vowels that were considered pleasant, especially α/αι. The thrice repeated ἅγιος (holy) serves an almost liturgical and climactic function, and the repetition of both the noun (ὁ παντοκράτωρ, "the almighty") and subsequent three participles, (ὁ ἦν, ὁ ὢν, ὁ ἐρχόμενος) all introduced with the article (ὁ) add to the climax. This is particularly felt with the single-syllable words that follow the article in cola four and five, followed by a four-syllable word in the sixth colon (ἐρχόμενος, "coming").

Period 8 (4:9–10)

1. Καὶ ὅταν δώσουσιν τὰ ζῷα δόξαν καὶ τιμὴν καὶ εὐχαριστίαν
2. τῷ <u>καθημένῳ</u> ἐπὶ τῷ <u>θρόνῳ</u>
3. τῷ ζῶντι <u>εἰς τοὺς αἰῶνας τῶν αἰώνων</u>,
4. πεσοῦνται οἱ εἴκοσι τέσσαρες πρεσβύτεροι

5. ἐνώπιον τοῦ καθημένου ἐπὶ τοῦ θρόνου

6. καὶ προσκυνήσουσιν τῷ ζῶντι εἰς τοὺς αἰῶνας τῶν αἰώνων

7. καὶ βαλοῦσιν τοὺς στεφάνους αὐτῶν ἐνώπιον τοῦ θρόνου λέγοντες·

Period 9 (4:11)

1. ἄξιος εἶ,

2. ὁ κύριος

3. καὶ ὁ θεὸς ἡμῶν,

4. λαβεῖν τὴν δόξαν καὶ τὴν τιμὴν καὶ τὴν δύναμιν,

5. ὅτι σὺ ἔκτισας τὰ πάντα

6. καὶ διὰ τὸ θέλημά σου ἦσαν

7. καὶ ἐκτίσθησαν.

Just as the previous two periods work together, so here. A regular use of both long ῷ, ου, ὁ vowels as well as the most pleasing α/αἰ vowels contribute to a euphonic meter that matches the tone and the content of the periods. Repeated elements (τοὺς αἰῶνας τῶν αἰώνων, δόξαν καὶ τὴν τιμὴν) further provide a sonorous echo, while the vowels within the spoken praise itself are open and wide (ὁ, α, ύ). Duvall notes that according to Suetonius, the phrase "you are worthy" was often used in welcoming and receiving the Roman emperor into a city, and that the title "our lord and god" was demanded by Emperor Domitian.[16] Four future tense verbs mirror the gravity of the doxology by mirroring sound and meter (δώσουσιν, πεσοῦνται, προσκυνήσουσιν, βαλοῦσιν).

Scene 2 (5:1–14)

Period 1 (5:1)

1. Καὶ εἶδον ἐπὶ τὴν δεξιὰν τοῦ καθημένου ἐπὶ τοῦ θρόνου βιβλίον

2. γεγραμμένον ἔσωθεν καὶ ὄπισθεν

3. κατεσφραγισμένον σφραγῖσιν ἑπτά.

---

16. Duvall, *Theology of Revelation*, 183.

The first scene that makes up chapter 4 of Revelation serves to establish the change of setting.[17] With the new setting now established (the heavenly throne room) and the characters within the room introduced (the one on the throne, the elders, and the four creatures), the action may now begin. In this next scene (Rev 5), the audience is directed again to the throne and introduced to a scroll. Several features combined to draw attention to the scroll. First, the period begins with Καὶ εἶδον (and I saw), which is a regular formula for introducing new material and marking discrete narrative elements in Revelation.[18] Second, the audience's mental picture is oriented back to the throne and the one seated on it, elements introduced at the beginning of the previous scene (Rev 4) that "help to organize the plot and facilitate the audience's visualization of narrated action."[19] Second, tail-head linkage of several words from the previous periods connect the material to follow with the prior worship scene. Third, John's variation of sound further aims attention at the scroll. The first colon is smooth and flowing, but that smooth meter gives way in the subsequent cola. The final colon contains two clusters of similar σφρ- sounds that are cacophonous and deliberately difficult to say. This is even more pronounced with the use of the difficult and cacophonous six-syllable word κατεσφραγισμένον (having been sealed), which is repeated immediately with the cacophonous σφραγῖσιν (seals). The sealed scroll will now function as the centerpiece for periods that follow.

Period 2 (5:2)

1. Καὶ εἶδον ἄγγελον ἰσχυρὸν κηρύσσοντα ἐν φωνῇ μεγάλῃ·
2. τίς ἄξιος ἀνοῖξαι τὸ βιβλίον
3. Καὶ λῦσαι τὰς σφραγῖδας αὐτοῦ;

This period is dominated with open ά/αι and ο/ω sounds throughout and has a pleasant meter as the syllables flow one to the next with few difficult clusters of consonants or hard stops, except for the reference to the previously introduced σφραγῖδας. These features would enable the announcement of the angel to be proclaimed clearly and with projection in public reading.

---

17. More will be said on this below.

18. Mathewson, "Verbal Aspect," 65. More will be explored regarding this structural device in the pages that follow.

19. Lee, *Sound Mapping*, 175.

Period 3 (5:3)

1. Καὶ <u>οὐδεὶς</u> ἐδύνατο ἐν τῷ οὐρανῷ
2. <u>οὐδὲ</u> ἐπὶ τῆς γῆς
3. <u>οὐδὲ</u> ὑποκάτω τῆς γῆς
4. ἀνοῖξαι τὸ βιβλίον
5. οὔτε βλέπειν αὐτό.

Period 4 (5:4)

1. Καὶ ἔκλαιον πολύ,
2. ὅτι οὐδεὶς ἄξιος εὑρέθη ἀνοῖξαι τὸ βιβλίον
3. οὔτε βλέπειν αὐτό.

Given the repetition of both sounds and words, periods 3 and 4 may be analyzed together. The diphthong οὐ permeates these periods, creating a dark meter that matches the content of these passages. This is further enhanced by the lack of harsh consonants, allowing the vowels to dominate the sound. In period 3, the triple negation powerfully responds to the question posed by the angel in the preceding period, and this negation is again reinforced in period 4.

Period 5 (5:5)

1. Καὶ εἷς ἐκ τῶν πρεσβυτέρων λέγει μοι·
2. μὴ κλαῖε,
3. ἰδοὺ ἐνίκησεν ὁ λέων
4. ὁ ἐκ τῆς φυλῆς Ἰούδα,
5. ἡ ῥίζα Δαυίδ,
6. ἀνοῖξαι τὸ βιβλίον καὶ τὰς ἑπτὰ σφραγῖδας αὐτοῦ.

The tone of lament gives way in this period to a more hopeful one, and the euphonic meter enhances the change. The dark οὐ sounds are mostly gone, replaced with the more pleasing α/αι vowels. Consonants are kept from clustering together, except for the again repeated and cacophonous σφρ- blend introduced in previous periods. Elongation serves to close the period as well as create suspense before the audience is shown the one who is finally able to open the scroll.

Period 6 (5:6)

1. Καὶ εἶδον <u>ἐν μέσῳ</u> τοῦ θρόνου
2. Καὶ τῶν τεσσάρων ζῴων
3. Καὶ <u>ἐν μέσῳ</u> τῶν πρεσβυτέρων
4. ἀρνίον ἑστηκὸς ὡς ἐσφαγμένον
5. ἔχων κέρατα <u>ἑπτὰ</u> καὶ ὀφθαλμοὺς <u>ἑπτὰ</u>
6. οἵ εἰσιν τὰ <u>ἑπτὰ</u> πνεύματα τοῦ θεοῦ
7. ἀπεσταλμένοι εἰς πᾶσαν τὴν γῆν.

John directs the attention back to the middle of the throne but doesn't immediately provide the audience with the anticipated answer to the question posed back in period 2. Instead, he restages the four creatures and the elders, employing a barrage of ου and ω vowels that provide a solemn and round sound. Then, as the lamb takes the stage, consonants cluster repeatedly. This has the effect of both adjusting the style but also forcing the reader to slow in order to rightly pronounce each syllable.

What is more, the deliberate "play" on sounds between ἐσφαγμένον (having been slain) and σφραγῖδας (seals) would be especially pronounced in oral performance. This "play" on sounds is a feature frequently missed by Revelation scholars.[20] In the first period of scene 2, the scroll was described as κατεσφραγισμένον σφραγῖσιν ἑπτά (sealed with seven seals). The σφρ- consonant blend[21] repeats again and again throughout the rest of this scene (S2:P2/Rev 5:2; S2:P5/Rev 5:5; S2:P9/Rev 5:9–10) making it noteworthy in and of itself,[22] but how it pairs with the description of the lamb is particularly remarkable.

The lamb is not merely a lamb, but it is said to be standing ὡς ἐσφαγμένον (as having been slain). This participle is repeated three times in the scene (Rev 5:6, 9, 12) and contains a σφ- consonant blend, making it nearly identical to the σφρ- blend, which introduced the sealed scroll. Indeed, to the ear, these two blends sound almost identical. Carefully, then, John weaves these two sounds into the scene. They are set in parallel

---

20. At least the present author has yet to come across a resource interacting with this concept.

21. This compound form of this verb is found only here in the New Testament. See Smalley, *Revelation to John*, 128.

22. de Waal, *Aural-Performance Analysis*, 7.

lines in the climactic song expressed at the end of the scene in S2:P9 (Rev 5:9–10):

καὶ ἀνοῖξαι τὰς **σφραγῖδας** αὐτοῦ,
ὅτι **ἐσφάγης**

Scholars have long noted the way in which John shifts the hearer's expectations from what John hears to what he then sees,[23] but have failed to also see how the sound choices reflected in the written text affect the listening audience. Techniques like this "play" on sound demonstrate John's creativity in composing his text for aural reception.[24]

Period 7 (5:7)

1. Καὶ ἦλθεν
2. καὶ εἴληφεν
3. ἐκ τῆς δεξιᾶς τοῦ καθημένου ἐπὶ τοῦ θρόνου.

Two verbs rush upon the audience almost rhythmically as the seventh period begins. While more will be said later in this chapter regarding the switch to the perfect in the second colon, it may be stated here that the more semantically marked perfect form of λαμβάνω provides a parallel in sound for the aorist in the first colon, enabling these two actions to smoothly flow together. The drama of the action is enhanced by the abruptness and simplicity of these two cola. The period is highly euphonic, with both liquid consonants that are smooth and flowing and voiceless stops that are clear and firm.

Period 8 (5:8–9)

1. Καὶ ὅτε ἔλαβεν τὸ βιβλίον,
2. τὰ τέσσαρα ζῷα καὶ οἱ εἴκοσι τέσσαρες πρεσβύτεροι
3. ἔπεσαν ἐνώπιον τοῦ ἀρνίου,
4. ἔχοντες ἕκαστος κιθάραν
5. καὶ φιάλας χρυσᾶς γεμούσας θυμιαμάτων,
6. αἵ εἰσιν αἱ προσευχαὶ τῶν ἁγίων,

23. More to follow concerning this, but for now, see Osborne, *Revelation*, 254–55; Barr, *Tales of the End*, 122–25; Gorman, *Reading Revelation Responsibly*, 108–9; Bauckham, *Theology of the Book*, 74; Resseguie, *Revelation of John*, 118.

24. These terms are woven throughout the book of Revelation, not just in the section currently under investigation (Rev 6:1, 3, 5, 7, 9, 12; 7:3, 4, 5, 6, 7, 8; 8:1; 10:4; 13:3, 8; 18:24; 20:3; 22:10). This would make an interesting study in its own right.

Period 9 (5:9–10)

1. καὶ ᾄδουσιν ᾠδὴν καινὴν λέγοντες·
2. ἄξιος εἶ λαβεῖν τὸ βιβλίον
3. καὶ ἀνοῖξαι τὰς σφραγῖδας αὐτοῦ,
4. ὅτι ἐσφάγης
5. καὶ ἠγόρασας τῷ θεῷ ἐν τῷ αἵματί σου
6. ἐκ πάσης φυλῆς
7. καὶ γλώσσης
8. καὶ λαοῦ
9. καὶ ἔθνους
10. καὶ ἐποίησας αὐτοὺς τῷ θεῷ ἡμῶν βασιλείαν
11. καὶ ἱερεῖς,
12. καὶ βασιλεύσουσιν ἐπὶ τῆς γῆς.

Period 10 (5:11–12)

1. Καὶ εἶδον,
2. καὶ ἤκουσα φωνὴν ἀγγέλων πολλῶν κύκλῳ τοῦ θρόνου
3. καὶ τῶν ζῴων καὶ τῶν πρεσβυτέρων,
4. καὶ ἦν ὁ ἀριθμὸς αὐτῶν μυριάδες μυριάδων
5. καὶ χιλιάδες χιλιάδων
6. λέγοντες φωνῇ μεγάλῃ·

Period 11 (5:12)

1. ἄξιόν ἐστιν τὸ ἀρνίον
2. τὸ ἐσφαγμένον
3. λαβεῖν τὴν δύναμιν
4. καὶ πλοῦτον
5. καὶ σοφίαν
6. καὶ ἰσχὺν
7. καὶ τιμὴν
8. καὶ δόξαν

9. καὶ εὐλογίαν.

Period 12 (5:13a)

1. καὶ πᾶν κτίσμα ὃ ἐν τῷ οὐρανῷ
2. καὶ ἐπὶ τῆς γῆς
3. καὶ ὑποκάτω τῆς γῆς
4. καὶ ἐπὶ τῆς θαλάσσης
5. καὶ τὰ ἐν αὐτοῖς πάντα ἤκουσα λέγοντας·

Period 13 (5:13b)

1. τῷ καθημένῳ ἐπὶ τῷ θρόνῳ καὶ τῷ ἀρνίῳ
2. ἡ εὐλογία
3. καὶ ἡ τιμὴ
4. καὶ ἡ δόξα
5. καὶ τὸ κράτος
6. εἰς τοὺς αἰῶνας τῶν αἰώνων.

Period 14 (5:14)

1. καὶ τὰ τέσσαρα ζῷα ἔλεγον· ἀμήν.
2. καὶ οἱ πρεσβύτεροι ἔπεσαν
3. καὶ προσεκύνησαν.

Given that exclamations of praise and worship drive the action of the remaining periods in Rev 5, the meter of each of these periods is similar throughout. Thus, these periods may be examined together. Each of these periods contain a highly pleasing and euphonic meter, undoubtedly to match the musical and liturgical imagery. Again, Duvall's reminder that the phrase "you are worthy" was often used in welcoming Roman emperors into a city[25] is noteworthy here, as the liquid consonants and vowel openness combined with a lack of harsh consonant clusters make this period breathy and open in oral recitation. In multiple cola, John employs structured lists that create a beat and a rhythm to the praise. The asyndeton repetition of καὶ in these lists carries the beat forward. All of these features work together to enable this entire section to be spoken

---

25. Duvall, *Theology of Revelation*, 183.

loudly and clearly, with a pleasing meter and rhythm throughout. The elongation of the sixth colon in period 13 provides a clear period boundary, marking the end of the praise of the creation, enabling the scene to close with the restaging of the elders and the creatures and their affirmation of honor to the one seated on the throne and to the lamb.

John's Grouping of Cola into Periods

After dividing the text into breath units, the next important step involves joining them with other cola to form complete discourse thoughts or periods. While this may be accused of being a rather subjective process, as noted in the methodology section above, ancient texts composed for performance[26] had many ways of signaling these discourse thoughts and grouping them together. To be sure, grammatical subordination of the sort evidenced in other texts included in the New Testament[27] must be acknowledged as lacking in the book of Revelation. Most of the cola form simple independent clauses. However, that does not mean that John's text is haphazard in its arrangement of cola. Rather, from the visual sound map arranged above and the data compiled in the accompanying tables, several features emerge.

First, it is clear that John employs καί (and)[28] at the start of the majority of the cola in these two chapters. This is a regular feature of the book of Revelation, displaying a continuous style[29] that flows from one cola and period to the next.[30] In fact, throughout the Apocalypse as a whole, this continuous style remains. Second, while John may not cluster cola by the use of grammatical subordination, it is demonstrated from the sound map arranged above that many of the lines of cola share sounds and repetition of words that makes forming them into periods more apparent.

---

26. See Horsley, *Text and Tradition*, 233.

27. See Eph 1:3–14 or 1 Pet 1:3–12 for an example of such intricacy in grammatical subordination.

28. All translations will be author's translation unless otherwise noted.

29. Aristotle, *Art of Rhetoric*, 1409a.

30. See Pattemore, "Revelation," 737. Pattemore notes that the use of καί is enormous and may indicate a Hebrew flavor. He suggests that it functions paratactically, but it is the contention of the present author that the use of καί more likely functions to create a continuous style, rather than a paratactic one.

Third, the pacing and plot of the narrative determines the arrangement of the cola and periods. Due in part to the style of John's storytelling, marked by simple independent clauses, sound and story generate the structure and arrangement of cola. For example, in scene 1, period 2 (Rev 4:2–3), John introduces the hearer to the vision of the heavenly throne. The pace moves rapidly following the introductory Εὐθέως (immediately), with four cola beginning with καί, and concluding with several descriptions of the one seated on the throne using the device of simile. The sound map above then suggests that period 3 (S1:P3 / Rev 4:4) begins when John announces new objects that make up the setting as well as new characters—the twenty-four thrones surrounding the central throne and the twenty-four elders. Thus, within the flow of the narrative, the introduction of new objects and characters establishes a period boundary. The fourth period in scene 1 (Rev 4:5–6a), then, reframes the center of attention of the hearer back to the central throne but introduces, yet again, new elements within the scene—ἀστραπαὶ καὶ φωναὶ καὶ βρονταί (lightning and noise and thunder [Rev 4:5]).[31] The combination of these new elements and the change to the dominant sound—αὶ again establish a narrative discourse thought. With these representative examples in mind, the sound map above visually represents the periods and numbers them accordingly.

Fourth, according to Margaret Ellen Lee and Bernard Brandon Scott, many ancient authors employed various techniques to also signal the boundary markers between periods. These techniques include rounding (where a sound or word is repeated at the beginning and end of a period to signal its close), balance (cola that are parallel or antithetical), and elongation (the lengthening of the final colon of a period or the use of multiple long vowel sounds in the final colon).[32] John's style will be analyzed in the pages below as well as the potential value for performance analysis, but for the present purposes it is clear from the following data that John employs several of these techniques in these chapters.

---

31. Beale notes what he refers to as the "allusive, progressively expanded paraphrastic refrain" of Exod 19:16 in this passage. See Beale, *Book of Revelation*, 124.

32. Lee, *Sound Mapping*, 171.

Table 1. Rounding and Elongation in Rev 4–5			
Rounding	Verse	Elongation	Verse
S1:P1 repetition of μετὰ ταῦτα (after this)	4:1	S1:P4	4:5–6a
S1:P8 (repetition of—ουσιν)	4:9–10	S1:P6	4:7–8a
S2:P1 (repetition of—ον endings)	5:1	S2:P5	5:5
S2:P3 (repetition of οὐ sounds)	5:3	S2:P7	5:7
S2:P6 (repetition of—ω in each cola)	5:6	S2:P12	5:13a
S2:P13 (repetition of—ω sounds).	5:13b		

Period Style

To speak of the style of John's composition requires analysis of both the nature in which periods and cola are arranged and interact, be it continuous or periodic, as well as the quality of the sound within the text, be it harmonious or cacophonous. Working from a more general overview to specific periods, it is clear that while John intentionally varies the way in which periods interact in other portions of the book of Revelation,[33] in this section, John employs a highly consistent continuous style with periods and cola running from one to the next. This is achieved by the regular use of καί in a majority of the cola within this section. Aside from the division between the first two periods in scene 1 (Rev 4:1–2), every period begins with this connective except periods that contain content introduced in the previous period (S1:P7/Rev 4:8b, S1:P9/Rev 4:11; S2:P12/Rev 5:13a, S2:P14/Rev 5:14), producing a fluid narrative of connected periods that quickly enable the audience to envision the setting and the participants depicted by the performance.

Since choice implies meaning, any deviation from such a regular formula is significant. While scholars overwhelmingly agree that Revelation 4:1 begins a new macro-segment of the book of Revelation,[34] they

33. This will be a highlighted feature of the analysis of the final representative section under investigation in this study (Rev 21:9—22:21). In both chapter 1 and chapter 22, John's style loses its continuous nature and instead betrays a much more periodic style, in which periods stand alone and are not connected with καί as frequently as they are in the narrative scenes of the book. This, it will be argued, suggests a performance technique called discourse "framing," in which the speaker often struggles to start and stop the performance. See Young, *Taleworlds and Storyrealms*, 1–68; Tannen, *Framing in Discourse*, 14–54; and Fox, "Worlds with Words," 43–71.

34. See Bauckham, *Climax of Prophecy*, 3–5; Fanning, *Revelation*, 58–64; Beale, *Book of Revelation*, 108–9; Aune, *Revelation*, c.

have failed to see how analyzing John's sound contributes. By utilizing several techniques, John signals these structuring cues to his audience: first, through the use of period rounding in S1:P1 (Rev 4:1), not simply with similar sounds but with an entire phrase μετὰ ταῦτα (after this); second, by the periodic noncontinuous style that transitions S1:P1 to S1:P2 (Rev 4:1-3) without the connective καί; and third, by changing the location entirely.[35] These cues are prominent and emphatic,[36] enabling both the speaker and the listener to divide the material of the narrative into units.[37] This prepares the audience to make a dramatic shift: from the series of seven letters spoken by Jesus concerning their real-world circumstances to the apocalyptic "taleworld"[38] to follow. It should be of no surprise, then, that these same devices are employed as John moves the audience from the "taleworld" and again directly addresses their real-world circumstances in Rev 22.[39]

Many of the individual cola also begin with καί. This repetition is often obscured in translation, but in an aural setting, this repetition would be apparent.[40] Two things are accomplished by this repetition, and this helps identify and articulate John's style: the first is that the continuity between periods as well as cola is enhanced and a narrative rhythm is established;[41] the second is that this repetition enables each individual item, object, or prop in the scene to receive proper attention by the listening audience.[42] This, with the addition of the repetition of words within periods, produces a balanced style that "zooms in" the mental conception of the audience to see and envision each participant or object. As a representative example, consider S1:P2 (Rev 4:2-3):

1. Εὐθέως ἐγενόμην ἐν πνεύματι,

2. καὶ ἰδοὺ θρόνος ἔκειτο ἐν τῷ οὐρανῷ,

---

35. Bauckham, *Climax of Prophecy*, 3-5; Barr, *Tales of the End*, 110-21.
36. Bauckham, *Climax of Prophecy*, 7.
37. Carruthers, *Book of Memory*, 7.
38. Young, *Taleworlds and Storyrealms*, 1-68.
39. To be analyzed in the pages to follow.
40. In the theophany scene that occurs in chapter 1, the redundant repetition of καί is present as well.
41. Ong, *Orality and Literacy*, 34-36.
42. While more will be said about this in the upcoming discourse analysis of the text, it is important to mention here a suggestion from James Resseguie, who notes that this technique allows John to make sentences thicker by this overt repetition as well as to enhance each feature within the list. See Resseguie, *Revelation of John*, 50.

3. καὶ ἐπὶ τὸν θρόνον καθήμενος,

4. καὶ ὁ καθήμενος

5. ὅμοιος ὁράσει λίθῳ ἰάσπιδι καὶ σαρδίῳ,

6. καὶ Ἶρις κυκλόθεν τοῦ θρόνου

7. ὅμοιος ὁράσει σμαραγδίνῳ.

In line 2, the audience is introduced to a θρόνος ἔκειτο ἐν τῷ οὐρανῷ (a throne standing in heaven). John's choice of repetition is seen in lines 3 and 4, as each subsequent element is introduced following the connective καί, and each line contains elements from the previous line. If objects were simply listed, one after another, the audience would certainly be given information, but John's choices suggest that mere information dissemination is not his aim. Instead, the audience is invited to consider each element. Like a master cinematographer, John moves the mental picture of his audience in and through the scene deliberately. The sound map above provides ample evidence of this feature by underlining repeated elements within periods.

Deviation from this pattern, again, indicates choice on the part of the author. Here, John's style is on display within this representative section of the book of Revelation. As stated above, every period begins with καί except those that contain content reported in the previous period. Thus, the content is continuous from a narrative perspective but distinct in style, producing rhetorical effect. This effect can be quickly ascertained as each example (S1:P7/Rev 4:8b, S1:P9/Rev 4:11; S2:P12/Rev 5:13a, S2:P14/Rev 5:14) contains content that expresses worship and praise.[43] The final three of these periods even begin with the same word (ἄξιος, "worthy")—with two (S1:P9/ Rev 4:11; S2:P9/Rev 5:9-10) sharing the exact formula of second-person address: ἄξιος εἶ (You are worthy). It is also worth noting that while S1:P7 (Rev 4:8b) does not begin with ἄξιος, it does begin with ἅγιος (holy) which, to the hearer, is very similar. This technique, involving a deviation from the established pattern of continuous periods introduced with καί, signals to both performer and audience to consider the significance of the content,[44] in this case the object of the hearer's worship. It is worthy of mention here and will be discussed later,

---

43. Gorman, *Reading Revelation Responsibly*, 102–15. See also Hurtado, *Ancient Jewish Monotheism*, 482.

44. Much more will be said concerning the "noise" in the book of Revelation in the next section.

but near the conclusion of both of these two scenes, there are repeated quotations of praise[45] introduced with λέγοντες (saying).

NARRATIVE DISCOURSE ANALYSIS OF REV 4–5

Markers of Orality

Structural Markers

INTRODUCTION

As noted in the methodology section in chapter 1, structural markers are embedded into texts—whether composed for the hearer or the reader—but that, for the listening audience, these structural markers must be recognized in real time and cued by the performer. Again, as a more recent example, Dr. Martin Luther King Jr.'s repetition of "I have a dream" marks units of thought and allows the audience to follow each successive thought clearly. This formula also invites the audience to capture the emotive force of the speech's conclusion, in effect, building each successive discourse thought on top of the previous.[46] John employs a number of these structural markers throughout the book of Revelation, and while scholars continue to debate the macrostructure of the book,[47] they all interact with these features in some way. What is often overlooked, however, is the way in which these structural markers function with the performance of Revelation in mind. Structural markers enable the composer to group periods together to form scenes within the narrative,[48] as well as introduce the hearer to new characters, objects, or important elements within the flow of the story. These markers include introductory formula, numbering sequences, repetition of phrases, and

---

45. See Smalley, *Revelation to John*, 140.

46. What is most impressive is the later reports that this part of the speech was largely done off-the-cuff and was not part of the original speech but created in real-time by combining elements of previous speeches and ideas. This performance betrays shocking parallels to the way in which ancient performers took material from memory and combined it to create the performance in real time. Thus, Dr. King was not working from a manuscript or a text at this point in the speech but rather creating the speech's conclusion. This creative act, however, was made possible by the way in which previously learned and articulated material were stored in the performer's repertoire, to be used appropriately here for rhetorical effect.

47. For a summary, see Bandy, "Layers of the Apocalypse," 469–99.

48. Ong, *Orality and Literacy*, 34–35, 139–46.

speech-acts and their introductory formula.[49] In this section of the book, the text bears the remaining imprint of these oral performances.[50]

Introductory Formula

First, chapter 4 (scene 1 in the present study) opens with a repeated formula that also functions as an introductory formula[51] for many of the pericope in the book of Revelation. The significance of this transition has been regularly noted by scholars,[52] but the impact such repetition would have on the listening audience is rarely considered. In the first chapter, John presents a familiar theophany that culminates in the one amidst the golden lampstands, presenting himself as one who was dead and now lives forever and ever (Rev 1:18). The character commands John to write ἃ εἶδες καὶ ἃ εἰσὶν καὶ ἃ μέλλει γενέσθαι μετὰ ταῦτα (what you have seen and what is and what is about to happen after these things [Rev 1:19]). Next, the one amidst the lampstands instructs John to write seven messages to seven churches (Rev 2–3), and the action of the narrative essentially grinds to a halt, making way for this lengthy didactic section. The narrative is not resumed until Rev 4:1,[53] and it is likely that John's use of rounding—not simply a repetition of sounds but a repetition of an entire phrase—serves as an aid for the audience to recognize that the narrative will now proceed.[54]

While Μετὰ ταῦτα (after this) occurs regularly throughout the book of Revelation (Rev 1:19; 4:1; 7:9; 9:12; 15:5; 18:1; 19:1; 20:3), it is only here that the phrase is repeated in this manner. This structural marker functions as an aural cue for the ancient listener.[55] This cue is enhanced by the combination of καὶ ἰδού (and behold), which grabs the attention of the ancient hearer. Fanning observes, "The expression εἶδον καὶ ἰδού (I looked and behold), followed by a nominative word frequently introduces

---

49. Lee, *Sound Mapping*, 66–68.

50. Rhoads, "Performance Criticism, Pt. I," 124.

51. de Waal, *Aural-Performance Analysis*, 7.

52. Some scholars see this as the key phrase to unlock the "outline" of the book of Revelation; Beale provides a lengthy argument in opposition to this technique. See Beale, *Book of Revelation*, 152–70.

53. See Koester, *Revelation*, 367.

54. Beale notes the significance of the Old Testament background for this expression. See Beale, *Book of Revelation*, 181–82.

55. Lee, *Sound Mapping*, 66–68.

visionary experiences in Revelation (4:1; 6:2, 5, 8; 7:9; 14:1, 14; 19:11)."[56] Again, the structural marker is evident in the text, but its effect for the gathered listening community must be properly appreciated,[57] as Charles suggested a century ago that the "restlessness, the troubles, the imperfectness and apprehensions pervading Rev 2–3 pass at once in Rev 4 into an atmosphere of perfect assurance and peace."[58]

Next, John dramatically shifts the setting from the island of Patmos to the heavenly throne room.[59] This shift draws the audience into the performer's mental construction of this new setting, in essence ushering them into a new existential world.[60] This is accomplished by the use of the prophetic-influenced[61] technical phrase: ἐγενόμην ἐν πνεύματι (I was in the Spirit). Bauckham and Fanning suggest that this repeated formula not only introduces the visionary experience of Revelation as a whole (Rev 1:10) but also serves to indicate transition to new settings within the narrative, creating three major transitions within the Apocalypse as a whole.[62] Again, this important transition point in the narrative is emphasized with the combination of καὶ ἰδοὺ[63] immediately following in Rev 4:2, with the demonstrative particle functioning as a way to call the hearer's attention to the scenes and figures therein.[64] While more will be stated in the discourse analysis section below, it is important at this point to note in agreement with Bauckham and Fanning that the new setting—the

56. Fanning, *Revelation*, 196.

57. Bauckham, *Climax of Prophecy*, 7.

58. Charles, *Critical and Exegetical Commentary*, 102–3.

59. For the rhetorical significance of this, see Barr, *Tales of the End*, 110–18. See also Hurtado, *Ancient Jewish Monotheism*, 469–71. This same dramatic shift in location occurs at key transitional moments throughout the narrative (Rev 1:10, 4:1, 17:1, 21:10). It is not simply the movement of the setting that is significant, but rather the repetition in the reporting of the event that creates a structural cue for the listening audience.

60. Lee, *Sound Mapping*, 77.

61. Bauckham, *Climax of Prophecy*, 3–5. See the influence of the book of Ezekiel and the parallel from the book of Ezekiel in Smalley, *Revelation to John*, 8–10; and Beale, *Book of Revelation*, 203–4. Hurtado notes how simplistically John depicts this compared to other apocalyptic literature. See Hurtado, *Ancient Jewish Monotheism*, 472.

62. See Rev 1:10; 4:1; 17:1–2; 21:9–10. See Bauckham, *Climax of Prophecy*, 3; Fanning, *Revelation*, 58–64. Fiorenza and Smalley disagree, noting the thematic structure is tighter than Bauckham and Fanning posit. See Fiorenza, *Book of Revelation*, 46–56; and Smalley, *Revelation to John*, 19–20.

63. Smalley notes that the demonstrative particle ἰδού is used twenty-six times in the Apocalypse. See Smalley, *Revelation to John*, 114.

64. Smalley, *Revelation to John*, 114.

heavenly throne room—creates a major division in the text.⁶⁵ This division, therefore, must be clearly and explicitly demarcated for the listening audience for two reasons. First, the shift is from the earthly realm to the heavenly realm. Second, since both visions contain experiences of divine figures, clarity that a new vision is underway is paramount. Thus, the audience needs prominent structural markers,⁶⁶ and that is precisely what John provides.⁶⁷ In Rev 1:10—3:22, the audience is told of John's vision of Jesus as one like of a Son of Man in glory. In Rev 4, however, the participants are presented differently, with one seated on a throne (God the Father) and with Jesus described symbolically as a slaughtered lamb. The audience must keep up, and these structural markers serve to guide the listener into the new setting.⁶⁸

In the present scene under investigation (Rev 4), all of the attention is oriented toward the newly established heavenly throne and the one seated on it.⁶⁹ The character is presented in the scene's second period (Rev 4:2), with the subsequent three periods (S1:P3/Rev 4:4; S1:P4/Rev 4:5–6a; S1:P5/Rev 6b-7) all oriented toward the throne.⁷⁰ This orientation is accomplished in two ways. First, each period introduces participants that are said to be either κυκλόθεν (around), ἐκ (out of), ἐνώπιον (before), or ἐν μέσῳ καὶ κύκλῳ (in the midst and around) the throne and the one seated on it.⁷¹ Second, the first cola of each period concludes with τοῦ θρόνου (the throne). Indeed, τοῦ θρόνου in the genitive case is repeated nine times in nine periods, with variations in case adding an additional two examples. Dooley and Levinsohn note that, in written language, there is a limit to how much repetition readers can tolerate, but, in

---

65. Barr, *Tales of the End*, 110–21. See also Hurtado, *Ancient Jewish Monotheism*, 471.

66. Bauckham, *Climax of Prophecy*, 7.

67. See Smalley, *The Revelation to John*, 126, where Smalley summarizes the debate concerning background influence on the structural layout of Rev 4–5. Beale suggests that scene 1 follows Daniel 7:9–28 and Ezekiel 1–2 in outline, with scene 2 following Daniel apart from Ezekiel. See Beale, *Book of Revelation*, 337. Bauckham however posits that both scenes, and much of the material in Rev 4–10, follows the outline of Ezekiel 1–3. See Bauckham, *Theology of the Book of Revelation*, 81–82.

68. Bauckham, *Climax of Prophecy*, 7.

69. Smalley suggests that in Rev 4–5, there are seventeen references out of its thirty-eight occurrences in Rev 4–22. See Smalley, *Revelation to John*, 114.

70. Koester, *Revelation*, 369. See also Hurtado, *Ancient Jewish Monotheism*, 473.

71. In similar fashion, in the theophany scene in Rev 1, the same technique is used, as John depicts the seven lampstands and then moves to closer to the center of the visionary setting. Again, the terms ἐν μέσῳ is employed.

spoken language, repetition abounds.[72] For the performer, this repetition would be helpful for recall.[73]

Imprinted on the written text of Revelation, the modern scholar can quickly discern that John frequently employs the phrase Καὶ εἶδον (and I saw),[74] often combining this with καὶ ἤκουσα (and I heard). Given that the book of Revelation is a visionary experience, it is not surprising that emphasis is given to what is seen. What is often underappreciated, however, is not *that* the phrase is used repeatedly but rather *how* it is used.[75] It is the perspective of the present writer that this technique functions much like a camera angle would in modern film, positioning the ancient audience's mental framework from one element to the next.

In Rev 4:1–11, as noted above, John introduces the section with careful attention, directing the hearer back to the opening chapter and the expectations presented in Rev 1:19. Revelation chapter 4 begins with Μετὰ ταῦτα εἶδον (after this I saw),[76] but then εἶδον is not used again in the rest of the chapter. However, in chapter 5 Καὶ εἶδον occurs four times (Rev 5:1, 2, 6, 11), marking four discrete units within the flow of the narrative.[77] Both chapters introduce new characters and elements, so why the difference? In chapter 4, the attention of the audience is to be focused squarely on the throne and the one seated on it. Other elements are brought in, but they are all oriented toward the throne. In this sense, it is almost as if the mental conception of the audience is meant to start "zoomed in" on the throne, then slowly panning back to take in the additional participants.[78] However, in chapter 5, the action increases[79] and thus it becomes necessary for the performer to guide the listener

72. Dooley, *Analyzing Discourse*, 15.

73. Ong, *Orality and Literacy*, 139–55. See Botha, *Orality and Literacy*, 109–10. Additionally, see Vansina, *Oral Tradition as History*, 39–47, 68–78.

74. Koester, *Revelation*, 382.

75. Mathewson notes that Καὶ εἶδον frequently marks discrete narrative units. See Mathewson, "Verbal Aspect," 65.

76. Again, it is worth stating how this connects this present section under analysis to the anticipation in Rev 1:19.

77. Mathewson, "Verbal Aspect," 65. See also Resseguie, *Revelation of John*, 115.

78. The same technique occurs in the theophany scene in Rev 1, as the narrative moves toward the one in midst of the lampstands, a lengthy description of the one like a son of man is reported. Just as in the theophany scene in Rev 4, repetition of ὡς and ὅμοιον occur.

79. This will be addressed in the analysis to follow, but for here, it must be noted that action verbs increase, contributing to the need to move the "camera angle" of the ancient hearer's mental projection of the scene.

through the events successively. In a sense (and again using modern film language), the pace of the action of the narrative moves quicker in scene 2 (Rev 5) requiring more deliberate structuring devices, and Καὶ εἶδον serves this function. Thus, careful analysis of John's use of Καὶ εἶδον enables the analyst to follow the way in which material is structured.

Repeated Formula

There are several other examples of structural markers that additionally aid the performer's memory.[80] Repeated formula consisting of words and phrases guided ancient speakers,[81] and John regularly employs them, leaving an imprint on the written text.[82] John introduces three vivid elements in Rev 4:5-6: ἀστραπαὶ καὶ φωναὶ καὶ βρονταί (lightning and sounds and thunderstrikes). Not only does the sound itself grab the hearer's attention,[83] but this formula will be repeated again and again in the book of Revelation,[84] often at important transition moments within the narrative itself.[85] In fact, the intensity of the formula builds as the narrative progresses,[86] but each example is ordered slightly different than the others. Much ink has been spilled attempting to adjudicate the meaning of these variations in order, but perhaps the order varies not due to some subtle and coded meaning but simply because, in oral performance, formula are repeated but often without precision.[87] Kelly Maxwell posits that "when oral texts were performed, whether as narrative or dialog, each speaker delivered the text in a unique manner. In fact, a word-for-word recitation of a text could not exactly replicate an earlier performance, even if the text were performed by the same person for the same audience."[88]

---

80. Lee, *Sound Mapping*, 60–70. Again, see pages 10–12 above in chapter 1. It is not necessary to establish that the book of Revelation was performed from memory. However, the characteristics that would be expected for a text composed to be memorized and recited from memory are explored and analyzed here.

81. Again, see Botha, *Orality and Literacy*, 109–10.

82. de Waal, *Aural-Performance Analysis*, 7.

83. The αἰ sound is repeated ten times in this period alone.

84. Again, likely a referent to Exod 19:16.

85. See Bauckham, *Climax of Prophecy*, 8.

86. Bauckham, *Climax of Prophecy*, 8.

87. Horsley, *Text and Tradition*, 26. For a survey of the way in which material in oral tradition was expected to be preserved, see Dunn, *Jesus Remembered*, 192–209.

88. Maxwell, "From Performance to Text," 169.

This same repetition of formula with slight variation occurs in Rev 4:8, where the four living beings ascribe praise to the one on the throne. Here, the formula is clearly the same as the one introduced in Rev 1:8, but the word order is different. Parts of this formula occur regularly in the book of Revelation,[89] but the pattern often varies slightly. Indeed, just two periods later, a part of it occurs in Rev 4:11, but again it is altered. Walter Ong posits that the repetition of formula without the need for exact precision is a mark of orality, as the performer is "remembering in a curiously public way—remembering not a memorized text, for there is no such thing, nor any verbatim succession of words,"[90] but rather themes and formulas.[91] This same feature is on display in Rev 5:9 with the grouping of πάσης φυλῆς καὶ γλώσσης καὶ λαοῦ καὶ ἔθνους (every tribe and tongue and people and nation). This fourfold formula symbolically represents universality and is a regular device in the book of Revelation,[92] but again the order varies.[93] Perhaps the simplest explanation for this variation is that the text was composed from oral performance for oral performance, and such precision was not necessary.[94] Bauckham suggests as much, revealing that precise verbal agreement of repeated formula typically only occurs in examples that are structurally significant, such as the repeated formula in Rev 1:1 and 22:6.[95]

Reported Speech

One final structural technique that requires attention is the introduction of spoken material. Often in Revelation, λέγω is used to mark the spoken word, and this device occurs in this section repeatedly (Rev 4:1, 8, 10; 5:5, 9, 12). It has often been stated that Revelation is a noisy book,[96] and one reason for this is the sheer volume of speech-acts reported within.

---

89. Rev 4:8; 11:17; 16:5; 17:8. See also Beale's comment regarding this recurring statement: *Book of Revelation*, 199–200.

90. Ong, *Orality and Literacy*, 145–46. See also Ong, *Presence of the Word*, 192–209. For yet another developed analysis, see Harvey, *Listening to the Text*, 35–60.

91. Lord, "Characteristics of Orality," 64.

92. Bauckham, *Climax of Prophecy*, 326–37.

93. For a complete list of the variations in the different formulae within the Apocalypse, see Bauckham, *Climax of Prophecy*, 22–29.

94. Vansina, *Oral Tradition as History*, 34–47, 95–100.

95. Bauckham, *Climax of Prophecy*, 22–23.

96. Resseguie, *Revelation of John*, 21.

In this section under investigation, the speech is largely in the form of exaltation and praise as opposed to dialogue. Rhetorically, this has the effect of presenting before the hearer one of the primary purposes of the book of Revelation itself: worship.[97] Moreover, since the prayers of God's people are specifically mentioned in cohort with this heavenly praise (Rev 5:8), the liturgical activity of worship[98] is emphasized with these repeated elements. Structurally, then, the performer is cued repeatedly for the anticipation of praise speech-acts by the repetition of the signal λέγω.

Style Markers

Introduction

While structural markers remain significant to scholars of Revelation and have received due attention in the history of Revelation studies,[99] style markers have gone underappreciated. Put simply, the characteristics typical of the style of oral performance differ from those on the written page.[100] These typical style markers are pervasive in John's Apocalypse, and they include additive rather than subordinate prose, aggregative rather than analytic prose, redundancy and repetition, an agonistic tone, empathetic and participatory tone, and a lack of sequential parallelism. Albert B. Lord proposes yet another characteristic of orality, namely that the action is oriented acoustically rather than visually.[101] Several other sections within the present investigation demonstrate the sheer noisiness of the book of Revelation, thus detailed analysis of this characteristic will not be discussed here. It is sufficient to simply note that the Apocalypse has a strikingly acoustic orientation. As stated in the methodology section in chapter 1, it is not that these characteristics occur which suggests an oral culture but rather the high frequency of their use. Such high frequency tends to dissipate in literate cultures adjusted to the written page.[102]

---

97. Barr, *Tales of the End*, 5. Gorman, *Reading Revelation Responsibly*, 35–38. See also Bauckham, *Theology of the Book*, 58–63; Koester, *Revelation*, 382–83.
98. Smalley, *Revelation to John*, 135.
99. Bauckham, *Climax of Prophecy*, 1–37.
100. Ong, *Orality and Literacy*, 36.
101. Lord, *Singer of Tales*, 33.
102. Ong, *Orality and Literacy*, 36–51, 117–35.

Additive Prose

First, according to Walter Ong, an oral culture tends to express thought using additive rather than subordinate prose. It is here that the aforementioned effusive use of καί becomes particularly relevant, for this sort of continuous additive repetition fades out of print culture.[103] Indeed, many of the uses of καί in the book of Revelation go untranslated in all of the modern English print versions or are rendered with more semantic range. This is almost certainly due to the sheer redundancy of uses, again eighty-nine, in just Rev 4–5.[104] If the oral tradition was represented faithfully in modern print versions, the redundancy would sound as follows:

> And I saw in the middle of the throne, and the four living creatures, and in the middle of the elders, a lamb standing as having been slain, having seven horns and seven eyes, which are the seven spirits of God sent into all the land. And he went. And he took out of the right hand of the one sitting on the throne. And when he took the scroll, the four living beings and the twenty-four elders fell before the lamb, each having a harp and golden bowls filled with incense, which are the prayers of the saints. And they sang a new song, saying, "You are worthy to take the scroll and to open its seals, because you were slain and purchased in your blood for God out of all the tribes and languages and people and nations and made them to be a kingdom to God, and priests. And they will reign on the earth."[105]

Several elements are repeated frequently in Rev 4–5: throne, the one seated on the throne, the four living creatures, the elders, the lamb, and the scroll. Scholars have suggested that the overwhelming repetition of the throne may suggest an editorial hand at work,[106] but perhaps the simpler explanation is that the book of Revelation was composed from oral performance and for oral performance.

Ong notes that

> written discourse develops more elaborate and fixed grammar than oral discourse does because to provide meaning it is more

---

103. Lord, *Singer of Tales*, 33.

104. In studies of traditional oral cultures, this sort of repetition is common in oral storytelling. See Vansina, *Oral History as Tradition*, 72–73.

105. Revelation 5:6–10. This pericope was chosen as a representative. The translation is the author's own. This redundancy will be even more explicit in Revelation chapter 6, to be analyzed below.

106. Charles, *Critical and Exegetical Commentary*, 118–19.

dependent simply upon linguistic structure, since it lacks the normal full existential contexts which surround oral discourse and help determine meaning in oral discourse somewhat independently of grammar.[107]

Given the sound map of Rev 4–5 detailed above, it is clear that the cola within each period progress in a rather straightforward, paratactic manner[108] with little grammatical subordination.[109] For a representative example, see S1:P5 (Rev 4:6b-7), cola 4 through 7:

καὶ τὸ ζῷον τὸ πρῶτον ὅμοιον λέοντι

καὶ τὸ δεύτερον ζῷον ὅμοιον μόσχῳ

καὶ τὸ τρίτον ζῷον ἔχων τὸ πρόσωπον ὡς ἀνθρώπου

καὶ τὸ τέταρτον ζῷον ὅμοιον ἀετῷ πετομένῳ.

Each line makes a simple assertion, each begins with καί, and each in parallel with the lines before and after. Consider also S2:P7 (Rev 5:7):

Καὶ ἦλθεν

καὶ εἴληφεν

ἐκ τῆς δεξιᾶς τοῦ καθημένου ἐπὶ τοῦ θρόνου.

Two short cola, each containing elements of the event-line of the narrative, each represented in dependent clauses, and each recalled in parallel two-word lines—the second of which is followed by a prepositional phrase.

Consider Tolkien's *Lord of the Rings* series again as a point of comparison. The following passage comes from the first volume, *The Fellowship of the Ring*:

> Away high in the East swung Remmirath, the Netted Stars, and slowly above the mists red Borgil rose, glowing like a jewel of fire. Then by some shift of airs all the mist was drawn away like a veil, and there leaned up, as he climbed over the rim of the

---

107. Ong, *Orality and Literacy*, 38. Smalley takes up the issue of John's use of the accusative tense in Rev 4:4 with seemingly no verb to govern them, but suggests that this grammatical irregularity displays a "further example of John's immediate and dramatic, if strictly ungrammatical, style." See Smalley, *Revelation to John*, 118.

108. Ong, *Orality and Literacy*, 38.

109. This same feature is evident when looking at the theophany scene in Rev 1, as the written page bears the marks of this additive prose just as it does in Rev 4–5.

world, the Swordsman of the Sky, Menelvagor with his shining belt. The Elves all burst into song.[110]

The stylistic differences become most evident by comparison. Tolkien's stylistic choices, both the sentence length, sentence complexity, and variation in sentence style is drastically different than the highly repetitive style of the book of Revelation. Consider another New Testament narrative that many scholars affirm as likely composed in an oral culture, the Gospel of Mark 5:21-29:[111]

> <u>Καὶ</u> διαπεράσαντος τοῦ Ἰησοῦ ἐν τῷ πλοίῳ πάλιν εἰς τὸ πέραν συνήχθη ὄχλος πολὺς ἐπ' αὐτόν, <u>καὶ</u> ἦν παρὰ τὴν θάλασσαν. <u>Καὶ</u> ἔρχεται εἷς τῶν ἀρχισυναγώγων, ὀνόματι Ἰάϊρος, <u>καὶ</u> ἰδὼν αὐτὸν πίπτει πρὸς τοὺς πόδας αὐτοῦ καὶ παρακαλεῖ αὐτὸν πολλὰ λέγων ὅτι τὸ θυγάτριόν μου ἐσχάτως ἔχει, ἵνα ἐλθὼν ἐπιθῇς τὰς χεῖρας αὐτῇ ἵνα σωθῇ <u>καὶ</u> ζήσῃ. <u>καὶ</u> ἀπῆλθεν μετ' αὐτοῦ. <u>καὶ</u> ἠκολούθει αὐτῷ ὄχλος πολὺς <u>καὶ</u> συνέθλιβον αὐτόν.
>
> <u>Καὶ</u> γυνὴ οὖσα ἐν ῥύσει αἵματος δώδεκα ἔτη <u>καὶ</u> πολλὰ παθοῦσα ὑπὸ πολλῶν ἰατρῶν <u>καὶ</u> δαπανήσασα τὰ παρ' αὐτῆς πάντα <u>καὶ</u> μηδὲν ὠφεληθεῖσα ἀλλὰ μᾶλλον εἰς τὸ χεῖρον ἐλθοῦσα, ἀκούσασα περὶ τοῦ Ἰησοῦ, ἐλθοῦσα ἐν τῷ ὄχλῳ ὄπισθεν ἥψατο τοῦ ἱματίου αὐτοῦ· ἔλεγεν γὰρ ὅτι ἐὰν ἅψωμαι κἂν τῶν ἱματίων αὐτοῦ σωθήσομαι. <u>καὶ</u> εὐθὺς ἐξηράνθη ἡ πηγὴ τοῦ αἵματος αὐτῆς <u>καὶ</u> ἔγνω τῷ σώματι ὅτι ἴαται ἀπὸ τῆς μάστιγος.

The parallel with the Apocalypse is quickly apparent as the style of both consists of simple cola, introduced by the redundant use of Καί, with little grammatical subordination.

In the book of Revelation, even where such subordination does occur, it is normally no more than one additional line. Grammatical subordination and sophistication of the sort revealed in the epistles of Paul[112] are notably absent in John's Apocalypse.[113] Instead, where subordinate clauses are present, they are normally rather brief. Again, for an example, consider S1:P9 (Rev 4:11): λαβεῖν τὴν δόξαν καὶ τὴν τιμὴν καὶ τὴν δύναμιν, ὅτι σὺ ἔκτισας τὰ πάντα καὶ διὰ τὸ θέλημά σου ἦσαν καὶ ἐκτίσθησαν (to

---

110. Tolkien, *Fellowship of the Ring*, 97.
111. Kelber, *Oral and Written Gospel*, 44-139.
112. Take Eph 1:3-14 as an example.
113. Perhaps Paul intended a greater sophistication on the part of both his reader and any hearers who would be present to listen. Paul frequently sent his letters with companions who had either helped him draft it or were close enough to him to interpret the letters once they arrived. While obviously this book is not an analysis of Pauline epistles, such questions arise. Perhaps it is simply a matter of genre and style.

receive glory and honor and power, because you created all things and through your will they are and were created). The dependent ὅτι clause introduces the cause of the praise that the twenty-four elders proclaim. This grammatical subordination is relatively simple and straightforward, and the text returns to the pattern of simple cola one after another in the line that follows. Perhaps John's discourse style is not rebellious or haphazard[114] but rather betrays the very characteristics of oral performance rather than print expression.

Aggregative Prose

Second, oral cultures are typified with aggregative rather than analytic prose. Here, again, John's style shows stylistic markers characteristic of orality. In nearly every instance where the word κύριος is applied to God, it is collocated with ὁ θεός (Rev 1:8; 4:8; 11:17; 15:3; 16:7; 18:8; 19:6; 21:22; 22:5, 6).[115] What is more, on seven occurrences, it is collocated also with ὁ παντοκράτωρ. This repetition would be significant to the ancient audience, as Aune suggests that such repetition may suggest that the use of these titles as such was in part "an antithetical reflection of the application of those titles to the Roman emperor."[116] Additionally, in the present section under investigation, John continuously addresses the one receiving praise as τῷ καθημένῳ ἐπὶ τῷ θρόνῳ[117] (to the one seated on the throne [Rev 4:9]). Just three lines later, again this character is noted as τοῦ καθημένου ἐπὶ τοῦ θρόνου.[118] This repeats again in Rev 5:1, 5:7, and 5:13b. Thought expressed in an oral culture "carries a load of epithets and other formulary baggage that high literacy rejects as cumbersome and tiresomely redundant because of its aggregative weight."[119] The repeated

---

114. It is beyond the scope of this present study to explore and analyze the solecisms in the book of Revelation. For a detailed analysis of these solecisms in the book, see Charles, *Critical and Exegetical Commentary*, cxliii–clvi.

115. Indeed, the exceptions (7:14; 11:4; 11:8, 15; 14:13; 15:4; 17:14; 19:16; 22:20; 22:21) may actually prove the rule, as these exceptions may be ascribed to persons other than God the Father, either Jesus or, even in 7:14, an angel.

116. Aune, *Revelation*, 310–312.

117. Or some variation in noun-case as seen in the next example.

118. The precise phrase τοῦ καθημένου ἐπὶ τοῦ θρόνου occurs precisely seven times in the book of Revelation. See Bauckham, *Climax of Prophecy*, 33.

119. Ong, *Orality and Literacy*, 38.

epithet τῷ ζῶντι εἰς τοὺς αἰῶνας τῶν αἰώνων (the one living forever and ever)[120] in Rev 4:9–10 likely also serves as another example.[121]

Redundancy and Repetition

Third, and again clearly demonstrated in the Apocalypse, oral cultures apply redundancy of the "just said"[122] in order to keep the speaker and the hearer together during the performance. This functions similarly to what other analysts refer to as "tail-head"[123] linkage, where the element of the previous main clause is repeated in subsequent subordinate clauses. Albert Lord finds a slightly different purpose for this repetition, noting that the repetition in oral cultures often occurs for ritualistic purposes. The repetition of details and of the "just said" point to the importance of the subject in the story.[124] Such redundancy of previously introduced elements is pervasive in the Apocalypse. Table 1 above suggests as much with the word θρόνος, for example, repeated nineteen times in two chapters and twelve times in scene 1 alone. It is not just volume, however, that indicates this sort of redundancy. It is rather the way in which the repetition occurs. Again, note the use of throne in Rev 4:5–6a:

1. Καὶ ἐκ τοῦ θρόνου
2. ἐκπορεύονται ἀστραπαὶ
3. καὶ φωναὶ
4. καὶ βρονταί,
5. καὶ ἑπτὰ λαμπάδες πυρὸς καιόμεναι
6. ἐνώπιον τοῦ θρόνου,
7. ἅ εἰσιν τὰ ἑπτὰ πνεύματα τοῦ θεοῦ,
8. καὶ ἐνώπιον τοῦ θρόνου ὡς θάλασσα ὑαλίνη ὁμοία κρυστάλλῳ.

---

120. Similar features occur in the theophany scene in Rev 1, with the one like a son of man introducing himself with several redundant titles that occur together frequently in John's Apocalypse.

121. The closest parallels to this come from the Greek Old Testament in Daniel 4:34. See Smalley, *Revelation to John*, 124.

122. Ong, *Orality and Literacy*, 40.

123. See Dooley, *Analyzing Discourse*, 15–16.

124. Lord, "Characteristics of Orality," 57–58.

Lines 6 and 8 repeat the very same formula for an element that has been introduced two periods earlier in Rev 4:2–3 and already repeated four times in scene 1 alone.[125]

Ong provides insight into why such repetition may occur:

> The public speaker's need to keep going while he is running through his mind what to say next also encourages redundancy. In oral delivery, though a pause may be effective, hesitation is always disabling. Hence it is better to repeat something, artfully if possible, rather than simply to stop speaking while finishing the next idea.[126]

In predominantly oral cultures, fulsomeness and volubility is encouraged, and this dissipates in a literate culture.[127] Ong even notes that rhetoricians had a formal name for this technique: copia.[128] While Ong may be correct in his assessment, it is the ritualistic implications suggested by Lord that may be even more insightful here. To Lord, this repetition functions not simply as a reminder—or even for fulsomeness—but rather as a way to mark the public and ritualistic setting that the story evokes.[129] This would be most significant here as the content of the story details John's approach to the throne of God. Lord refers to this as ritual elaboration, which is evidence of the oral residue left behind in the written text.[130]

This same characteristic surfaces again and again. In scene 2, the repetition of βιβλίον (scroll), newly introduced in Rev 5:1, keeps the audience's attention trained on the scroll. John accomplishes this by his use of redundancy, particularly at the end of periods. In scene 2, periods 3 and 4 (Rev 5:3, Rev 5:4), the same formula occurs with the exact same wording: ἀνοῖξαι τὸ βιβλίον οὔτε βλέπειν αὐτό (to open the scroll or to look inside it). Given Ong's suggestions above concerning the way in which ancient performers would rather repeat than hesitate, this redundancy should not be surprising. In fact, the collocation of ἀνοῖξαι and βιβλίον occur twice more (Rev 5:5, 9).

---

125. This excludes the additional two plural uses of thrones, upon which the twenty-four elders sit.
126. Ong, *Orality and Literacy*, 40–41.
127. Ong, *Orality and Literacy*, 40–41.
128. Ong, *Orality and Literacy*, 40–41.
129. Lord, "Characteristics of Orality," 57–62.
130. Lord, "Characteristics of Orality," 57.

Agonistic Tone

Fourth, since oral storytelling is not mediated through the written page but rather spoken person to person, interpersonal relations, both positive and negative, receive added significance. Thus, in telling a story, the speaker is directly addressing his audience. Since the human social setting forms the setting in which all stories play out in an oral culture, orality often situates the content of the message within a context of struggle.[131] Evidence of this struggle pervade the book of Revelation.[132] From the onset, John notes that he is exiled because of his allegiance to Jesus (Rev 1:10). Each of the seven churches receives commendation and rebuke for their ability to bear up in the midst of the struggle (Rev 2:2–3, 6, 9–10, 13–14, 20–25; 3:2–4, 9–11, 15–17). This is further confirmed by the repeated refrain to overcome (Ὁ νικῶν, Rev 2:7, 11, 17, 26; 3:5, 12, 21). Elements of conflict and struggle are too ubiquitous to continue to list, as they comprise the entire backdrop of the story of the Apocalypse.[133]

Ong further notes that this struggle may be presented through the back-and-forth expressions of bragging and name-calling between antagonists, enthusiastic depictions of physical violence, and effusions of praise for the heroes.[134] Depictions of physical violence is a regular feature of the Apocalypse, again too numerous to list here. In the two scenes presently observed, however, it is the fulsome expressions of praise for the one on the throne and the lamb that are most apparent. In oral cultures, this is not evidence of insincerity or verbosity but rather belonging to the "highly polarized, agonistic, oral world of good and evil, virtue and vice, villains and heroes."[135] This polarized context will only grow clearer as the Apocalypse develops further.

---

131. Ong, *Orality and Literacy*, 43–45.

132. For comparison, John clarifies that the very occasion that generated this visionary experience was his exile to Patmos because of his commitment to Jesus.

133. Collins, *Crisis and Catharsis*, 141–61. See also Collins, *Combat Myth*, 57–100, 207–45; Fiorenza, *Book of Revelation*, 1–140; Barr, *Tales of the End*, 1–25, 101–50; Bauckham, *Climax of Prophecy*, 210–37.

134. Ong, *Orality and Literacy*, 43–45.

135. Ong, *Orality and Literacy*, 45.

Empathetic and Participatory Tone

A fifth characteristic of orality is the empathetic and participatory tone of the narrator.[136] As opposed to the objective tone of many modern print texts, ancient performers wanted to place the narrator in the midst of the action. Unlike perhaps any other New Testament narrative text,[137] John's Apocalypse places the narrator squarely in the midst of the action. In the first scene, John is in the spirit and receives direct speech from a heavenly voice.[138] All of the events to follow in chapters 4 and 5 are oriented to what John saw himself and reported to the audience. In scene 2, John's subjective experience is front and center, with the text even noting John's emotional response to the unmet request of the angel: καὶ ἔκλαιον πολύ (and I wept much).[139] In oral performance, often the narrative voice is buried completely in the text, as the narrator participates throughout.[140] After weeping, John records receiving comfort personally as one of the participants speaks directly to him. Later in the narrative, John's dialogue with one of the elders is recorded (Rev 7:13–17), it is John himself who takes and eats a βιβλαρίδιον (scroll) from the hand of an angel (Rev 10:8–11), a voice from heaven speaks with him again (Rev 14:13), he is carried into the wilderness (Rev 17:1–2), again he is instructed to write (Rev 19:9), he is carried onto a high mountain (Rev 21:9–10), and again is instructed (Rev 22:6–7). While personal first-person visionary depictions are a regular feature of apocalyptic literature,[141] the participatory nature of the experience also betrays a regular feature of oral culture as well. Perhaps the genre of apocalyptic literature as a whole was developed

---

136. Ong, *Orality and Literacy*, 45–46.

137. Even the "we" sections of Acts pale in comparison to the involvement of John in Revelation.

138. This is precisely the same as the events depicted in Rev 1:10, as John reports the entirety of the visionary experience within the Apocalypse as something he participated in. Not only that, but John also greets his readers by acknowledging that he is receiving this vision while exiled to Patmos because of his commitment to Jesus. This sort of empathy would have been well received in an oral reception.

139. This dramatic scene is depicted in such a way to highlight the emotional element and may be influenced by Isaiah 29:11. See Aune, *Revelation*, 349; as well as Smalley, *Revelation to John*, 130.

140. Ong, *Orality and Literacy*, 148.

141. See Blackwell, *Reading Revelation in Context*, 19–36; Bauckham, *Climax of Prophecy*, 38–91.

with the listening audience in mind, as the vivid nature and agonistic style lend itself to oral performance.[142]

Lack of Sequential Parallelism

One further characteristic of orality is definitively present in the book of Revelation, particularly in the present section under review, which is the lack of sequential parallelism.[143] Scholars have debated the way in which the various scenes within the book of Revelation are related, with many suggesting some sort of chronological ordering of events in a linear fashion[144] and others suggesting a cyclical retelling of the same events again and again, recapitulating previously covered material.[145] It is beyond the scope of the present section to wade into this weighty and important debate, but what must be recognized here is the way in which John's style varies throughout. Different scenes are told with a different pace, some following a brisk linear progression[146] and others seemingly with little to no chronological progression at all.

Since oral performers often rely on memory, as their memory guides them through each retelling of the story, temporal linear progression often falls by the wayside.[147] Ong then notes that the poet reciting from memory frequently gets caught up with lengthy descriptions, noting the colors of the hero's shield or the vividness of a character's outfit. These descriptions essentially form a digression where the narrator loses track of the narrative entirely.[148] Scholars who study the way that folk stories are told and retold within oral cultures acknowledge this characteristic,[149] and this characteristic is on display in Revelation chapter 4. After the lengthy recitation of the seven letters to the churches, John moves the

---

142. Indeed, this would be a welcome advance in the study of apocalyptic literature given the methodology and findings of the present book.

143. Ong, *Orality and Literacy*, 147.

144. See Fanning, *Revelation*, 61–63; Morales, "Discourse Analysis," 46–123.

145. Beale, *Book of Revelation*, 108–16; Smalley, *Revelation to John*, 19–20; Fiorenza, *Book of Revelation*, xci–ci.

146. Rev 6, to be studied in the section to follow, serves as an example here.

147. Ong, *Orality and Literacy*, 147.

148. Ong, *Orality and Literacy*, 147.

149. Vansina, *Oral Tradition as History*, 42–47; Ong, *Orality and Literacy*, 139–55. See also Bauman, *Story, Performance, and Event*, 1–115.

setting of the narrative to the heavenly throne room.[150] The resumption of the narrative storyline is expected by the repetition of Μετὰ ταῦτα εἶδον (after these things, Rev 4:1), with added urgency by the use of Εὐθέως (immediately) and ἰδοὺ (behold). What follows, however, is a series of lengthy descriptions of the new setting.[151] The same feature occurs in the first chapter of Revelation as John follows the apocalyptic tradition, providing a lengthy description of the heavenly messenger.[152] This characteristic is not simply a matter of rhetorical effect, rather it serves to illustrate the way in which ancient oral performers could rely on the mention of a place, image, or person to trigger their memories to retrieve an established pattern for talking about said place or image or person.[153] Again, Lord agrees that this reveals evidence of the oral culture behind the text; he disagrees with Ong regarding the way in which this sort of technique functioned within oral cultures. Lord suggests a ritual repetition behind such lengthy and elaborate descriptions,[154] and perhaps Lord's explanation is more appealing. In any case, however, both scholars acknowledge the technique as a characteristic of oral culture.

Narrative Discourse Features

Given that the Apocalypse of John contains agent orientation and continent temporal succession (albeit not always in a strictly linear fashion), the discourse is therefore a narrative.[155] As such, the tools for analyzing narrative discourse must be employed. In the subsequent analysis of Rev 4–5, it is important not simply to articulate the findings of the analysis

---

150. Barr, "Apocalypse as Oral Enactment," 244–47.

151. Again, see the comparison in Rev 1:10–19 as John introduces the voice that speaks to him with imperative force. The narrative however pauses to describe the one like a son of man in great detail, only to pick up the same imperative ten verses later.

152. See Reynolds, "Parables of Enoch," 37–44; Bauckham, *Climax of Prophecy*, 38–91. Perhaps these sorts of lengthy descriptions, as characteristic of oral culture, are often used in apocalyptic literature because the genre was best performed out loud to the gathered audience and not on the written page read silently.

153. Again, see Vansina, *Oral Tradition as History*, 42–47; Barr, "Apocalypse as Oral Enactment," 244–47. More to be said concerning this technique in the "mnemonic device" section below.

154. Lord, "Characteristics of Orality," 57.

155. Longacre, *Holistic Discourse Analysis*, 35. While there are multiple types of narratives, particularly among traditional oral cultures, it is still important to recognize that the Apocalypse is, in essence, a narrative.

but rather to note the way in which these narrative discourse techniques are relevant to the text of Revelation as a narrative intended for performance. The application of the methodology provided in chapter 1 should not be applied looking for something that is not there but rather carefully exploring the imprints of orality left on the text itself. The text is all the modern student has available for such a purpose. Aspects of storyline, participants and participant rank, narrative pacing, and events will be studied in turn.

Verbal Aspect and Storyline

Gerard Genette makes a simple observation about narratives in that they tell events that happen to characters, thus the exploration of the verbal elements of any story is critical.[156] A list of persons, items, or objects one after another may very well be important for a merchant or a statistician, but such a listing would make for a terrible story. Stories involve events. These events typically are told in a sequential manner so that the "situation at the end is subsequent to what it was at the beginning,"[157] otherwise the story is difficult to follow. Careful attention to the storyline (or the event-line) of the narrative is required, with proper recognition of the difference between the storyline and support material. In narrative, given the reality that the telling of an event must be subsequent to the event itself, the past tense is expected as well as the perfective aspect.[158] In Greek, the aorist verb functions to accomplish both of these expectations[159] and is therefore the most basic or default choice.[160] In Revelation, this default choice is employed extensively, creating the basic storyline of the narrative.[161] The pervasive use of the καί + aorist construction forms the backbone of the Apocalypse,[162] which Mathewson refers to as background events.[163]

---

156. Genette, *Narrative Discourse*, 30.
157. Ong, *Orality and Literacy*, 147.
158. Longacre, *Grammar of Discourse*, 21.
159. Porter, *Idioms*, 22–23.
160. Runge, *Discourse Grammar*, 11.
161. Mathewson, "Verbal Aspect in the Apocalypse," 65.
162. The aorist can also be used in a grammatically subordinate clause, thus functioning to expound and develop supporting material contained in the subordinate clause.
163. Mathewson, "Verbal Aspect in the Apocalypse," 65.

Deviation from this default choice signal, or "mark," prominence or some unique quality—a quality that would not have been marked if the default option was used.[164] The imperfective verbal aspects and perfect verbs, then, function as marked options within the book of Revelation. They differ from the default aorist verb as well as from each other. Following markedness theory, therefore, Mathewson proposes that the imperfective verb (both present and imperfect) serves to indicate foregrounded events, with frontgrounded events reserved for the perfect tense.[165] He posits that foregrounded material would be utilized in signaling to the reader important characters within the story and stand out as central to the themes of the overall narrative, while frontgrounded material would draw attention to material that stands out as surprising or unexpected, marking them for consideration.[166] Mathewson's "markedness" proposal provides a functional guide to analysis of the book of Revelation and is not meant to be understood as the decisive verdict regarding the complex scholarly debate about the Greek verb.[167]

Since this book assumes an emphasis on examining the text of John's Apocalypse for its oral features, these marked events would be important not only to signal prominence in the written text itself but also for the public performer. Thus, application of this markedness theory provides valuable interpretive insight. In Revelation scene 1 (Rev 4), John uses his fewest amount of aorist verbs per one thousand words than any other chapter in the entire book, as indicated in the graph below.

---

164. Mathewson, "Verbal Aspect in the Apocalypse," 65.

165. Mathewson, "Verbal Aspect in the Apocalypse," 65.

166. Mathewson, "Verbal Aspect in the Apocalypse," 65. Smalley notes that when the future tense is combined with ὅταν, as in Rev 4:9, the actions should be best understood as simultaneous to the present scene and not to be understood as a grammatical error. See Smalley, *Revelation to John*, 123. For additional support of Mathewson's proposal, see Campbell, *Basics of Verbal Aspect*, 197; as well as Porter, *Verbal Aspect*, 207.

167. See Porter, *Idioms*, 302–3. Mathewson builds much of his methodology following Porter's suggestion from this resource.

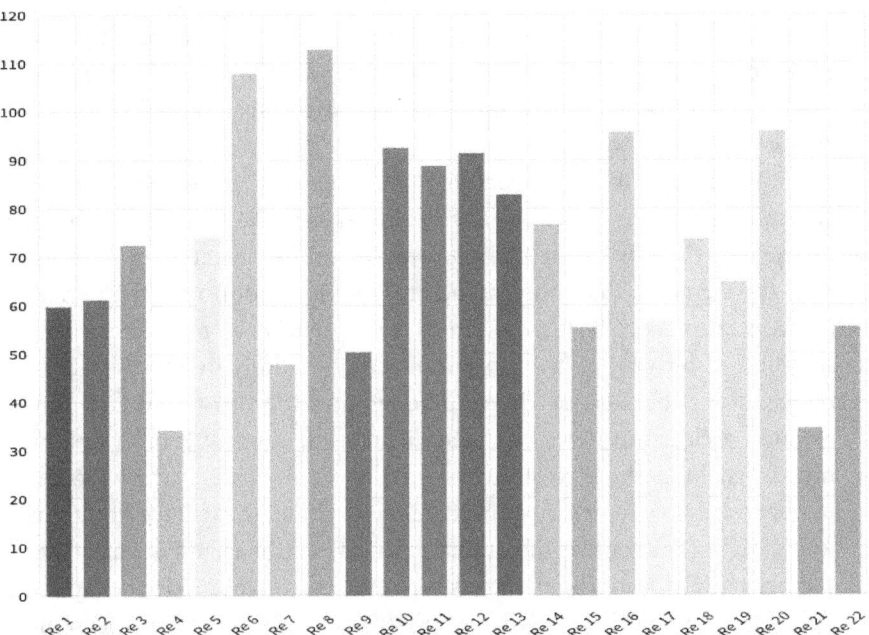

Aorist verb use (all moods, including participles) per one thousand words per chapter in Revelation

Little temporal sequential progression or action occurs within this chapter. Given the amount of material devoted to description mentioned in the previous section, this lack of event-line material should not be surprising. Additionally, chapter 4 has the second highest[168] count of imperfective verbs (present and imperfect) per one thousand words per chapter than any other. For many scholars, both Revelation chapters 4 and 17 function as transitions to new macro-sections of the book.[169] In each, the setting is dramatically changed and each employ the repeated introductory formula stating that John was in the spirit. Given that both introduce new settings and characters, these introductions require adequate space and time devoted to such a task, thus taking the narrative away from the main event-line. Additionally, the characters introduced in both of these chapters play prominent roles in the subsequent storyline to follow. Thus,

---

168. Rev 17 has the highest but only slightly more than chapter 4. Additionally, it is noteworthy that chapter 1 is the third highest, which certainly serves as a transition from outside the narrative to inside.

169. Bauckham, *Climax of Prophecy*, 3–5; Fanning, *Revelation*, 58–64.

these elements are highlighted as central to the overall theme of the narrative and are therefore semantically marked with the imperfective aspect. To only follow the traditional understanding of verbs representing time and tense would obscure the way in which this material functions rhetorically in the text itself.[170]

This data corroborates Mathewson's proposal that the verb in John's Apocalypse serves as a tool to mark prominence in the text. What is more, the way in which material is frontgrounded using the perfect aspect unveils the elements that John intends to highlight. John uses the perfect twice in chapter 4 (Rev 4:1, 4). The θύρα ἠνεῳγμένη ἐν τῷ οὐρανῷ (door standing in heaven) is given prominence not simply by the use of the perfect aspect but also by virtue of being introduced with καὶ ἰδού (and behold), a clear motivator of the audience's attention.[171] It must first be noted that John chose to shift from the aorist indicative εἶδον[172] to the perfect participle to describe the state of the door. This choice functions to highlight the event, as the dramatic shift from the island of Patmos to the heavenly throne room requires careful rhetorical guidance for the audience.[173] Second, John also employs this technique with the same perfect participle in Rev 19:11 at yet another significant moment in the narrative. Again, the pragmatic choice in both instances to deviate from the default option requires explanation, and here Mathewson's proposal proves satisfying.

The second use of the perfect aspect highlights the way in which the twenty-four elders are clothed: περιβεβλημένους ἐν ἱματίοις λευκοῖς (dressed in white clothes [Rev 4:4]). While much attention has been given in scholarship to the identification of the twenty-four,[174] few note the

---

170. It is here that a break with the traditional understanding of the Greek verb depicting different types of action encoded in time has less explanatory value than the proposal put forward by Mathewson. To be sure, one could apply categories like "the historical present" or "progressive imperfect," but these may be less helpful in explaining John's use of verbs than verbal aspect guiding markers of prominence. Since this is not a study on the verb system of Koine Greek, much more could be said. Sufficient for the present purposes is this: Mathewson's suggestion proves helpful in its application to the book of Revelation.

171. Smalley, *Revelation to John*, 114.

172. Mathewson notes that εἶδον is often used to frame a discrete visionary segment within the book of Revelation. Mathewson, "Verbal Aspect in the Apocalypse," 65.

173. Bauckham, *Climax of Prophecy*, 7. As noted above, these major structural seams in the narrative require clear and pronounced markers. Koester, *Revelation*, 367.

174. See Beale, *Book of Revelation*, 322–26. It is worth noting here that the elders are also described as seated. This is an unusual feature in apocalyptic literature, as

prominence established by the use of the perfect aspect here. Osborne, for example, notes that white garments signify purity and holiness as perhaps part of a priestly function,[175] but few scholars seriously consider the adjustment in verbal aspect. In the context surrounding this clause, the imperfective aspects are regularly employed to introduce new elements or characters, yet here the pattern varies.

In scene 2 (Rev 5), variation and placement of verbal aspect and storyline are even more pronounced. In fact, Mathewson applied his methodology to this chapter specifically in an article published in 2008 in *Novum Testamentum*. First, he notes the backgrounding function of the aorist, with the introductory Καὶ εἶδον construction again serving to frame segments of the vision itself, thus dividing Rev 5:1 from 5:2-5, 5:2-5 from 5:6-10, 5:6-10 from 5:11-14.[176] Background material is advanced in summary fashion, utilizing the aorist verb in both indicative and infinitive mood, as well as in participle form.[177] The storyline advances more substantially in chapter 5 than in chapter 4, yet chapter 5 still retains a high variation of verbal aspect.[178]

Second, Mathewson notes that "in contrast to the background aorist tense, the present and imperfect aspects occur throughout the vision to add descriptive color and highlight or foreground certain events and features."[179] For the purposes of validating and appreciating the oral performance intention of the book, it is particularly noteworthy that the speeches, announcements, songs, and hymns of this scene are introduced with verbal forms in the present tense.[180] The angel speaks κηρύσσοντα ἐν φωνῇ μεγάλῃ (proclaiming in a loud voice [Rev 5:2]), the elder speaks to John using a present aspect verb λέγει (he says [Rev 5:5]),[181] the living creatures and the elders καὶ ᾄδουσιν ᾠδὴν καινὴν λέγοντες· (and a

---

frequently it is only God on the throne who sits while the other participants stand. See Hurtado, *Ancient Jewish Monotheism*, 475-78.

175. Osborne, *Revelation*, 229.

176. Mathewson, "Verbal Aspect in the Apocalypse," 65.

177. Mathewson, "Verbal Aspect in the Apocalypse," 66.

178. Mathewson, "Verbal Aspect in the Apocalypse," 67-70.

179. Mathewson, "Verbal Aspect in the Apocalypse," 67.

180. Again, see Dooley, *Analyzing Discourse*, 128.

181. This same feature emerges in examination of Rev 1, as the present tense introduces speech-acts there as well (Rev 1:8, 11, 17). This is also true in Rev 2-3, as each of the messages to the seven churches are introduced with the present verb (2:1, 8, 12, 18; 3:1, 7, 14).

new song they sing saying [Rev 5:9]), the myriad of angels[182] λέγοντες φωνῇ μεγάλῃ (are saying in a loud voice [Rev 5:12]), the entire creation are heard λέγοντας (saying [Rev 5:13]), and the four living creatures ἔλεγον· ἀμήν[183] (saying "amen" [Rev 5:14]). Mathewson's methodology provides clarification, enabling the student to see how these speech-acts are highlighted, since they are critical in establishing a liturgical directive as the lamb takes the scroll.[184] The prominence of these speech-acts not only stands out in the written text but would be significant for both the oral performer as well as the listening audience,[185] facilitating the hearer with the ability to discern elements that John intends to stand out and the speaker with the knowledge of which elements to accentuate in performance.

Additionally, John noted his own emotional response to the report from the angel by again departing from the default verb choice. As suggested above, a participatory tone is common among oral cultures, and John marks his own experience of weeping by choosing to present the event with the imperfect verb καὶ ἔκλαιον (and I was weeping [Rev 5:4]). This is further highlighted by the modification of the verb with the adjective πολύ (much). Lastly, the inability of anyone to open the scroll is brought to the foreground by the imperfective aspect in this scene, as John states that οὐδεὶς ἐδύνατο ἐν τῷ οὐρανῷ οὐδὲ ἐπὶ τῆς γῆς οὐδὲ ὑποκάτω τῆς γῆς . . . οὔτε βλέπειν αὐτό (no one was able in the heavens or on the earth or under the earth . . . or *even* look at it). The change from aorist ἀνοῖξαι (to open) to present βλέπειν (to look) likely indicates that John is bringing intensity to the scene: not only is no one able to open the scroll, but no one is able to *even* look at it.[186]

Finally, which elements are frontgrounded in scene 2 by the use of the perfect aspect? Mathewson notes that the perfect verb is not used haphazardly, but when used as a participle, it clusters "around the two most significant features of the vision in two of the discreet units of the vision:

---

182. Likely taken from Dan 7:10.

183. Thus, the four living creatures who began the effusion of praise in scene 1 close the doxology in scene 2. See Smalley, *Revelation to John*, 141.

184. Mathewson, "Verbal Aspect in the Apocalypse," 67.

185. Lord, *Singer of Tales*, 33; Vansina, *Oral Tradition as History*, 13–25, 34–43.

186. Mathewson suggests that this shift suggests that the looking is the more "salient activity of the two," whereas Osborne suggests that they are part of the same action and should be seen together. See Mathewson, "Verbal Aspect in the Apocalypse," 68. See also Osborne, *Revelation*, 252.

the scroll (Rev 5:1) and the Lamb (Rev 5:6)."[187] In Rev 5:1, the scroll is noted as having two significant characteristics, each marked with perfect participles: γεγραμμένον ἔσωθεν καὶ ὄπισθεν κατεσφραγισμένον σφραγῖσιν ἑπτά (having been written inside and out and having been sealed with seven seals). While scholars continue to disagree over the function of the perfect verb, perhaps Mathewson's contribution sheds valuable light on the way in which the verbs function within the discourse of Revelation.[188] Following Mathewson, by choosing two perfect verbs here, thus deviating from the default option, John marks the action in some way. As the scroll is brought front and center, with no one able to open its seals, John builds suspense and tension within the narrative. Later, the lamb in Rev 5:6 is introduced with two perfect participles: ἀρνίον ἑστηκὸς ὡς ἐσφαγμένον (a lamb standing as having been slain). The choice of both of these pairs[189] of perfect participles necessitate functional explanation, and Mathewson's application of markedness theory provides a satisfactory account. Thus, these perfects mark prominence in the narrative, elevating the rank of these participants (the scroll and the lamb).

While these participles certainly lend credibility to Mathewson's proposal, it is the one perfect verb that is in the indicative case that is most provocative in scene 2. The lamb moves to the throne and καὶ εἴληφεν (and takes) the scroll from the hand of the one on the throne.[190] Indeed, the shift from aorist καὶ ἦλθεν (and he went) to the perfect requires clarification,[191] since the aorist form of λαμβάνω is used elsewhere in Revelation, even in the immediate context (5:8, 9, 12). Why the switch to the perfect here? Scholars disagree, of course. Charles views this as an example of a semitism in the text.[192] Beale and Fanning agree that the

---

187. Mathewson, "Verbal Aspect in the Apocalypse," 70.

188. Again, see the summary in Campbell, *Advances*, 117–19.

189. As an exception to the case currently being presented, ἵστημι is almost always used in the perfect in Revelation. More will be said regarding the perfect use of ἵστημι in the subsequent sections under investigation. Since it is almost always set in the perfect aspect, it may perhaps reflect more about the nature of the action itself rather than an intention on the part of the author.

190. Again, the references to Dan 8:26 and 12:4 are unmistakable. See Smalley, *Revelation to John*, 129.

191. This construction is used also in Rev 3:3; 8:3, 5; 19:3–4. Smalley, *Revelation to John*, 133.

192. Charles, *Critical and Exegetical Commentary*, 143–44.

verb functions as an aorist verb.[193] Smalley views the switch to the perfect as indicating an abiding result, presented sequentially after the lamb's movement toward the throne.[194] Mounce and Aune argue in a similar fashion to Mathewson's proposal, suggesting that the switch to the perfect is an intentional one that highlights and dramatizes the action.[195]

Mathewson posits that the shift to the perfect frontgrounds the event[196] in order to "focus attention on the process of the reception of the scroll."[197] Here, Mathewson's proposal that the pragmatic variation between the choices of verbs at John's disposal provides explanatory power for the often-shifting verb tenses in the book of Revelation.[198] This book assumes an emphasis on the orality of the book of Revelation, and these functional discourse markers of prominence, utilizing the grammatical and morphological features of the various Greek verbs, would be relevant for ancient readers of the book of Revelation. Put simply, if John intended certain events and participants to be signaled as prominent within his discourse, then skilled readers would be forced to recognize such prominence and render it obvious to the audience as well.[199] As discussed in the analysis of the sound map in the pages above, the switch to the perfect also serves to create parallel sounds between the aorist ἦλθεν and the perfect εἴληφεν in the same period.

In summary, while this is not a book about verbal aspect theory, the markedness theory may clarify the way in which background and foreground material is utilized in John's Apocalypse. Furthermore, structural features, such as the higher accumulation of imperfective aspects in comparison to aorist verbs, bolster the position of scholars who have understood chapters 4 and 17 to be key structural indicators within the

---

193. Beale, *Book of Revelation*, 357; Fanning, *Verbal Aspect*, 302–3.

194. Smalley, *Revelation to John*, 133.

195. Aune, *Revelation*, 324. Mounce, *Book of Revelation*, 146.

196. It is here that Mathewson's article is most profitable, as he provides a summary of the scholarly debate regarding the use of the perfect here, particularly in such close collocation with the aorist that precedes it. It is the opinion of the present writer that Mathewson's methodology brings an added clarity to the functional discourse use of the perfect in the book of Revelation. See Mathewson, "Verbal Aspect in the Apocalypse," 72–73.

197. Mathewson, "Verbal Aspect in the Apocalypse," 73–74.

198. Mathewson, "Verbal Aspect in the Apocalypse," 61.

199. Vansina, *Oral Tradition as History*, 34–54. See also Iverson, "Oral Fixation or Oral Correctiven," 183–200; Rhoads, "Performance Criticism, Pt. I," 124–27.

book.[200] In addition, featured elements are signaled by the use of verbal aspect, enabling the hearer and performer alike to give attention to the most prominent participants of the narrative. This prominence will be accounted for in chapter 4 of the book, as a performance commentary suggesting prosody in the public telling of the narrative of John's Apocalypse.

Participants and Rank

One of the difficulties in interpreting the book of Revelation is the way in which characters are presented differently throughout the narrative. For example, in Rev 1, Jesus was introduced as one like a son of man (1:13), walking among seven golden lampstands. However, in chapter 5, the symbolic imagery of a lamb is used to describe Jesus (5:6). Later, Jesus appears in heaven riding a white horse (19:11–16). In this way, Jesus is "restaged" again and again throughout the narrative and depicted by a variety of means. Other participants leave the scene almost as quickly as they emerge,[201] thus suggesting that they rank lower in prominence than characters who participate in multiple scenes.

Participant and participant rank go hand in hand with the storyline, or the event-line noted above, because action happens to and by participants.[202] That is what creates a story: actors and actions. In any story, certain actors take more prominent roles while others take a more secondary or background role.[203] Careful attention to these elements in studying narrative enables the modern analyst to perceive how the text's composer intended the story to be understood. Additionally, one point of view often overlooked when considering participants in a story is the narrator himself.[204] As noted in the methodology proposed above, narrators may position the perspective of the story around a character's point of view as well as present the material from an internal or an external perspective.[205] In regard to both of these available options, John himself takes center stage as the story is told from his point of view as the narrator, and the story is told from an internal, first-person perspective. Often,

---

200. Bauckham, *Climax of Prophecy*, 3–7. Fanning, *Revelation*, 58–64.

201. This will be particularly clear in the next section to be studied (Rev 6:1—8:1).

202. Longacre, *Holistic Discourse Analysis*, 81–92.

203. Longacre, *Holistic Discourse Analysis*, 81–92. See also Dooley, *Analyzing Discourse*, 109–27; Genette, *Narrative Discourse*, 25–32.

204. Genette, *Narrative Discourse*, 10.

205. Genette, *Narrative Discourse*, 10.

this feature is overlooked in Revelation scholarship, with few commentators even giving it much of a mention but in passing,[206] but appreciation of this requires placing John as the most prominent participant in the narrative as a whole. From the opening lines of the book to the closing lines, John's voice is the one the audience must follow, for his voice has been divested with authority from on high.[207] This participatory, internal, and subjective storytelling was noted above as a feature more widely acceptable in oral cultures rather than print.[208]

In Rev 4:1—5:14, then, which other participants show prominence, and which rank lower in importance? Longacre and Hwang suggest a methodology for analyzing these features as noted in the proposed methodology in chapter 1. With their approach in mind, combined with the markers for prominence noted in the previous section regarding verbal aspect, the student is able to rank the participants appropriately. Again, it must be recognized that 4:1–2 introduce a new setting to the narrative, namely the heavenly throne-room. The first participant brought onto the staging of this new scene is the one seated on the throne. Much of the subsequent material (Rev 4:4–11) is oriented to the throne and the one seated on the throne, and each additional group of characters is also oriented to the throne, with the twenty-four elders said to be κυκλόθεν τοῦ θρόνου (around the throne), the four living creatures ἐν μέσῳ τοῦ θρόνου καὶ κύκλῳ τοῦ θρόνου (in the midst of the throne and around the throne), the lightning, sounds, and thunderstrikes ἐκ τοῦ θρόνου ἐκπορεύονται (coming out of the throne).[209] Expressions of adoration are made to the one sitting on the throne (4:9–10; 5:13) and attention is again focused to the scroll ἐπὶ τὴν δεξιὰν τοῦ καθημένου ἐπὶ τοῦ θρόνου (in the right hand of the one sitting on the throne) in the opening line of scene 2. Thus, in these chapters, the highest participant rank belongs to the throne and the

---

206. For a notable exception, see Resseguie, *Revelation of John*, 47–53.

207. See the discussion among commentators regarding the chain of transmission of the material in the narrative. This feature is regularly noted, but again it is suggested in this book that many scholars then fail to note how John's participation in the story betrays a kind of storytelling found more prominently among oral cultures. See Ong, *Orality and Literacy*, 37.

208. Ong, *Orality and Literacy*, 37.

209. Again, this is highly similar to the theophany scene in Rev 1:10–17, as the audience is directed to the one walking among the golden lampstands.

one seated on it,[210] highlighting the universal sovereignty of the one seated on the throne, which is "enhanced by its central location on the stage."[211]

Additionally, the four living creatures and the twenty-four elders figure prominently in this section.[212] They are introduced largely with verbs in the imperfective aspect, noting their prominence grammatically. As stated above, the garments worn by the twenty-four elders is highlighted by the perfect participle that accompanies the description of their clothing. Each group is routinely tracked throughout chapters 4 and 5, members of each group reappear outside of these two scenes (Rev 6:1, 6; 7:11, 13; 11:16; 14:3; 15:7; 19:4), and their purpose in the narrative never wavers in that they consistently point the audience back to the throne, thus requiring the analyst to assign them a place of prominence within the book of Revelation. Indeed, Smalley notes that the function of the elders is more important than their identity, as their chief task is to "participate fully in the worship of God."[213] In chapter 6, the four horsemen come and go quickly, but not so with the four living creatures and the twenty-four elders. Perhaps it is the need to invest time and energy in introducing these weighty and significant characters that necessitates chapter 4's lack of event-line progression. Again, such lengthy descriptions of participants were regular in oral cultures,[214] but these descriptions also serve an important function of marking prominence on these characters so that the listening community recognizes their significance.

In chapter 5, additional participants are brought onto the stage. An ἄγγελον ἰσχυρὸν (strong angel) is introduced, who shouts in a loud voice. This participant comes onto the scene with a dramatic question, which establishes the tension that persists until the lamb appears. This angel incites the conflict to follow with his announcement, and John highlights this by placing the participle κηρύσσοντα (he proclaims) in the present aspect, thus foregrounding the angel and his message. This technique

---

210. Barr, *Tales of the End*, 112–15; Bauckham, *Climax of Prophecy*, 33.

211. Smalley, *Revelation to John*, 115.

212. See Aune, *Revelation*, 288. Aune notes the likely Old Testament influence on John's characterization of these elders but goes as far as to note that John likely creates these participants from a combination of sources. Again, the proposal of this book is that such "creation" may be a marker of oral composition, as the performer works from a shared prophetic background but not necessarily from a written text.

213. Smalley, *Revelation to John*, 115. See also Hurtado, *Ancient Jewish Monotheism*, 478.

214. Ong, *Orality and Literacy*, 37.

enables the angel and the question to move to the center of the audience's mental representation, thus taking center stage in the narrative.

It is not incidental that John then introduces the lamb in the most semantically marked way available to him. John employs two perfect participles that describe the lamb—ἀρνίον ἑστηκὸς ὡς ἐσφαγμένον (a lamb standing as slain)—followed by two dependent clauses, the first adding further depiction of the lamb and the second introduced by a relative clause that further clarifies the meaning. The lamb then moves front and center: first, as part of the main event-line as John articulates the action of the lamb in the aorist aspect (καὶ ἦλθεν, and he went); second, the lamb then dispels the tension created by the angel's announcement by taking (εἴληφεν) the scroll himself. Again, this is the only use of the perfect indicative in either of these two scenes, thus moving the lamb and this action to the place of peak prominence on the mental "stage" of the audience.[215] Every other participant, even those that were previously foregrounded, must now move to a secondary position to the lamb. As a result of this action, in the remainder of chapter 5 τῷ καθημένῳ ἐπὶ τῷ θρόνῳ καὶ τῷ ἀρνίῳ (to the one seated on the throne and to the lamb [Rev 5:13]) are collocated on several occasions. Thus, the lamb is elevated to the prominent participant rank enjoyed by the one seated on the throne,[216] which directly challenges the audience to right belief about and loyalty to the person of Jesus with corresponding conduct in life.[217]

That several significant characters are introduced in Revelation 4:1—5:14 is not novel, but the way in which these participants are tracked throughout the rest of the book is often overlooked. The twenty-four elders reappear in Rev 7:11, 13; 11:16; 14:3; and 19:4. The four living creatures appear in Rev 6:1, 6; 7:11; 14:3; and 15:7. Barr notes that characters that appear within the different settings or "staging" of John's Apocalypse are marked for prominence,[218] and these characters are restaged in different settings and scenes throughout the book. Indeed, while John certainly experiences things from different vantage points within the narrative,

---

215. Mathewson, "Verbal Aspect in the Apocalypse," 70.

216. Many scholars refer to this as the investiture of the lamb and also note the significance of this scene. What is important to the present investigation, however, is how this significance is accomplished functionally within the grammar of Revelation. *That* the lamb is highlighted is beyond dispute. *How* the lamb is highlighted is the present question. See Beale, *Book of Revelation*, 350–57; Fanning, *Revelation*, 220–21. Osborne, *Revelation*, 257–58; Gorman, *Reading Revelation Responsibly*, 102–15.

217. Smalley, *Revelation to John*, 6.

218. Barr, *Tales of the End*, 27–30.

moving the mental picture of the audience from earth to heaven and back again (see the events in chapters 6 through 18), it is as if the throne and the throne's attendants are always in the background.[219] Many scholars have noted that this may even suggest that the staged Greek drama performed publicly in theaters may have had influence on the Apocalypse.[220]

Pace, Event, and Nonevent

Developing alongside the previous two sections, the pacing of these two scenes (Rev 4:1—5:14) requires brief attention. Since narratives normally involve actors and actions, nonevents become important for orienting the audience to participants in the story. These non-events function to create a mental representation of the story's setting (or stage), to explain elements of the story, to evaluate characters and their actions, to provide information to the audience, and to reporting speech-acts or dialogue within the story.[221] This nonaction does not necessarily carry the event-line of the story forward but plays a crucial role in making the story intelligible.

Since scene 1 (Rev 4:1–11) introduces a new setting as well as new participants, it is not surprising that much of the material in this scene would be categorized as nonevent.[222] John provides the hearer with details regarding the color and vividness of the setting, likening the throne and its surroundings to beautiful jewels, a rainbow, and a lake of glass. Additionally, here the four living creatures and the twenty-four elders are introduced with accompanying description. These details are all at once vivid, colorful, noisy, similar and yet dissimilar to things available to the audience (thus the frequent use of simile),[223] and full of praise to the one on the throne. Such details enable the hearer to picture and imagine the stage upon which the action begins to unfold in scene 2 (Rev 5:1–14).

Again, numerous speech-acts are preserved in chapter 5 (Rev 5:2, 5, 9–10, 12, 13, 14), constituting nonevents that report the content of each. While the similarities between these scenes were noted above—each

---

219. Janse van Rensburg, "All the Apocalypse," 1–8. This is where Barr's suggestion that those characters that are restaged retain prominence within the text is so helpful.

220. Janse van Rensburg, "All the Apocalypse," 1–8.

221. Grimes, quoted from Dooley, *Analyzing Discourse*, 82.

222. Dooley, *Analyzing Discourse*, 79–85.

223. Vansina, *Oral Tradition as History*, 12. The frequent use of the simile also serves to introduce the one like a son of man in Rev 1.

ending with dual proclamations of praise—what must be stated in the present is the sheer volume of speech reported in these scenes. Following the suggestion of Albert B. Lord, narratives in a predominantly oral culture are often oriented acoustically rather than visually.[224] These speech-acts are similar, and it is the redundancy of these that invites the hearer to respond and even join.[225] Again, scholars making comparison to the Greek drama theater receive corroboration, as live audiences were expected to respond appropriately to the performance.[226]

A final note on the pacing of this section of Revelation is warranted. When compared with chapter 6 (to be explored in detail below), chapters 4 and 5 contain a relatively infrequent use of the καί + aorist construction, with chapter 4 employing very few aorist verbs in comparison to the rest of the book and chapter 5 following suit. The frequency of nonevents combined with the infrequency of event-line aorist verbs creates a slowed pace to these two scenes. Elements are carefully placed on the stage, oriented to the throne, and given appropriate time for consideration, while the audience takes in the bombardment of reported speech. As will be seen in the analysis of chapters 6 and 7, this pace will be completely abandoned for a rapid-fire series of event-line actions utilizing the aorist tense, then slowed significantly again in chapter 7. This technique would be particularly effective in performance, where prosody would make the impact of these features even more pronounced.

BIBLICAL PERFORMANCE CRITICISM OF REV 4–5

Introduction

Performance criticism begins with the assumption that ancient cultures experienced stories out loud, publicly performed before the listening audience.[227] Most people were incapable of reading lengthy epics on the written page, and even those who read from the page were expected to read out loud. In addition, public performances of texts were expected to be done from memory. Compositions were organized and presented with this in mind, and the various cues which signaled to the ancient

---

224. Lord, *Singer of Tales*, 33.
225. Rhoads, "Performance Criticism, Pt. I," 128–29.
226. Janse van Rensburg, "All the Apocalypse," 1–8; and Rhoads, "Performance Criticism, Pt. I," 128–29. See also Vansina, *Oral Tradition as History*, 34–35.
227. Vansina, *Oral Tradition as History*, 3–54; Ong, *Orality and Literacy*, i.

performer remain in the printed text for the modern scholar to explore. They just have to know where to look.²²⁸

Mnemonic Devices

Numbered Sequences

One of the things consistently noted by scholars is the way in which the book of Revelation employs a repeated cycle of seven numbered events.²²⁹ Some even propose the presence of additional unnumbered seven-fold series at various parts.²³⁰ While it is beyond the scope of this book to corroborate the macro-structure of the book and their constitutive features, one significant element of the numbered sequencing often goes overlooked in Revelation scholarship and that is the way in which numbering aids memory for public storytelling.²³¹ This rather obvious observation contributes further evidence in support of the thesis of this book, that the book of Revelation was indeed composed with the listening audience in mind and is structured for its public performance.²³² These memory aids guide the ancient performer to repeat the story again and again from memory.²³³ They will receive attention in the next section to be evaluated, as Rev 6:1—8:1 specifically articulates one of the numbered sequences.

Place and Location

In Rev 4:1—5:14, another feature common to ancient performance is imprinted onto the written text, and that is the way that place and location aided memory in performance.²³⁴ The value of this device, however,

---

228. Rhoads, "Performance Criticism, Pt. I," 124; Horsley, *Text and Tradition*, 223.
229. Fanning, *Revelation*, 58–164; Bauckham, *Climax of Prophecy*, 7–15.
230. Collins, *Combat Myth*, 32–43.
231. Barr, "Apocalypse as Oral Enactment," 244–47.
232. The episodic structuring device (such as the numbered sequences) is matched with a consistent repetition of elements within each scene. As stated above, the four-fold repetition (although frequently different in order) of ethnic groups, the seven-fold repetition of praise (see Rev 5:11), and the triple use of ἅγιος in Rev 4:8 all at least suggest that devices such as this may indicate performance mnemonic aids imbedded in the written text.
233. Again, Botha notes that composition in the ancient world was a "memory-based activity." See Botha, *Orality and Literacy*, 34–51; 116.
234. Vansina, *Oral Tradition as History*, 44–47, 124–28.

is rather intuitive due to the fact that events happen at places, creating memories and stories. Frequently just passing by or mentioning a location can spring forth a story that is associated with that place.[235] The images and elements associated with that place then become necessary and important in the telling of the story.[236] Thus, the movement to the new location in Rev 4:1–2 acts as a mnemonic cue for the ancient performer.[237]

Perhaps John has employed such a device here in Rev 4:1–2. With the first numbered sequence (Rev 2–3) complete, John has guided his performer through the first large section of the book. Given Botha's assertion that in the ancient world even the composition of performances was a memory-based activity,[238] this study proposes that the introduction of the heavenly throne room then serves as a mnemonic aid, triggering the host of images and participants that follow.[239] These images and participants are combined from a shared literary and prophetic tradition,[240] coming together to enable easy recall here. Vansina suggests that this cluster of stock-images, combined with the setting, enables the performer to create the public performance from memory.[241] This may provide sufficient explanation for why the four living creatures are described using a blend of elements from several prophetic traditions,[242] thus baffling scholars for generations. While most scholars agree that elements from

---

235. The theophany scene introduced in Rev 1:10 begins by John not only recognizing the place he is located, but also the reason for his placement there: he has been exiled because of his commitment to Jesus. Patmos, however, receives no further attention. Instead, John directs his audience to a scene that shows comparison with the vision recorded in Zech 4. In Rev 2–3, Jesus moves about the room, speaking directly to each group that is symbolically represented by the seven lampstands.

236. Barr, "Apocalypse as Oral Enactment," 244–47; as well as Bauman, *Story, Performance, and Event*, 1–10, 112–17.

237. Vansina, *Oral Tradition as History*, 43.

238. Botha, *Orality and Literacy*, 116.

239. In my own work on this book, I memorized the book of Revelation 1:1—14:5 before moving on to other tasks that needed more urgent attention. (I hope to go back and finish at some point.) In memorizing the book, the importance of place was essential. I found this mnemonic device crucial in mentally adjusting from the numbered sequences in chapters 2–3 and 6:1—8:1 to the setting established here. With the "trigger" of the heavenly throne room, essentially all of chapters 4 and 5 unfolded more effortlessly in recall.

240. Vansina, *Oral Tradition as History*, 12. Collins, *Apocalyptic Imagination*, 256–79; Reynolds, "Parables of Enoch," 37–44.

241. Vansina, *Oral Tradition as History*, 12, 35.

242. Smalley, *Revelation to John*, 120.

Isaiah and Ezekiel are prominent,[243] it is the transformation and blending of these descriptive components that may indicate that John is not strictly quoting from a particular Old Testament passage but rather combining from memory stock-elements from the Hebrew prophetic tradition to describe these heavenly beings.[244] The same feature may be on display with the introduction of the twenty-four elders. Aune notes the likely influence on the text of Revelation but concedes that John's description of these participants is likely a combination or blending of elements from various sources and may even be a creation of John himself.[245] Thus, all the public speaker needs to remember is the place—the heavenly throne room—and essentially the rest of the scene would follow, from the props and staging to the participants themselves.[246] With that in mind, then, scene 2 (5:1–14) flows naturally from scene 1 with the stage now set for the introduction of the angel and the lamb. In short, to recall merely the location—the heavenly throne room in Rev 4:1–2—unlocks the next two scenes, which then anticipate the next numbered sequence of seven, enabling even further aid for the performance from memory.

The Use of Scrolls

One final mnemonic device that requires attention is the way in which the three scrolls mentioned in the book of Revelation correspond to a sequence of events and actions.[247] Barr notes that the first mentioned scroll contains the letters to the churches, depicting the events that occur on the earthly island of Patmos; the second scroll—the sealed scroll mentioned in Rev 5:1–7—corresponds to events that occur in heaven around the heavenly throne; and the third scroll that John eats then (10:9) adjusts the mental representation of the events to the earth.[248] While Barr disagrees with Bauckham and Fanning regarding the macro-structure of the book, they both share a willingness to acknowledge the significance of the scrolls for structuring the book. Neither note, however, the way in which these elements would facilitate recall in performance, though Barr

243. See Beale, *Revelation of John*, 87; Smalley, *Revelation to John*, 8–10.
244. Vansina, *Oral Tradition as History*, 12.
245. Aune, *Revelation*, 288.
246. Barr, "Apocalypse as Oral Enactment," 244–47.
247. Barr, "Apocalypse as Oral Enactment," 246–47; Collins, *Combat Myth*, 19–31; Bauckham, *Climax of Prophecy*, 13–15.
248. Barr, "Apocalypse as Oral Enactment," 246–47.

does posit that "the orality of the Apocalypse is an essential element in its interpretation."[249] While Barr provides a few cues to look for when analyzing the book of Revelation as an oral composition,[250] it is the aim of the present study to validate this claim in a more robust manner.

Episodic Storytelling

This book has consistently referred to the narrative units that comprise chapters 4 and 5 of Revelation as scenes and that has been done intentionally. Scenes combine to form episodes and, as noted in the proposed methodology, ancient storytelling betrays an episodic style as opposed to a climactic linear plot. This is due to the difficulty of following lengthy and detailed plots, which often require the ability to move forward and backward in a written text. Ong maintains that an ancient oral culture would not recognize a lengthy, novel-size linear plot.[251] Instead, themes are repeated in a redundant and episodic style, allowing the performer to memorize and recall a scene at a time without creating a strict linear progression.[252]

This feature will be more readily apparent in the comments on the next section to be explored below, but for the present section, it is sufficient to simply identify redundancy in episodic theme.[253] Many modern crime investigation television shows follow a similar pattern: the crime is found and reported, the police arrive and face initial confusion, the police work to solve the crime using whatever means available, they hand the case to the prosecutors, the courtroom drama unfolds, and the audience is provided with a fitting conclusion—and all in one hour.[254] The audience does not need prior information to make sense of each episode, however, significant characters occur across multiple episodes; and the more the audience watches, the more familiar they become to these main characters. In the same manner, in Rev 1:9–16, John invites his audience

---

249. Barr, "Apocalypse as Oral Enactment," 246–47.

250. Barr, "Apocalypse as Oral Enactment," 246–47.

251. Ong, *Orality and Literacy*, 143.

252. Ong, *Orality and Literacy*, 143.

253. Collins, *Combat Myth*, 207–17. She sees a recapitulation theory based around scenes, each related in some way to the ancient near eastern mythology of cosmic warfare.

254. This describes every scene of *Law and Order* and its derivatives that have been on the air for decades.

to partake in his theophany experience by describing it in detail. Then John interacts with one of the characters who speaks directly with him (Rev 1:17–19). Then a numbered series of messages are presented to the ancient audience (Rev 2–3). This pattern emerges again in Rev 4:1—5:10, as John invites his audience to partake in his theophany experience (Rev 4:1–11). John then depicts the characters' interactions, particularly through recorded speech-acts and the movement of the lamb (Rev 5:1–14). Then again, a numbered sequence follows (Rev 6:1—8:1). This redundancy aids the performer's memory in the public recitation of the story, and it will be suggested in the analysis in the subsequent sections that these corresponding episodes may have been composed separately and performed as individual narratives that were later compiled together to form the anthology of the book of Revelation as a whole.[255]

Prosody Features in Rev 4:1—5:14

The book of Revelation has been cited as the noisiest book in all of Scripture.[256] All of this noise provided opportunity for the ancient reader to dramatize the action of the story for the listening audience. Scholars debate the way in which ancient readers would have addressed their audience,[257] and it is beyond the scope of this paper to settle the matter. However, it must be stated that the text would have been read skillfully, and that the reader/performer had a significant responsibility in the communication of the story. This is evident by the public commendation and blessing that starts the book (Rev 1:3). Thus, even if the written manuscript was used, the reader/performer had ample opportunity to bring the text to life in their recitation. Of course, if the reader/performer was working from memory, this enhanced their ability to bring the text to life. Thus, the function of all of the noise in the oral performance event of the book's reception has gone underdeveloped. First, John creates urgency with

---

255. This would certainly run counter to many of the proposals that try and bring a climactic linear chronological progression to the macro-structure of Revelation. In a fascinating thesis, Morales suggests applying Longacre's methodology concerning plot structuring in *The Grammar of Discourse* to the book of Revelation as a whole. However, given Ong's caution that many ancient "readers" would not be reading the text at all but rather hearing it aloud, such complex and linear plots are difficult to maintain. See Morales, "Discourse Analysis," 46–123.

256. Resseguie, *Revelation of John*, 21.

257. See the "Four Founding Assumptions" sections of chapter 1 for a summary of the discussion.

his repetition of καὶ ἰδού (and behold [4:1, 2; 5:5]). Second, numerous times John directs his audience's mental representation—from Patmos, for example, to a door ἠνεῳγμένη ἐν τῷ οὐρανῷ (having been opened in heaven). This statement would even prompt the performer to point upwards.[258] In a previous section, it was stated that all the action in Rev 4:2–8 is oriented to the throne and the one seated on it; John introduces other participants as either κυκλόθεν τοῦ θρόνου (around the throne), ἐκ τοῦ θρόνου (out of the throne), ἐνώπιον τοῦ θρόνου (before the throne), or ἐν μέσῳ τοῦ θρόνου καὶ κύκλῳ τοῦ θρόνου (in the midst of the throne and around the throne). Each of these provide opportunity for the performer to gesture, helping the audience picture the scene appropriately.

Additionally, and perhaps most significantly, John's use of reported speech clearly signals the performer's vocal pitch.[259] It is not simply that speech is reported, but the speaker is cued to the way the speech should be read: καὶ εἶδον ἄγγελον ἰσχυρὸν κηρύσσοντα ἐν φωνῇ μεγάλῃ (and I saw a strong angel proclaiming in a loud voice . . .), καὶ ᾄδουσιν ᾠδὴν καινὴν λέγοντες (and they sang a new song saying), the myriad of angels are said to be λέγοντες φωνῇ μεγάλῃ (speaking in a loud voice).[260] These clear instructions inform the performer's prosody. Other signals, while perhaps not as clearly identifiable, also remain imprinted on the text: the strong angel asks an important question τίς ἄξιος ἀνοῖξαι τὸ βιβλίον καὶ λῦσαι τὰς σφραγῖδας αὐτοῦ; (Is anyone worthy to open the scroll and loose its seals?). In reading silently on the page, the necessary pause may be hard to conceptualize, but in public performance, the speaker would rightly pause after this question in order to build suspense for what follows. John breaks into tears upon learning that no one is found worthy to open the scroll[261] or even look inside (Rev 5:3–4), requiring a change in tone and voice on the part of the performer. He is then comforted by one of the twenty-four elders (Rev 5:5a), but this comfort then turns into an announcement to behold the lion who has conquered and is worthy to open the scroll. A flat and monotonous tone would not do for such a speech-act.[262] Prosody in the performer's voice and gesturing enable a

---

258. Vansina, *Oral Tradition as History*, 34–35. See Hearon and Ruge-Jones, *Bible in Media*, 51–59; Rensburg, "All the Apocalypse a Stage," 4–5.

259. Vansina, *Oral Tradition as History*, 34–35.

260. In Rev 1:10, the speaker is introduced similarly, again likened to a particularly noisy instrument: φωνὴν μεγάλην ὡς σάλπιγγος.

261. Likely a reference to Ezek 2:9–10. See Smalley, *Revelation to John*, 127.

262. Vansina, *Oral Tradition as History*, 34–35; Rhoads, "Performance Criticism, Pt. I," 126–27.

more engaging and inviting experience of hearing the book of Revelation as John intended it to be heard.

SUMMARY OF ANALYSIS OF REV 4–5

This study has thus far provided analysis of two chapters of John's Apocalypse, working first from a sound map and the way in which repetition of sounds form individual cola and periods. Working from the period, John's style can be evaluated as largely a plain style that employs a continuous movement from period to period—several structural markers as well as style markers that are common in oral cultures of the ancient world. These guided the audience as the plot developed and may have facilitated the recitation of the text from memory. Careful analysis of the choice of verbs used, participants, event and nonevent, and narrative pacing guide the analyst to see which events and characters should be brought to the foreground in the performance of the story. This enabled the performer to highlight elements and participants, bringing them to the front of the mental stage of the hearers, while also maintaining the background storyline of the narrative. Finally, several devices that aid the performer's telling of the story remain imprinted on the story, from mnemonic devices to cues for prosody. Since stories were not read with a flat, monotone voice, these cues imprinted on the text are helpful for interpretation, enabling the modern scholar to hear the text again as it was intended. With two more sections left to be explored, the thesis of this book—that the book of Revelation was composed for an aural performance—finds many points of corroboration.

4

Performance Analysis of a Numbered Sequence Scene

INTRODUCTION TO REV 6:1—8:1

REPRESENTATIVE SECTIONS OF THE book of Revelation were chosen for their variation in order to validate the central claim of the study. Put simply, if the proposed methodological approach only provides exegetical insight to certain portions of Revelation but fails to yield similar results when applied to the rest of the book, then the method may be inadequate, and the thesis of this investigation would not be proven. The theophany scene analyzed in the previous chapter gives way to the rush of activity in the "opening of the seals" episode to be explored in this chapter. While Rev 4, for example, has the fewest amount of aorist verbs per chapter by percentage, Rev 6 is the complete opposite. Chapters 4 and 5 center the attention on the throne and the one seated on it, and every character is essentially oriented "throneward," while in Rev 6 and 7, the action, participants, and pacing change dramatically. What is more, Rev 6:1—8:1 contain one of the four seven-fold numbered sequences, a technique that John employs regularly. It is imperative to apply the methodology suggested to this next large section of the book in order to verify that the methodology is sound. Thus, attention to this section provides a framework for analyzing the other numbered sequences found in the Apocalypse, making the careful investigation of this chapter relevant for broader scholarly work on the book as a whole. Points of comparison with the other numbered sequences will be noted in the footnotes in this chapter.

THE SCIENCE OF SOUND IN REV 6:1—8:1

Sound Map of Rev 6:1—8:1 with Analysis

Scene 3 (Rev 6:1-8)

Period 1 (Rev 6:1)

1. Καὶ εἶδον ὅτε ἤνοιξεν τὸ ἀρνίον μίαν ἐκ τῶν ἑπτὰ σφραγίδων,
2. καὶ ἤκουσα ἑνὸς ἐκ τῶν τεσσάρων ζῴων
3. λέγοντος ὡς φωνὴ βροντῆς·
4. ἔρχου.

Period 2 (Rev 6:2)

1. καὶ εἶδον,
2. καὶ ἰδοὺ ἵππος λευκός,
3. καὶ ὁ καθήμενος ἐπ' αὐτὸν ἔχων τόξον
4. καὶ ἐδόθη αὐτῷ στέφανος
5. καὶ ἐξῆλθεν νικῶν
6. καὶ ἵνα νικήσῃ.

Period 3 (Rev 6:3)

1. Καὶ ὅτε ἤνοιξεν τὴν σφραγῖδα τὴν δευτέραν,
2. ἤκουσα τοῦ δευτέρου ζῴου λέγοντος·
3. ἔρχου.

Period 4 (Rev 6:4)

1. καὶ ἐξῆλθεν ἄλλος ἵππος πυρρός,
2. καὶ τῷ καθημένῳ ἐπ' αὐτὸν ἐδόθη αὐτῷ
3. λαβεῖν τὴν εἰρήνην ἐκ τῆς γῆς
4. καὶ ἵνα ἀλλήλους σφάξουσιν
5. καὶ ἐδόθη αὐτῷ μάχαιρα μεγάλη.

Period 5 (Rev 6:5a)

1. Καὶ ὅτε ἤνοιξεν τὴν σφραγῖδα τὴν τρίτην,
2. ἤκουσα τοῦ τρίτου ζῴου λέγοντος·
3. ἔρχου.

Period 6 (Rev 6:5b)

1. καὶ εἶδον,
2. καὶ ἰδοὺ ἵππος μέλας,
3. καὶ ὁ καθήμενος ἐπ' αὐτὸν
4. ἔχων ζυγὸν ἐν τῇ χειρὶ αὐτοῦ.

Period 7 (Rev 6:6)

1. καὶ ἤκουσα ὡς φωνὴν ἐν μέσῳ τῶν τεσσάρων ζῴων λέγουσαν·
2. χοῖνιξ σίτου δηναρίου
3. καὶ τρεῖς χοίνικες κριθῶν δηναρίου,
4. καὶ τὸ ἔλαιον καὶ τὸν οἶνον μὴ ἀδικήσῃς.

Period 8 (Rev 6:7–8)

1. Καὶ ὅτε ἤνοιξεν τὴν σφραγῖδα τὴν τετάρτην,
2. ἤκουσα φωνὴν τοῦ τετάρτου ζῴου λέγοντος·
3. ἔρχου.

Period 9 (Rev 6:8a)

1. καὶ εἶδον,
2. καὶ ἰδοὺ ἵππος χλωρός,
3. καὶ ὁ καθήμενος ἐπάνω αὐτοῦ ὄνομα αὐτῷ θάνατος,
4. καὶ ὁ ᾅδης ἠκολούθει μετ' αὐτοῦ

Period 10 (Rev 6:8b)

1. καὶ ἐδόθη αὐτοῖς ἐξουσία ἐπὶ τὸ τέταρτον τῆς γῆς
2. ἀποκτεῖναι ἐν ῥομφαίᾳ
3. καὶ ἐν λιμῷ
4. καὶ ἐν θανάτῳ
5. καὶ ὑπὸ τῶν θηρίων τῆς γῆς.

Given the volume of repeated elements, words, and phrases that make up this scene, they may rightly be analyzed together. Overall, the pleasant α/αί and weightier ου sounds dominate these periods. These vowel sounds are also part of the repeated introductory formula for each of the four horsemen (καὶ, σφραγῖδα, ἔρχου, ἰδού), thus giving them even greater emphasis. The repeated imperative ἔρχου with its ending vowel sound provides a dark and solemn tone, which matches the content. Additionally, these periods have a larger quantity of hiatus, which is caused by ending a word with a vowel and beginning the following word with a vowel. Hiatus was not preferred,[1] causing a deliberate stop in the flow of the spoken word. The hiatus in these periods is also part of the introductory formula for each of the horsemen (καὶ εἶδον καὶ ἰδοὺ ἵππος), creating suspense as each character is introduced.

While each period contains a high distribution of liquid and nasal consonants that enable the meter to flow smoothly, it is the injection of harsh consonant blends and harsh consonant sounds at key junctures that warrants remark. In the second period, the repetitive κ- sound provides a marshal crispness, which balances out the otherwise smooth meter. The difficult σφρ- blend, which introduces each of the horsemen, continues the "play" on sounds discussed in chapter 3 above. In fact, this sound play is applied again in period 4 as the highly similar σφ- (σφάξουσιν) is used in close proximity. Hiatus is pervasive in the fourth period, forcing the speaker to be especially deliberate in oral communication. Also, aspirates (φ, χ) and double consonants (ξ) make period 4 quite distinct, matching the harshness of the content. Similar patterns occur in the remaining periods in this passage, creating a variation and tone that facilitates both briskness and harshness in the sound's meter.

Scene 4 (Rev 6:9–17)

Period 1 (Rev 6:9)

1. Καὶ ὅτε ἤνοιξεν τὴν πέμπτην σφραγῖδα,
2. εἶδον ὑποκάτω τοῦ θυσιαστηρίου
3. τὰς ψυχὰς τῶν ἐσφαγμένων
4. διὰ τὸν λόγον τοῦ θεοῦ
5. καὶ διὰ τὴν μαρτυρίαν ἣν εἶχον.

---

1. From Quintilian, *Institutio Oratia*, 9.4.10.

Now that the four horses and their riders have come and gone, the fifth seal introduces the audience to a new collective character, and yet again the "play" on sounds is utilized (σφραγῖδα and ἐσφαγμένων). It is worth noting that this is now the third character referenced with the verb σφάζω (I slaughter): the lamb, the second horseman, and now the martyred souls. Additionally, sibilant sounds and voiceless aspirates create a harsh sounding style tone that serves to amplify the introduction of these characters. This is likely deliberate, as the souls of the martyrs will linger on the mental "stage" longer than the horsemen in the previous pericope and will also speak directly to the Lord. The description of the martyrs has a pleasant abundance of liquid consonants and pleasant ἀ sounds.

Period 2 (Rev 6:10)

1. καὶ ἔκραξαν φωνῇ μεγάλῃ λέγοντες
2. ἕως πότε,
3. ὁ δεσπότης ὁ ἅγιος καὶ ἀληθινός,
4. οὐ κρίνεις καὶ ἐκδικεῖς τὸ αἷμα ἡμῶν
5. ἐκ τῶν κατοικούντων ἐπὶ τῆς γῆς;

The spoken word recorded in the second period begins with an address directly to the Lord, using a nice sounding mixture of liquid consonants. This gives way, however, in cola 4 and 5, as the respectful address of colon 3 moves into the specific prayer request of the martyrs. Here, as the martyrs question the Lord's timing, consonant clusters emerge and more voiced and voiceless stops created by the use of dental consonants alters the tone. The four-syllable κατοικούντων rounds off the period with the open and dark ω/ού sounds.

Period 3 (Rev 6:11a)

1. καὶ ἐδόθη αὐτοῖς ἑκάστῳ στολὴ λευκὴ
2. καὶ ἐρρέθη αὐτοῖς
3. ἵνα ἀναπαύσονται ἔτι χρόνον μικρόν,
4. ἕως πληρωθῶσιν
5. καὶ οἱ σύνδουλοι αὐτῶν
6. καὶ οἱ ἀδελφοὶ αὐτῶν
7. οἱ μέλλοντες ἀποκτέννεσθαι ὡς καὶ αὐτοί.

Repetition of sounds and words marks this period, particularly the repetition of αὐτος. The period begins with a καὶ + aorist construction in the first two cola, and both aorist verbs have almost identical sounding syllables at the beginning and end of the words (ἐδόθη, ἐρρέθη). Both are also followed with αὐτοῖς. The smooth and pleasant consonant sounds, coupled with the voluminous use of open α vowels, combine with this repetition to form the euphonic response to the martyr's question. The response may be euphonic in tone, but that hits an abrupt halt as the period closes. Elongation and the five-syllable ἀποκτέννεσθαι alters the otherwise pleasing response with a more somber note. The dental consonants that make up this multisyllabic word are crisp and hard, matching the message.

Period 4 (Rev 6:12)

1. Καὶ εἶδον ὅτε ἤνοιξεν τὴν σφραγῖδα τὴν ἕκτην,
2. καὶ σεισμὸς μέγας ἐγένετο
3. καὶ ὁ ἥλιος ἐγένετο μέλας ὡς σάκκος τρίχινος
4. καὶ ἡ σελήνη ὅλη ἐγένετο ὡς αἷμα

Period 5 (Rev 6:13)

1. καὶ οἱ ἀστέρες τοῦ οὐρανοῦ ἔπεσαν εἰς τὴν γῆν,
2. ὡς συκῆ βάλλει τοὺς ὀλύνθους αὐτῆς ὑπὸ ἀνέμου μεγάλου σειομένη,

Period 6 (Rev 6:14)

1. καὶ ὁ οὐρανὸς ἀπεχωρίσθη ὡς βιβλίον ἑλισσόμενον
2. καὶ πᾶν ὄρος καὶ νῆσος ἐκ τῶν τόπων αὐτῶν ἐκινήθησαν.

Since each of these periods work together thematically and share many grammatical features, they are suited for combined analysis. In the period 4, the repetition of ἐγένετο enables the action to take center stage. Additionally, multiple simile introduced with ὡς serve to further depict the vivid imagery. What is striking in these periods, however, is the increased use of the sibilant consonant (σ). The sibilant is shrill and hissing, and oftentimes, its use was limited if possible. Here, with the devastating apocalyptic imagery, the sibilant works perfectly to depict the sounds of the creation, particularly the repeated wind/air/sky elements in the passage.

Additionally, careful attention to the variation in rhythm combined with the manipulation of sounds demonstrates intentionality on the part of the author. Since choice implies meaning, it is noteworthy that each of the comparisons that follow the similes are relatively short, except for period 5. Here, the comparison persists for nine words, significantly longer than the other three similes in these periods. The length is not all. The simple comparison, ὡς συκῇ, would have been sufficient and matched the other similes in length and style. However, this one continues, and as it does, the description is loaded with long and dark ου diphthongs. These mimic the heavy sound of figs falling in the strong wind.

Period 7 (Rev 6:15–16a)

1. Καὶ οἱ βασιλεῖς τῆς γῆς
2. καὶ οἱ μεγιστᾶνες
3. καὶ οἱ χιλίαρχοι
4. καὶ οἱ πλούσιοι
5. καὶ οἱ ἰσχυροὶ
6. καὶ πᾶς δοῦλος καὶ ἐλεύθερος
7. ἔκρυψαν ἑαυτοὺς εἰς τὰ σπήλαια
8. καὶ εἰς τὰς πέτρας τῶν ὀρέων
9. καὶ λέγουσιν τοῖς ὄρεσιν καὶ ταῖς πέτραις·

Period 8 (Rev 6:16b–17)

1. πέσετε ἐφ' ἡμᾶς
2. καὶ κρύψατε ἡμᾶς
3. ἀπὸ προσώπου τοῦ καθημένου
4. ἐπὶ τοῦ θρόνου
5. καὶ ἀπὸ τῆς ὀργῆς τοῦ ἀρνίου,
6. ὅτι ἦλθεν
7. ἡ ἡμέρα ἡ μεγάλη τῆς ὀργῆς αὐτῶν,
8. καὶ τίς δύναται σταθῆναι;

The martyrs introduced with the opening of the fifth seal are contrasted with the peoples of the land and their kings introduced in the sixth seal. (Again, the characters and their request are considered together here.) This contrast is made even more explicit by John's careful manipulation of sound, in that the kings of the earth are characterized by an overall dissonant sound quality. Each of these characters is introduced through the technique of anaphora, or the repetition of a word or phrase at the beginning of successive clauses. As the peoples of the land are recorded, the tone starts euphonic (οἱ βασιλεῖς τῆς γῆς), but as the list builds it, becomes increasingly cacophonous (καὶ οἱ χιλίαρχοι, οἱ πλούσιοι, οἱ ἰσχυροί). What is more, the verbal element in period 7, ἔκρυψαν, contains a consonant cluster as well as a double consonant, ψ. Thus, the verb's difficult sounds matches the context as the peoples of the land hide from the wrath to come. What is remarkable about the eighth period is the overall euphonic quality to the period, with few consonant clusters and a high degree of liquid consonants, besides two notable exceptions. The first is the repetition of the main verb in period 7, marking the imperative request κρύψατε in colon 2. The second is in the final colon and serves as a powerful structural marker in the overall book, as the peoples of the land ask a question of no little significance: καὶ τίς δύναται σταθῆναι. This στ- cluster gives a final stop to their spoken word but also invites the audience to ponder the question, as the content will change in the section that follows.

Scene 5 (Rev 7:1–8)

Period 1(Rev 7:1)

1. Μετὰ τοῦτο εἶδον τέσσαρας ἀγγέλους
2. ἑστῶτας ἐπὶ τὰς τέσσαρας γωνίας τῆς γῆς,
3. κρατοῦντας τοὺς τέσσαρας ἀνέμους τῆς γῆς
4. ἵνα μὴ πνέῃ ἄνεμος ἐπὶ τῆς γῆς
5. μήτε ἐπὶ τῆς θαλάσσης
6. μήτε ἐπὶ πᾶν δένδρον.

This period has a highly euphonic meter with abundant ἀ and ή sounds that were preferable for harmony and rhythm. What is more, the repetition of several words and phrases provide a steady beat-like pattern to the period. While the sibilant consonant was to be used sparingly, if possible, here the multiple sibilants match the content, as the restraining of the winds is in view. The movement of air through the mouth and over the tongue would mimic the sound of wind and, as the period closes, the final colon contains no sibilant consonant; indeed, the following period has very few.

Period 2 (Rev 7:2a)

1. Καὶ εἶδον ἄλλον ἄγγελον
2. ἀναβαίνοντα ἀπὸ ἀνατολῆς ἡλίου
3. ἔχοντα σφραγῖδα θεοῦ ζῶντος,

Period 3 (Rev 7:2b)

1. καὶ ἔκραξεν φωνῇ μεγάλῃ
2. τοῖς τέσσαρσιν ἀγγέλοις
3. οἷς ἐδόθη αὐτοῖς ἀδικῆσαι τὴν γῆν
4. καὶ τὴν θάλασσαν λέγων·

Period 4 (Rev 7:3)

1. μὴ ἀδικήσητε τὴν γῆν
2. μήτε τὴν θάλασσαν
3. μήτε τὰ δένδρα,
4. ἄχρι σφραγίσωμεν τοὺς δούλους τοῦ θεοῦ ἡμῶν
5. ἐπὶ τῶν μετώπων αὐτῶν.

Period 5 (Rev 7:4–8)

1. Καὶ ἤκουσα τὸν ἀριθμὸν τῶν <u>ἐσφραγισμένων</u>,
2. ἑκατὸν τεσσεράκοντα τέσσαρες χιλιάδες,
3. <u>ἐσφραγισμένοι</u> ἐκ πάσης φυλῆς υἱῶν Ἰσραήλ·
4. ἐκ φυλῆς Ἰούδα δώδεκα χιλιάδες <u>ἐσφραγισμένοι</u>,
5. ἐκ φυλῆς Ῥουβὴν δώδεκα χιλιάδες,
6. ἐκ φυλῆς Γὰδ δώδεκα χιλιάδες,
7. ἐκ φυλῆς Ἀσὴρ δώδεκα χιλιάδες,
8. ἐκ φυλῆς Νεφθαλὶμ δώδεκα χιλιάδες,
9. ἐκ φυλῆς Μανασσῆ δώδεκα χιλιάδες,
10. ἐκ φυλῆς Συμεὼν δώδεκα χιλιάδες,
11. ἐκ φυλῆς Λευὶ δώδεκα χιλιάδες,
12. ἐκ φυλῆς Ἰσσαχὰρ δώδεκα χιλιάδες,

13. ἐκ φυλῆς Ζαβουλὼν δώδεκα χιλιάδες,
14. ἐκ φυλῆς Ἰωσὴφ δώδεκα χιλιάδες,
15. ἐκ φυλῆς Βενιαμὶν δώδεκα χιλιάδες ἐσφραγισμένοι.

Periods 2 through 5 all contain the introduction of yet another angel and his accompanying action and the narrator's recording of it, so they will be covered together. The angel is welcomed to the mental "stage" of the audience in the first two cola of period 2 with a beautiful collection of liquid consonants and pleasant vowel sounds. The pleasant tone gives way, however, in the third colon, as the task of the angel comes into view. Yet again, the σφρ- cluster is utilized, and this final colon of period 2 has multiple aspirate consonant sounds, varying the meter established in the first part of the scene. This continues into period 3, as the angel begins to take action by crying out (ἔκραξεν). The combination of the final colon in period 2 and the opening colon of period 3 provides a sudden harshness that cues the action of this important character. Again, the content of the angel's speech is mostly euphonic except the intrusion of the σφρ- cluster, once again breaking up the meter with this now familiar and difficult sound grouping. This pattern emerges in period 5 as the overly pedantic listing of the tribes of Israel and the repetition of δώδεκα χιλιάδες (twelve thousand) dominates the narrative.[2]

Scene 6 (Rev 7:9—8:1)

Period 1 (Rev 7:9)

1. Μετὰ ταῦτα εἶδον,
2. καὶ ἰδοὺ ὄχλος πολύς,
3. ὃν ἀριθμῆσαι αὐτὸν οὐδεὶς ἐδύνατο,
4. ἐκ παντὸς ἔθνους
5. καὶ φυλῶν
6. καὶ λαῶν
7. καὶ γλωσσῶν
8. ἑστῶτες ἐνώπιον τοῦ θρόνου
9. καὶ ἐνώπιον τοῦ ἀρνίου

2. More to be said on this in the pages that follow.

10. περιβεβλημένους στολὰς λευκὰς

11. καὶ φοίνικες ἐν ταῖς χερσὶν αὐτῶν,

The repetitive voiceless stops (τ) in the first colon require careful articulation, slowing the smooth meter and helping signal a transition. This period has a weightiness with the application of full open ω sounds and more solemn ου sounds. The majority of the passage contains liquid consonants with the occasional dental consonant, but overall, the meter is pleasing and euphonic. Again the one on the throne and the lamb are positioned as both receiving the effusive praise, and the collection of long vowels that describe each one mirrors the two's equal status.

Period 2 (Rev 7:10)

1. καὶ κράζουσιν φωνῇ μεγάλῃ λέγοντες·

2. ἡ σωτηρία τῷ θεῷ ἡμῶν

3. τῷ καθημένῳ ἐπὶ τῷ θρόνῳ

4. καὶ τῷ ἀρνίῳ.

With the exception of the opening κρ- cluster, this mini-doxology contains a beautifully euphonic tone established with the repetition of full and grand ω sounds and the open ἡ and α sounds. The consonants are also beautifully spaced and the meter flows nicely one word to the next. All of this matches the content of the period perfectly.

Period 4 (Rev 7:11–12a)

1. Καὶ πάντες οἱ ἄγγελοι εἱστήκεισαν κύκλῳ τοῦ θρόνου

2. καὶ τῶν πρεσβυτέρων

3. καὶ τῶν τεσσάρων ζῴων

4. καὶ ἔπεσαν ἐνώπιον τοῦ θρόνου ἐπὶ τὰ πρόσωπα αὐτῶν

5. καὶ προσεκύνησαν τῷ θεῷ λέγοντες·

Period 5 (Rev 7:12b)

1. ἀμήν,

2. ἡ εὐλογία

3. καὶ ἡ δόξα

4. καὶ ἡ σοφία

5. καὶ ἡ εὐχαριστία

6. καὶ ἡ τιμὴ
7. καὶ ἡ δύναμις
8. καὶ ἡ ἰσχὺς τῷ θεῷ ἡμῶν
9. εἰς τοὺς αἰῶνας τῶν αἰώνων·
10. ἀμήν.

These periods also enjoy a pleasing harmony and meter, particularly the fifth period as liturgical praise breaks out yet again. The weight of the scene lifts as the long ω and ου sounds restage the various characters introduced in the previous scenes in the fourth period. The consonants comprise a blend of labials, liquids, and dentals, while avoiding consonant clusters, difficult gutturals, and double consonants. What is most appealing is the open ἀ vowels that characterize the fifth period. This is doubly effective when combined with the repetition of καὶ ἡ that precedes each element of praise. The flowing meter, balanced cola, and pleasing vowel sounds work together to create a beautifully euphonic hymn of praise, closed perfectly with the sonically appealing ἀμήν.

Period 6 (Rev 7:13)

1. Καὶ ἀπεκρίθη εἷς ἐκ τῶν πρεσβυτέρων λέγων μοι·
2. οὗτοι οἱ περιβεβλημένοι τὰς στολὰς τὰς λευκὰς
3. τίνες εἰσὶν
4. καὶ πόθεν ἦλθον.

Period 7 (Rev 7:14a)

1. καὶ εἴρηκα αὐτῷ·
2. κύριέ μου, σὺ οἶδας.

Again, since the context warrants, periods 6, 7, and 8 will be examined in unison. The harmony of period 5 adjusts slightly as one of the elders poses a question to the narrator. Elements of hiatus and a higher employment of sibilants and consonant clusters arrests the otherwise pleasing meter established in the previous context. This is necessary, however, as the narrator may desire to slow the pace of the liturgical praise and prepare the audience for the dialogue to follow. The repetition of hiatus in period 7 is especially striking, given the general lack of it in many of John's periods thus far examined.

Period 8 (Rev 7:14b)

1. καὶ εἶπέν μοι·
2. οὗτοί εἰσιν οἱ ἐρχόμενοι
3. ἐκ τῆς θλίψεως τῆς μεγάλης
4. καὶ ἔπλυναν τὰς στολὰς αὐτῶν
5. καὶ ἐλεύκαναν αὐτὰς ἐν τῷ αἵματι τοῦ ἀρνίου.

Period 9 (Rev 7:15–16)

1. διὰ τοῦτό
2. εἰσιν ἐνώπιον τοῦ θρόνου τοῦ θεοῦ
3. καὶ λατρεύουσιν αὐτῷ
4. ἡμέρας καὶ νυκτὸς ἐν τῷ ναῷ αὐτοῦ,
5. καὶ ὁ καθήμενος ἐπὶ τοῦ θρόνου σκηνώσει ἐπ' αὐτούς.
6. οὐ πεινάσουσιν ἔτι
7. οὐδὲ διψήσουσιν ἔτι
8. οὐδὲ μὴ πέσῃ ἐπ' αὐτοὺς ὁ ἥλιος
9. οὐδὲ πᾶν καῦμα,

Period 10 (Rev 7:17)

1. ὅτι τὸ ἀρνίον τὸ ἀνὰ μέσον τοῦ θρόνου ποιμανεῖ αὐτοὺς
2. καὶ ὁδηγήσει αὐτοὺς ἐπὶ ζωῆς πηγὰς ὑδάτων,
3. καὶ ἐξαλείψει ὁ θεὸς πᾶν δάκρυον ἐκ τῶν ὀφθαλμῶν αὐτῶν.

The answer provided by the elder is given in periods 8 through 10 with impressive sonic repetition. In period 8, οἱ, εἶ and αἰ diphthongs all mirror each other in sound[3] and work well with the ἀ vowels and mostly pleasant consonants. John employs yet another "play" on sound in period 8, mirroring the sound of (ἔπλυναν, they washed) with (ἐλεύκαναν, they whitened). This "play" on sounds serves a didactic function in that the manner in which the robes of the martyrs is washed is through the blood of the lamb. This "play" on sounds also mirrors the one already noted in chapter 5. The long ου vowel sound permeates the rest of the periods in this section, giving gravity and weight to the tone. The final three cola that

---

3. Caragounis, *Development of Greek*, 352.

make up period 10 are longer, rounding out the dialogue and providing the necessary instruction to the audience in the process. This rounding technique is particularly effective with John's clustering of consonants and the heavier use of double consonants and voiceless aspirates in the final colon. Certainly, these harsh and difficult consonants would necessitate a deliberate and slow pronunciation on the part of the speaker, enabling the audience to focus on the contents of the message.

Period 11 (Rev 8:1)

1. Καὶ ὅταν ἤνοιξεν τὴν σφραγῖδα τὴν ἑβδόμην,
2. ἐγένετο σιγὴ ἐν τῷ οὐρανῷ
3. ὡς ἡμιώριον.

In order to create the movement toward silence in the scene, John decelerates the use of consonantal energy, moving from multiple consonant clusters and double consonants in colon 1 to liquids in the final colon. Additionally, the length of each cola shortens, slowing the rhythm of the narration to match the silence. It is probable that the narrator would provide a lengthy pause here to mark the occasion.

John's Grouping of Cola into Periods

Structurally, the scenes that make up Rev 6:1—8:1 share similar patterns with the previous two scenes (Rev 4–5 studied above). First, most of the cola in scenes 3 and 4 start with καί. These scenes resume the continuous style pattern[4] with cola flowing one to the next. The cola stack paratactically, relying on the profusive use of καί to connect them with very little grammatical subordination. For a representative example, see S3:P2 (Rev 6:2):

1. καὶ εἶδον,
2. καὶ ἰδοὺ ἵππος λευκός,
3. καὶ ὁ καθήμενος ἐπ' αὐτὸν ἔχων τόξον
4. καὶ ἐδόθη αὐτῷ στέφανος
5. καὶ ἐξῆλθεν νικῶν
6. καὶ ἵνα νικήσῃ.

---

4. Aristotle, *Art of Rhetoric*, 1409a.

All six cola are stacked paratactically, connected by καί. Three lines contain indicative verbs; one contains an imperative (ἰδού, behold). Even where the dependent ἵνα clause is present, it still follows καί. This redundancy is often obscured in translation but characteristic in oral recitation.[5] In scenes 5 (Rev 7:1–8) and 6 (Rev 7:9–17), the pattern is adjusted dramatically[6] as καί begins significantly fewer cola (to be addressed in subsequent sections).

What remains consistent throughout all four scenes, however, is that John refrains from employing exclusive grammatical subordination. Most of the periods within these scenes continue John's use of balance, as John employs repetitive sounds and phrases frequently in order to produce a cadence and rhythm by which the audience can follow.[7] The text shows some use of rounding and very little elongation. Given that period boundaries in ancient composition were often marked by either grammatical subordination (with dependent clauses connected to the main independent clause in the period), rounding, or elongation, period divisions must be established another way.

How, then, does John signal these period boundaries? In these scenes, John's decision to employ a numbered sequence structural technique guides the way. As the seals are opened one by one, the cola structurally cluster within the boundaries of the numbered sequencing, making these scenes markedly different than the previous two. Indeed, the numbered sequencing makes the use of typical period boundary markers, such as rounding and elongation, unnecessary.[8] The structural markers are "baked into" the text via the numbered sequencing.[9] As will be seen below, such numbered sequencing enabled both the performer and the audience to follow the narrative and aided the performer working

---

5. Ong, *Orality and Literacy*, 34.

6. And style variation must be investigated, as variation does not simply occur for variation's sake. Longacre, *Holistic Discourse Analysis*, 15.

7. Longacre, *Holistic Discourse Analysis*, 15.

8. Bauckham goes as far as to suggest that the numbering sequences are intentionally obvious and emphatic due to the complexity of the arrangement of the material in this section of Revelation. See Bauckham, *Climax of Prophecy*, 7.

9. This same technique is used in each of the numbered sequences of seven. Obvious structural markers, such as introductory formula and concluding formula, make the boundary markers between elements clear. While this is certainly true at the macro-level above the individual cola, several of the numbered sequences contain more than one period. These period boundaries, then, are marked with rounding, elongation, and balance, as well as introduction of new characters or movement of the setting.

from memory.[10] The numbered sequence is accompanied by pronounced structural devices, making the division between periods (and scenes) emphatic.[11] Character introductions, dialogue, description, and repetition signal the beginning and end of thought-units.[12]

The Style of Sound in Rev 6:1—8:1

Period Style

As previously stated, John's style is marked by continuous flow both between cola within periods as well as between periods. Again, this is achieved with the abundant use of καί to begin clauses. While translation may not always directly translate each of these (for stylistic purposes), to the listening audience, this repetition would certainly be obvious. The rhythm of John's style, therefore, is grounded by this repetition. Since translation often obscures this redundancy, the following provides an explicit rendering into English from scene 3 (Rev 6:1–8):

> And I saw when the lamb opened the first out of the seven seals. And I heard one out of the four living creatures saying as a voice like thunder, "Come." And I saw. And behold, a white horse. And the one sitting on it had a bow. And it was given to him a sword. And he went out conquering and in order to conquer. And whenever he opened the second seal, I heard the second living creature saying, "Come." And out came another horse. And it was given to the one sitting to take peace from the earth, and in order that they would slaughter one another. And he was given a great sword. And whenever he opened the third seal, I heard the third living creature saying, "Come." And I saw. And behold, a black horse. And the one sitting on it had scales in his hand. And I heard as a sound from the midst of the four living creatures saying, "A quart of wheat for a denarius. And three quarts of barley for a denarius. And the wine and the oil do not harm." And whenever he opened the fourth seal, I heard a sound from the fourth living creature saying, "Come." And I saw. And behold a pale horse. And the one sitting on it, its name is death, and hades following him. And power was given to him

---

10. Botha, *Orality and Literacy*, 102–25.
11. Botha, *Orality and Literacy*, 102–25.
12. Lee, *Sound Mapping*, 168–76.

on a fourth of the land to kill by sword, and by famine, and by plague, and by the beasts of the land.

The style of the book of Revelation demonstrates this consistent pattern, with the redundant repetition of καί to introduce many of its cola.[13] This paratactic style enables the action to move quickly but is also typical of oral storytelling.[14]

As seen in the above translation (and to be demonstrated in the subsequent analysis), the pace of scene 3 (Rev 6:1–8) quickens to an almost breathtaking speed, as the καί + aorist verb formula drives the action forward. Here, John bombards the audience with new characters, action, violence, and speech-acts, each appearing on the mental "stage" and then exiting in rapid succession.[15] The pace is rapid, marking the disintegration of order into chaos, while also depicting that this swift and decisive judgment is all the while in the hands of the lamb, as it is the lamb who breaks each seal.[16]

Any variation in this pattern must be recognized as a deliberate choice on the part of the author.[17] This pattern slows slightly[18] in scene 4 (Rev 6:9–17), as the καί + aorist verb formula is utilized less extensively.[19] As will be noted below, John also moves the audience's attention to a new

---

13. For a point of comparison, see the redundant use of καί to introduce individual colas in Rev 2–3. Here, the pattern continues even though the narrative event-line largely vanishes, giving way to the series of messages for the seven churches. What is crucial to see is that the style stays consistent, even though the narrative slows to a crawl.

14. As will be seen below. See Ong, *Orality and Literacy*, 38, 40. Jan Vansina, *Oral Tradition as History*, 40–56.

15. In the three numbered sequences of seven that make up the series of judgments (Rev 6:1—8:2; 8:6—11:19; 16:1–21), the first series are presented to the audience with this same rapid pace. For comparison, see Rev 8:6–13 and Rev 16:1–7. The first numbered sequence of seven in Rev 2–3 follows a clear 3+4 pattern, with the alteration coming in the commendation to the victorious in Rev 2:22. The middle two series of sevens follow a 4+3 pattern, with the pace of the first four swiftly depicted, and the pacing of the subsequent three in the series slowed significantly. The final numbered series of seven again follows the 3+4 pattern with the first three bowl-judgments presented swiftly, while the final four receive additional attention.

16. Resseguie, *Revelation of John*, 126.

17. Runge, *Discourse Grammar*, 5. See also the helpful introduction to a manual of sorts for discourse analysis of the New Testament: Scacewater, *Discourse Analysis*, 1–30.

18. Resseguie, *Revelation of John*, 129.

19. Like here, in the other two numbered sequences of seven that comprise scenes of judgment (Rev 8:6—11:19; 16:1–21), the repetition of the καί + aorist continues, as seen in the graph below.

location as seals five and six are opened. This adjustment to the "camera angle" of the story, from the lamb at the center of the throne to the altar in seal five and the earth in seal six, necessitates an adjustment in pattern. As pertains to style, however, the text remains consistent, enlisting a flowing continuous style with nearly every cola in this scene beginning with καί.

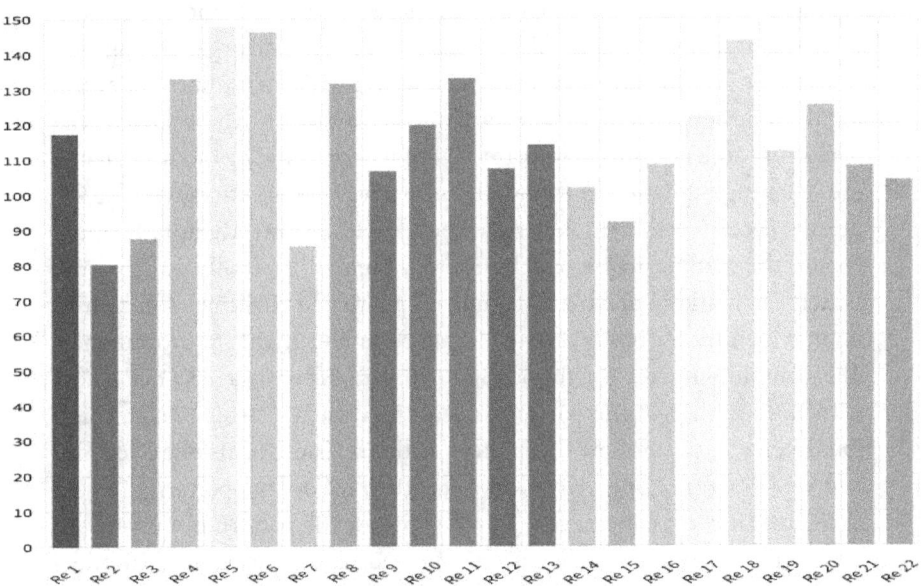

Use of καί per chapter per thousand words in Revelation

As noted in the graph above, scenes 5 (Rev 7:1–8) and 6 (Rev 7:9–17) are drastically different than the previous two. The dramatic decrease in the use of καί alters the pace of the narrative considerably. Resembling the pattern established in scene 1 (Rev 4:1–11), here period boundaries are established primarily by the introduction of new characters or objects. Three of the periods still begin with a καί + aorist formula (S5:P2–P3/Rev 7:2; S5:P5/Rev 7:4), but the majority of the cola in this scene do not begin with καί, thus breaking the pattern. Since choice implies meaning, analysis of John's variation in style enables the modern student to recognize the way in which the pace and structure are adjusted in chapter 7. It is then possible to propose suggestions as to why John decided to employ this technique within the flow of his narrative. Several such suggestions will be made in the analysis to follow.

NARRATIVE DISCOURSE ANALYSIS OF REV 6:1—8:1

Markers of Orality

Structural Markers

INTRODUCTORY FORMULA

Again, Walter Ong's maxim must be stated: "Thought and expression in oral cultures is often highly organized but calls for organization of a sort unfamiliar to and often uncongenial to the literate mind."[20] Several regularly used patterns emerge within Rev 6:1—8:1. These enable the performer to learn and memorize material accordingly as well as enable the listening audience to follow the narrative's progression. Within the present section,[21] the numbering sequence with its introductory formula creates the scaffolding on which the story builds.[22] Not only that, but the structural markers are obvious and emphatic,[23] providing a backdrop upon which the author is able to elevate certain elements to prominence. The scaffolding takes the following form: Καὶ ὅτε ἤνοιξεν τὴν σφραγῖδα, with the number of the particular seal listed next.[24] Seals two through four (Rev 6:3, 5, 7) follow this pattern with precision. Seals one (Rev 6:1) and six (Rev 6:12) open with Καὶ εἶδον, then follow the pattern directly. Seals five (Rev 6:9) and seven (Rev 8:1) follow the pattern but invert the word order, with the seal's number preceding τὴν σφραγῖδα. In addition, the final seal exchanges ὅταν for ὅτε. The introductory formula for the first four seals is even more robust, noting that it is the lamb who is the one opening each of these seals.[25] Each of the first four seals also includes John's report of what he heard, noted with the aorist verb ἤκουσα as well as the invitation ἔρχου from one of the living creatures. Seals five

---

20. Ong, *Orality and Literacy*, i.

21. Each of the numbered sequences of seven in the book of Revelation contains repeated introductory formula that varies little. When totaled, these four series comprise nine of the twenty-two chapters in the book of Revelation. It is for this reason that one of these episodes was chosen for analysis in the present book.

22. Aune, *Revelation*, xcvi–xcvii; Bauckham, *Climax of Prophecy*, 7–15. See also Fiorenza, *Book of Revelation*, 167.

23. Bauckham, *Climax of Prophecy*, 7.

24. Fanning, *Revelation*, 236–39.

25. Aune, *Revelation*, 389.

through seven do not include this part of the formula, yet they do record speech-acts.[26]

What is the analyst to make of such striking similarity with such subtle variation? Indeed, every scholar of the book of Revelation notes this regularity of the pattern, but few account for the ever-so-slight variation within the pattern itself.[27] Bauckham notes that the numbered sequences within the book frequently demonstrate a 4+3 structure, with the first four forming a set and marked off intentionally from the remaining three.[28] In the seven messages to the seven churches in Rev 2–3, this pattern is inverted (3+4).[29] In a later scene in John's Apocalypse, the trumpet judgments (Rev 8:2—11:19) follow this pattern, with the latter three each introduced with a proclamation of "woe." Bauckham suggests that this technique enabled the ancient listening community to maintain their awareness of the sequencing of the narration while it was performed aloud.[30]

While Bauckham's proposal may indeed be correct for structuring the numbered sequences into a 4+3 pattern, it still does not account for the variation that remains. Why exchange ὅταν for ὅτε?[31] Why include Καὶ εἶδον sometimes to begin the formula, while other times omit εἶδον altogether or move it to a subsequent cola? Why note within the introduction to the fourth seal not only that John heard something (ἤκουσα, as is the case in seals one through three), but only include the direct object φωνὴν here with the fourth seal?[32] Perhaps these questions may be adjudicated by manuscript evidence. Perhaps John had a provocative reason simply impossible to unearth. Or perhaps this sort of slight variation contributes to the thesis of the present investigation, as it

---

26. Aune, *Revelation*, 391.
27. Bauckham, *Climax of Prophecy*, 11. Also Aune, *Revelation*, 389.
28. Bauckham, *Climax of Prophecy*, 10–11. Smalley, *Revelation to John*, 145–46.
29. Bauckham, *Climax of Prophecy*, 10–11.
30. Bauckham, *Climax of Prophecy*, 11.

31. This variance may be best accounted for by the choice of manuscript adopted by the SBL editors. Indeed, there is an early parchment manuscript (ℵ) that includes ὅτε in 8:1. However, most commentators agree that the adjustment to ὅτε is more likely to have been done by a scribe, thus leaving ὅταν as most likely part of the original text. Aune, *Revelation*, 483.

32. Again, it is possible that textual criticism will be able to solve this slight variation, but there is ample evidence in the manuscript tradition that indicates that the pattern was broken here, φωνὴν was included, and that later scribes adjusted the text in order to make the pattern more uniform. Aune, *Revelation*, 381.

is precisely this kind of slight variation[33] that one would expect in a text transcribed from performance and intended for performance. Indeed, as later scribes inherited the manuscripts of Revelation, it seems most likely that they attempted to smooth out some of these irregularities so that the pattern would be more uniform.[34] This verbatim regularity, again, is a hallmark of culture moving toward the reading of a written text as opposed to a text publicly read aloud from memory.[35]

The text also includes other introductory formula that enable the audience to follow the structure of the narrative. Twice (Rev 7:1, 9) within the narrative, John employs the same formal introductory phrase that began scene 1 (Rev 4:1) above: Μετὰ ταῦτα εἶδον. In the book of Revelation, this formula alerts the listener to new material or characters, inviting them to advance their mental projection with the speaker.[36] In the second of these instances (7:9), just as in Rev 4:1 above, the formula is made even more emphatic with the combination of καὶ ἰδοὺ,[37] arresting the attention of the audience. As will be seen later, the collocation of the repetitive formula joined with the injunction to look/behold (ἰδοὺ) likely signals the ancient performer for prosody and inflection, heightening the urgency in the narrative for what follows next.[38]

Additionally, John also employs the repeated formula Καὶ εἶδον, that, as has been stated, is used regularly to introduce visionary experiences or new elements within the vision already underway.[39] Perhaps nowhere is this formula more pronounced than here in these chapters.[40] This formula is explicitly used six times (Rev 6:1, 2, 5, 8, 12; 7:2) in thirty-five verses—and used with slight variation once more (Rev 6:9). In the four scenes that make up the "opening of the seals" episode of John's Apocalypse, the movement and the pace changes drastically.[41] Particularly in scene 3 (Rev

33. Bauckham, *Climax of Prophecy*, 11.

34. Ong, *Orality and Literacy*, 78–115; Dooley, *Analyzing Discourse*, 15–18.

35. Ong, *Orality and Literacy*, 117–38.

36. Aune, *Revelation*, 450; Smalley, *Revelation to John*, 178; Pattemore, "Revelation," 730.

37. Pattemore, "Revelation," 737.

38. Vansina, *Oral Tradition as History*, 34–35.

39. Mathewson, "Verbal Aspect in the Apocalypse," 65. See also Pattemore, "Revelation," 730.

40. This pattern continues in the rest of the numbered sequence episodes (Rev 8:2, 13; 9:1, 17; 10:1; 16:13).

41. More will be said below, but for now, much of the pace is determined by aorist verbal form, particularly as part of the storyline of the narrative.

6:1–8), the characters move onto the mental "stage" of the audience and exit almost as fast as they appeared. Thus, the repetition of καὶ εἶδον functions to mark discrete narrative units,[42] helping the audience recognize that the narrative is moving forward, albeit at a brisk pace.[43] Without such structuring devices, it would be difficult to understand which characters should stay front and center and which are merely "bit players." The four horses with their four riders, for example, do not linger long on the stage, and the repeated formula aids the hearer in following along with the speed of the plot as it is narrated publicly. The formula varies little, forming a simple yet powerful tool for performance, moving the audience's attention throughout the narrative with as little effort as possible. A print culture frequently requires significantly more stylistic variation, as the repetition can become tedious and monotonous,[44] but for an oral culture, such techniques benefit the hearer.[45]

Repeated Formula

While much of the repeated material in this section comprises introductory formula, still other repetition must be explored.[46] As stated above, repeated formula consisting of words and phrases guide the ancient hearer, and it is the imprint of these formula on the written text that concerns the present section. Three of the four horse riders in scene 3 (Rev 6:1–8)

---

42. Mathewson, "Verbal Aspect in the Apocalypse," 65. See also Pattemore, "Revelation," 730.

43. As will be noted later, scholars comment on the Old Testament background of the horsemen, their colors, their riders, their purposes, their interpretation, etc. Yet none of the commentators or scholars reviewed for this book acknowledge the sheer speed at which these characters move onto and then off the main storyline of the narrative. Could it be that they receive more attention than they deserve given their prominence (or lack thereof) in the text?

44. Ong, *Orality and Literacy*, 117–38; Dooley, *Analyzing Discourse*, 15–18.

45. Ong, *Orality and Literacy*, i, 39–41; Harvey, *Listening to the Text*, 41.

46. For a point of comparison, see this same technique on display in the other numbered sequences of seven. In Rev 2–3, each message to the seven churches includes an admonition to hear the message as well as commendation to the one who overcomes (Rev 2:7, 11, 17, 26–29; 3:5–6, 12–13, 21–22). In the third sequence (Rev 8:6—11:19), the first four judgments involve devastation measuring one-third the total of the object in view. The next three each involve a repeated declaration of woe with accompanying anticipation of subsequent judgment. In the final sequence (Rev 16:1–21), the first three judgments all repeat the verb ἐγένετο in precisely the same manner. Each of the final four judgments in the final sequence depict the ongoing rebellion of the peoples of the world, even in the face of such tremendous judgment.

are given something (ἐδόθη). As terrifying as the actions surrounding these four horsemen may be, the audience is reminded that even these actions are ultimately under the sovereign hand of God.[47] The four riders have authority, but it is a derivative authority. The pattern is only broken with the third rider, as the call from one of the living creatures rings out instead of the report of the rider's gift.

John again groups people from among the nations in S6:P1 (Rev 7:9): παντὸς ἔθνους καὶ φυλῶν καὶ λαῶν καὶ γλωσσῶν (every nation and tribe and people and language). This four-fold formula represents universality[48] and is used extensively in the book of Revelation, but again, the order varies. Revelation 5:9, for example, reads: πάσης φυλῆς καὶ γλώσσης καὶ λαοῦ καὶ ἔθνους (every tribe and language and people and nation). Verbatim precision is not necessary in oral performance,[49] as this device is not primarily for the printed text (in which case, one may expect to find each of these mirroring with exact precision) but rather for the performer working from memory.[50] Put simply, ancient performers could call to mind the formula,[51] recognizing that it was always four-fold and always with the same words, but did not feel the necessity to repeat the order with precision.[52]

As John narrates the number of those sealed by God, he provides within the performed text yet another repeated pattern. Each clause within the pericope follows this pattern precisely: ἐκ φυλῆς _____ δώδεκα χιλιάδες (Rev 7:5–8). This repetition serves two primary aims: first, it allows the speaker to rely on the pattern, thus only requiring memorization of the particular tribes themselves;[53] second, as will be explored below, this pattern slows the pace of the narrative down dramatically.[54] This listing of the twelve tribes from Israel is also bracketed by an inclusio, with

---

47. Smalley, *Revelation to John*, 151.

48. Bauckham, *Climax of Prophecy*, 326–37.

49. Ong, *Orality and Literacy*, 145–46.

50. Harvey, *Listening to the Text*, 41.

51. See Bauckham's note regarding the sheer variation in these repeated formulas. Bauckham does not, however, recognize the way in which working from memory in oral performance would contribute to this variation. Bauckham, *Climax of Prophecy*, 22–29.

52. Bauckham, *Climax of Prophecy*, 22–29. See also Botha, *Orality and Literacy*, 34–51, 116; Ong, *Orality and Literacy*, 145–46.

53. It is beyond the scope of this paper to address why John chose these particular twelve and in this order. For a detailed overview, see Beale, *Book of Revelation*, 417–23.

54. Resseguie, *Revelation of John*, 137–38.

the first and last tribe enclosed within the narration by the repetition of ἐσφραγισμένοι (Rev 7:5, 8).[55] In fact, this word alone occurs four times within this period, and this repetition is sometimes eliminated in translation, likely for its sheer redundancy (see the NIV translation as an example). This redundancy, however, aided the speaker's recall during public performance and is a hallmark of oral culture.[56]

Reported Speech

It is difficult to overstate the significance of reported speech within the book of Revelation—and in this section particularly.[57] Nearly every period contains some speech-act, and many of them are introduced in exactly the same manner. In scene 3 (Rev 6:1–8), all but one of the periods describe what John heard using the same aorist verb: ἤκουσα (I heard). Each then similarly introduce the content of the speech but with slight variation. In periods 3 through 5 (Rev 6:3, 5, 7), the speech-act of one of the living creatures is introduced with λέγοντος (saying), with only the first period in the scene (Rev 6:1) altering the pattern. The same pattern follows within the same periods, as periods 3 through 5 also share the repetition of the first words from the living creatures: ἔρχου (come!). In performance, this pattern enables the speaker to dramatize each imperative in a way that is difficult to replicate in written form.[58]

Scene 4 (Rev 6:9–17) contains reported speech-acts as well, but in this scene, they are introduced differently. As noted above, the introductory pattern changes with the opening of seals five through seven, with seals five and six introducing new characters and elements onto the stage.[59] In

55. Beale, *Book of Revelation*, 421–22. Beale goes further, noting that the appropriate case in the context of the sentence should be the genitive, but the nominative is used instead. Beale suggests that this change of case is deliberate, with the awkwardness serving to highlight these participles. This awkward but deliberate choice would be perceptible to hearers and readers alike, thus drawing attention to the inclusio and the contents within. Beale also suggests that the form of these participles may also echo the numbering of the tribes of Israel in Num 1:19 and 44.

56. Ong, *Orality and Literacy*, 37–38.

57. Reported speech pervades each of the numbered sequences in the book. Rev 2–3 is predominantly a series of speeches given by the one like a son of man to the churches. In Rev 8:6—11:19, speech-acts occur regularly (Rev 8:13; 9:14; 10:3, 4, 6, 8, 9, 11; 11:1–4, 12, 15, 17–18). In the final sequence (Rev 16), reported speech is again a regular feature (Rev 16:1, 5–6, 7, 15, 17).

58. Vansina, *Oral Traditional as History*, 34–35.

59. As will be seen later, the pacing of the narrative changes as well, slowing slightly

both, however, the newly introduced characters speak. In the opening of the fifth seal, the souls of those who had been slain ἔκραξαν φωνῇ μεγάλῃ λέγοντες (cry out in a loud voice [Rev 6:10]). This pattern—spoken word shouted in a loud voice—is a regular one in the book of Revelation (Rev 5:2, 12; 6:10; 7:2, 10; 8:13; 10:3; 14:7, 9, 15, 18; 16:17; 18:2; 19:17). Again, it must be stated that such formulaic repetition betrays a text composed for performance,[60] and within the next scene under review (Rev 7:1–8), this same phrase is used in exactly the same way (Rev 7:2). The second group, introduced with the opening of the sixth seal, also speaks, with their speech-act introduced simply with λέγουσιν (Rev 6:16).

In scene 5 (Rev 7:1–8), the text again depicts recorded speech, with John reporting the number of those sealed from the tribes of Israel. This report returns to the pattern utilized in scene 3 (Rev 6:1–8), which introduced each message with the aorist ἤκουσα (Rev 7:4). In scene 6 (Rev 7:9–17), many of the elements already established emerge again[61]—first, those from among the four-fold gathering from the nations κράζουσιν φωνῇ μεγάλῃ λέγοντες. Here, the words selected to report the action are precisely the same as before, but the aspect of the action is viewed differently as John describes this speech-act using the present aspect (see below). Second, in period 4 (Rev 7:12), the gathered multitudes around the throne worship the one on the throne with their speech-act introduced in the present tense by λέγοντες, matching the tense established in period 2 above (Rev 7:10). Scene 6, however, varies from the previous ones in that, in this scene, John includes a dialogue. As will be seen below, this dialogue serves to clarify for the audience many of the elements that were developed in the previous scene[62] as well as alter the pacing of the narrative itself.[63] For the present section, however, it is worth simply noting that these periods again contain reported speech.

All in all, within the various periods that make up scenes 3 through 6 in the book of Revelation (Rev 6:1—8:1), reported speech occurs in sixteen of the twenty-seven periods. Perhaps this onslaught of speech-acts creates the need for the silence reported in the last period of this

---

here. See Resseguie, *Revelation of John*, 129–31.

60. See Horsley, *Text and Tradition*, 223. See also Barr, "Apocalypse as Oral Enactment," 244–47; Bauman, *Story, Performance, and Event*, 1–10, 112–17; Ong, *Orality and Literacy*, 38–39.

61. Harvey, *Listening to the Text*, 41.

62. Dooley, *Analyzing Discourse*, 81–84.

63. Resseguie, *Revelation of John*, 137–38.

PERFORMANCE ANALYSIS OF A NUMBERED SEQUENCE SCENE 157

present section (Rev 8:1). As the final seal is opened, after the flurry of noise and sound, John notes ἐγένετο σιγὴ ἐν τῷ οὐρανῷ ὡς ἡμιώριον (there was silence in heaven as half an hour). This is a surprising turn, as the previous seal-openings were each loud. Here, the absence of noise would be particularly unexpected and dramatic.[64] Commentators explore many of the possible reasons for this silence,[65] and many indeed note the literary or dramatic effect.[66] Few, however, recognize that, in an oral performance, this technique enables the audience to catch its breath and meditate on the story up to this point.[67] This would be particularly important if the performer employed prosody (to be discussed later) in the telling of the story, adjusting the pace and the pitch of the oral speech regularly,[68] which was done intentionally to affect the audience.[69]

Style Markers

As noted above, the redundancy of καὶ within the book of Revelation, coupled with the continuous style, betrays an additive style common in oral culture.[70] It is again clear within the scenes explored in this section that the style of the Apocalypse is not one of complex grammatical subordination but rather simple cola introduced with καί one after another.[71] Where there is grammatical subordination, such as the second period in scene 3 (Rev 6:2), the ἵνα clause is introduced with καί and is itself only one word in length: καὶ ἵνα νικήσῃ (and in order that he might conquer). This same feature occurs in scene 5, period 1 (Rev 7:1) with three subordinate clauses within the ἵνα clause. Again, these features are worth noting here simply for their irregularity within the book of Revelation,

---

64. Fanning, *Revelation*, 279.

65. Resseguie, *Revelation of John*, 141. See also Smalley, *Revelation to John*, 211–13; Aune, *Revelation*, 507–8; Osborne, *Revelation*, 336–37; Beale, *Book of Revelation*, 446–60; Bauckham, *Climax of Prophecy*, 70–83; Barr, *Tales of the End*, 149–50.

66. Fanning, *Revelation*, 279; Resseguie, *Revelation of John*, 141.

67. Aune, *Revelation*, 507. Aune notes that this retards the narrative action.

68. Resseguie, *Revelation of John*, 141; Bauckham, *Climax of Prophecy*, 12.

69. Vansina, *Oral Tradition as History*, 34–35. See also Rhoads, "Performance Criticism, Pt. II," 173–80.

70. Resseguie, *Revelation of John*, 50.

71. This style continues throughout the seven numbered sequences, with the redundant use of καί followed by the aorist.

suggesting a continuous style familiar to a culture steeped in orality as opposed to literacy.⁷²

The aggregative prose typical in oral culture continues with these scenes as well.⁷³ In scenes 1 and 2 (Rev 5–6, analyzed in the previous section), the story builds to the climactic moment when the lamb moves to the center of the stage and takes the scroll from the one seated on the throne. This decisive act demonstrates that the lamb is worthy to be worshiped alongside the one seated on the throne, as the narration depicts. Again, within these scenes, the one on the throne is addressed repeatedly with a version of the formula ὁ καθήμενος ἐπὶ τοῦ θρόνου (the one seated on the throne [Rev 6:16; 7:10, 15]). Here, however, the lamb is repeatedly collocated with the throne, cementing the point established by the lamb's taking of the scroll. This collocation was first established in Rev 6:13, as John reports the praise of the creatures of the earth addressed to τῷ καθημένῳ ἐπὶ τῷ θρόνῳ καὶ τῷ ἀρνίῳ (To the one seated on the throne and to the lamb). This combination occurs three times in scenes 4 through 6 (Rev 6:16; 7:9, 10).

Redundancy and repetition are common in oral cultures,⁷⁴ and the structuring device of the numbered sequencing creates a redundancy in scenes 3 and 4.⁷⁵ Other instances of redundancy, particularly of the "just-said," are worth noting. In introducing new participants, which begins scene 5 (Rev 7:1–3), the copious redundancy of elements is unnecessary:

> Μετὰ τοῦτο εἶδον τέσσαρας ἀγγέλους ἑστῶτας ἐπὶ τὰς τέσσαρας γωνίας τῆς γῆς, κρατοῦντας τοὺς τέσσαρας ἀνέμους τῆς γῆς, ἵνα μὴ πνέῃ ἄνεμος ἐπὶ τῆς γῆς μήτε ἐπὶ τῆς θαλάσσης μήτε ἐπὶ πᾶν δένδρον. ² καὶ εἶδον ἄλλον ἄγγελον ἀναβαίνοντα ἀπὸ ἀνατολῆς ἡλίου, ἔχοντα σφραγῖδα θεοῦ ζῶντος, καὶ ἔκραξεν φωνῇ μεγάλῃ τοῖς τέσσαρσιν ἀγγέλοις οἷς ἐδόθη αὐτοῖς ἀδικῆσαι τὴν γῆν καὶ τὴν θάλασσαν, ³ λέγων· Μὴ ἀδικήσητε τὴν γῆν μήτε τὴν θάλασσαν μήτε τὰ δένδρα, ἄχρι σφραγίσωμεν τοὺς δούλους τοῦ θεοῦ ἡμῶν ἐπὶ τῶν μετώπων αὐτῶν.

---

72. Again, it is worth noting that these may indicate a paratactic style; this works together in order to create a flow to the narrative, made up of short paratactic sentences and/or clauses, woven together by the repetition of καί.

73. See the continual use of this aggregative style used in the other numbered sequences of seven (Rev 10:6; 11:17; 16:5, 7, 14).

74. Ong, *Orality and Literacy*, 39–41. Harvey, *Listening to the Text*, 41. Dooley, *Analyzing Discourse*, 15–18.

75. Aune, *Revelation*, xcvi–xcvii. Bauckham, *Climax of Prophecy*, 7–15. See also Fiorenza, *Book of Revelation*, 167.

Repeated elements are bolded in the paragraph above, stylistically suggestive of a text composed for performance. Ong suggests that this characteristic often fades in literate cultures, as the redundancy becomes too overwhelming.[76]

The agonistic tone characteristic of orality continues in the "Opening the Seals" episode (Rev 6:1—8:1). In each of the scenes that comprise this episode, conflict abounds. The four horsemen ride out, bringing destruction. The martyred souls cry out for vengeance. Celebratory songs of victory pervade the book of Revelation,[77] as well as taunt-songs against the defeated foe.[78] With common apocalyptic stock sourced for symbolic imagery, the enthusiastic descriptions of the violence of God's wrath break forth in Rev 6:12–17. Just as the previous episode (Rev 4–5), fulsome praise explodes in Rev 7:9–17. Much of the material of scene 6 consists of declarations of worship oriented yet again to the one seated on the throne and the lamb. This provides continuity with the previous material found in chapters 4 and 5 and again demonstrates features "found everywhere in connection with orality."[79]

In addition, John's participatory tone is evident throughout.[80] Each of the elements reported within these scenes is narrated through the eyes John himself. Not only that, but John even notes his interaction with one of the characters, recording a dialogue between himself and one of the elders introduced in chapter 4. This participatory and experiential tone was a common choice for author's writing for the gathered listening audience in the ancient world, as it brought the audience into the telling of the story.[81] This is combined with Lord's additional suggestion, that action in texts were often depicted acoustically, not visually.[82] It is not worth restating in full here, but given the sheer volume of reported speech-acts, sounds, and noise in the present section under investigation (Rev 6:1—8:1), this characteristic is certainly evident. Often, John reports the action in the scene in speech-acts, rather than merely describing the action outright.

---

76. Ong, *Orality and Literacy*, 38, 40. Again, see Horsley, *Text and Tradition*, 223.
77. See Rev 7:10, 12; 11:15, 17–18; 12:10–12; 14:3; 15:3–4; 19:1–2, 3, 4, 5, 6–8.
78. Rev 6:15–17; 8:13; 12:10–12; 14:8, 11; 18:2–3, 4–8, 10, 16–17, 19–20, 21–24.
79. Ong, *Orality and Literacy*, 45.
80. Ong, *Orality and Literacy*, 36.
81. Ong, *Orality and Literacy*, 36.
82. Lord, *Singer of Tales*, 33.

Finally, one of the characteristics of oral culture is lacking in this section, namely the lack of sequential parallelism. As noted above, strict linear progression is not always present within a mostly illiterate society adapted for aural hearing of texts out loud.[83] In this section, however, the action of the story progresses clearly and linearly throughout. While the pace certainly varies and the mental projection of the audience shifts between characters and elements, these scenes move forward in a clear and linear way. The numbering sequences enables the "opening of the seals" macro-unit of the narrative to join together, forming a single episode. While the characteristic of a lack of linear progression is absent within these scenes (Rev 6:1—8:1), this is likely due to the author's decision in structuring the story.[84]

Narrative Discourse Features

Verbal Aspect and Storyline

Again, following the tools provided for rightly analyzing narrative discourse, primacy in narration belongs to the storyline.[85] The event-line carries the story forward, enabling the author to supplement the basic plot with background and support material.[86] As noted above, in the book of Revelation, the event-line is marked with the frequent use of the aorist verb, forming the backbone of the story.[87] The aorist serves as the default option for John's narrative, with other options of verb tense marked as unique or prominent.[88] Mathewson proposes that imperfective verbs (both the perfect and imperfect verbs) bring the action to the foreground of the mental "stage" of the hearer, while perfect verb marks even more unique or unexpected material (frontgrounded).[89] This variation in the choice of verbs used functions to mark prominent elements in the narrative as well as adjust the conceptual pace of the story. The aorist

---

83. Ong, *Orality and Literacy*, 144–46.

84. While it is certainly possible to attribute these features to other aims on the part of the author, the combination of features contributes to the working thesis of this book—that the text of Revelation was composed for oral performance.

85. Genette, *Narrative Discourse*, 30.

86. Dooley and Levinsohn, *Analyzing Discourse*, 79–86.

87. Mathewson, "Verbal Aspect in the Apocalypse," 65.

88. Runge, *Discourse Grammar*, 11.

89. Runge, *Discourse Grammar*, 11.

functions as the drumbeat of the narrative, while the foregrounded and frontgrounded material invites reflection and additional attention. Such analysis is crucial for the performance-analyst of the book of Revelation, as prominent features of the written text would be appropriate to highlight in the oral recitation of the text.[90]

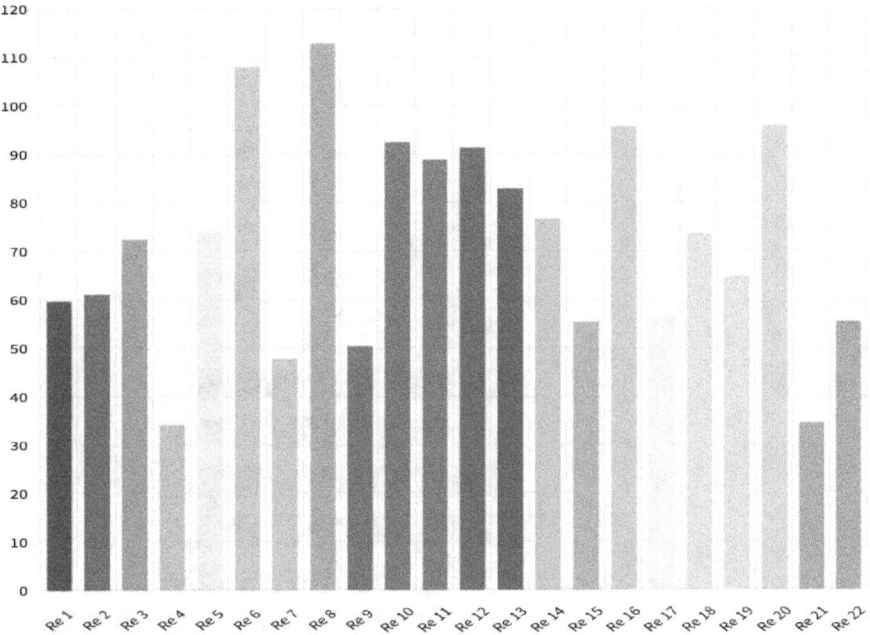

Aorist verbs (all moods, including participles, per one thousand words in Revelation

---

90. Again, this is the basic assumption noted by Bauckham but rarely explored in sufficient detail: that the text was meant to be heard (Bauckham, *Climax of Prophecy*, 1–2).

Present, imperfect, and perfect verbs (all moods, including participles) per one thousand words in Revelation

PERFORMANCE ANALYSIS OF A NUMBERED SEQUENCE SCENE   163

As seen in the two charts above, chapter 6 contains the second highest amount of aorist verbs per one thousand words per chapter in the book of Revelation. Scene 3 (Rev 6:1–8) unfolds with a quick-succession of aorist verbs, presented one after another in successive cola. The elements and characters presented within this scene bombard the audience, moving quickly from one to the next.[91] The storyline progresses without pause, as each character—in this case, the four horsemen[92]—move onto the mental "stage" of the hearer and then leave almost as quickly as they appeared. These characters are not introduced again in the book of Revelation, thus marking them as part of the background storyline with little prominence within the text. It is as if the action of these four figures is meant to be experienced quickly, with the narrative steadily marching forward. In this scene, the aorist is the predominant verb employed in the indicative mood. As seen in chart 3, the use of the non-aorist verb is less extensive in chapters 6 through 8 than the previous two, and in scene 3 (Rev 6:1–8), John omits the perfect verb altogether. Present participles supply support material or introduce speech. Scene 3, therefore, advances the storyline of the narrative event by event without marking any for prominence.

The aorist remains the dominant tool for establishing the backbone of the narrative in the next scene (Rev 6:9–17) but with one notable exception. In this pericope, John highlights a group of newly introduced participants by his use of the perfect participle: τῶν ἐσφαγμένων (the ones who had been slaughtered). Given the significance of the play on words between ἐσφαγμένων (slaughter) and σφραγῖδας (seal) evident in Rev 5 and throughout the Apocalypse, combined with the choice of perfect verbs introducing the lamb (ἑστηκὸς ὡς ἐσφαγμένον; standing as slain), highlighting these new participants is not surprising.[93] Following Mathewson's application, then, careful attention to the choices John made regarding the use of verbs functionally serves to reveal elements meant to receive prominent rank in the audience's mind. This scene ends with one group of participants asking a significant question in Rev 6:17: καὶ τίς δύναται σταθῆναι (and who is able to stand?). This question serves as

---

91. Aune, *Revelation*, 389.

92. It is beyond the scope of the present book to explore the OT background and interpretation of these four figures. For a summary, see Beale, *Book of Revelation*, 372–89.

93. Again, see Mathewson for the use of the perfect to frontground material in the narrative. Mathewson, "Verbal Aspect in the Apocalypse," 67–68.

a rhetorical device,[94] setting up the next two scenes, and will be explored in more detail subsequently.

In scene 5 (Rev 7:1–8), the repetition of καί, as well as the use of the aorist aspect decreases dramatically.[95] Given the axiom from discourse analysis that variety never simply occurs for variety's sake but reflects an author's choice,[96] this change requires analysis. In the previous table, the decrease in backgrounded event-line aorist verbs is clear, as chapter 7 contains nearly the fewest aorist verbs in the entire book. To put it simply, from chapter 6 to chapter 7, the narrative moves from one of the chapters with the most aorist verbs to one of the chapters with the least in the Apocalypse. Thus, the pace of the storyline grinds to a slow crawl, often with several cola in a row without an indicative verb at all.[97] New participants move onto the stage with accompanying description, and these are summarily reported with the regular formulas Μετὰ τοῦτο εἶδον (after this I saw [Rev 7:1]) and Καὶ εἶδον (and I saw [Rev 7:2]).[98]

Following Mathewson's proposal, two sets of participants are introduced with participles in the perfect tense in this scene. The question remains: does the use of the perfect function to frontground these participants in any way? The first set is the four angels announced in 7:1. They are announced as standing (ἑστῶτας) on the four corners of the earth. This perfect participle, however, is set parallel to a present participle in the subsequent cola. When coupled with the nature of the act of the verb itself, this particular participle's function likely does not indicate prominence.[99]

This leaves another group of participants to explore: τῶν ἐσφραγισμένων (the ones sealed) from the tribes of Israel. Here, the perfect participle is used four times in one period (Rev 7:5–8), with one functioning as substantival and the other three functioning as adverbially and sharing the same form, sound, and syllables. This repetition in sound

---

94. Fanning, *Revelation*, 252; Bauckham, *Climax of Prophecy*, 11.

95. Two other chapters in Revelation contain a significant drop in aorist verbs, as noted in graph 2 above (Rev 9 and 15). Both chapters introduce new participants, with one in the midst of a numbered sequence of seven and another introducing a numbered sequence of seven. In each case, the rapid pace slows. In neither case, however, does the pace slow to the same level as in Rev 7:1–8.

96. Longacre, *Holistic Discourse Analysis*, 15.

97. Resseguie, *Revelation of John*, 135.

98. Mathewson, "Verbal Aspect in the Apocalypse," 65.

99. In nearly every instance in the book of Revelation, John employs the perfect tense for ἵστημι. For an additional example, the verb "to know" is almost always set in the perfect tense, which may indicate more about the action of the verb than the prominence of the verb.

and syllable,[100] as well as the theme of sealing, signals prominence. Remember in chapter 5, the scroll was introduced with a perfect verb (Rev 5:2), the lamb was introduced as slain using a perfect participle as a play on words (Rev 5:6), and in chapter 6, the slain souls under the altar were introduced with a similar substantival perfect participle (Rev 6:9). Here, then, it betrays intentionality on the part of the author that ἐσφραγισμένων is again used in the perfect tense and is also repeated four times (not to mention one more time as a subjunctive in Rev 7:3).[101] As will be seen, this dramatic move on the part of the author moves this group front and center on the mental stage of the audience. When combined with the pacing variation in the story already noted, with the decrease in the action of the storyline, this becomes an effective rhetorical device that sets up the scene that follows, heightening the narrative tension.[102]

In the next scene (scene 6: Rev 7:9–17), the backbone of the event-line remains strikingly slowed, as indicative verbs appear in only two of the first five periods of the scene (Rev 7:9, 11). In the remaining six periods, there are only three aorist indicative verbs, apart from those that are part of the content of speech-acts. Dialogue, description, and spoken words of praise dominate this scene, much like Rev 4:1–11. Yet there is variation in the use of verbal aspect in this scene. Again, following Mathewson, which participants are highlighted by this variation?

One group of participants is introduced in somewhat surprising fashion: the multitude from every nation, tribe, people, and language. This group's introduction not only follows the major structuring device Μετὰ ταῦτα εἶδον (After this I saw [Rev 7:9]), but in the subsequent description, they are depicted using two perfect participles: ἑστῶτες (having stood [Rev 7:9]) and περιβεβλημένους (having been dressed [Rev 7:9]). Given the nature of the action of the first participle and John's consistent choice to use the perfect aspect when utilizing ἵστημι,[103] what should the analyst make of these participles? To the present author, it is the combination of the two in conjunction with the other structural

---

100. Harvey, *Listening to the Text*, 41.

101. Rowland, *Open Heaven*, 418–19. See also, Aune, *Revelation*, 434. While a silent reader of a written text may certainly observe this repetition, it is the rhetorical effect of it on the listening audience under analysis here.

102. Resseguie, *Revelation of John*, 136.

103. ἵστημι is frequently put in the perfect tense in Revelation, which may simply indicate the type of action is viewed best with this verbal aspect and not as a marker for prominence.

features that serve to bring prominence to this group of participants. In the previous scene, John's four-fold repetition of the perfect participle ἐσφραγισμένων frontgrounded the twelve tribes of Israel in the mind of the audience. Here, then, the choice of verbal aspect enables the student of the Apocalypse to see the dramatic and ironic reversal presented in the text,[104] as the same frontgrounding technique elevates the nations to the front of the stage in the same manner as the tribes of Israel. The perfect participle περιβεβλημένους is repeated in the dialogue between John and one of the elders (Rev 7:13), further emphasizing this group. The rhetorical effect of this is striking[105] and would provide the performer with an opportunity to elevate his tone of voice and pause for dramatic effect.[106]

Scholars of the book of Revelation often note the way in which the seven numbered judgments are structured, noting the literary breaks or interludes in the action.[107] That John inserts these breaks into the flow of the action is undeniable, but the way in which the variation of the verbal aspect affects the pacing of these stories is often overlooked. Yet these changes in structure, repetition, style, and verbal aspect all combine to adjust the pacing, focus, and themes under consideration.[108] What is more, the way in which this variation affects the ancient hearer is almost never explored. These grammatical features left in the printed text must be rightly appreciated, for the author made choices to tell this story this way.[109]

Participants and Rank

As noted above, actors and actions create stories.[110] Participants and the events in which they partake combine to form a story worth telling. Yet, in any given story, not all participants are equal, with some receiving

---

104. Smalley, *Revelation to John*, 189–90; Resseguie, *Revelation of John*, 137–38; Aune, *Revelation*, 434.

105. See Resseguie, *Revelation of John*, 137–38.

106. Vansina, *Oral Tradition as History*, 34–35; Rhoads, "Performance Criticism, Pt. II," 173–80.

107. Bandy, "Layers of the Apocalypse," 469–99; Fiorenza, *Book of Revelation*, 159–80; Beale, *Book of Revelation*, 108–10.

108. Resseguie, *Revelation of John*, 125.

109. Longacre, *Holistic Discourse Analysis*, 15.

110. Genette, *Narrative Discourse*, 30.

significantly more prominence than others.[111] In a first-person account, such as the book of Revelation, the narrator himself takes the central role as every action and actor is literally depicted through his eyes.[112] This is compounded when the narrator involves himself in the plot of the story, as is the case in the Apocalypse.

Through the first two scenes explored above (Rev 4–5), John himself was noted as the most prominent participant, as his personal experience is the vehicle through which the narrative's action moves. This continues in the four scenes analyzed in the present section (Rev 6:1—8:1), as John remains the eyes and ears by which the audience partakes in the drama. John not only narrates the events of the story but he also participates personally in the story. In the previous section, the variation in verbal aspect and the application of the perfect verb was noted for its use in marking prominence among events in the text. In Rev 7:9, the great multitude from among the nations was marked by two perfect participles. The prominence assigned to these participants is only intensified by John's gathering of the participants from the previous scenes (Rev 4–5)—the angels around the throne, the twenty-four elders, and the four living beings—to join in the worship of this great multitude.[113] At this critical juncture in the narrative, with all the actors brought onto the mental stage of the audience, John chose to insert a dialogue (Rev 7:13–17). This explanatory conversation[114] involves one of the twenty-four elders and none other than John himself. The back-and-forth between these two places John again in the central role of all the participants. In effect, John's central role invites the audience onto the stage through John's eyes and ears and voice. For scholars of Revelation, however, the literary effect of this participatory narrative is too often overlooked.[115]

Other actors move on and off the mental stage in these scenes, with some enjoying only a brief moment in the "spotlight" before moving aside quickly. The four horsemen in scene 3, for example, make barely

---

111. Longacre, *Holistic Discourse Analysis*, 81–92; Dooley, *Analyzing Discourse*, 109–27.

112. Genette, *Narrative Discourse*, 10.

113. Restaging a previously introduced member demonstrates their importance to the narrative.

114. Dooley, *Analyzing Discourse*, 82.

115. Ong, *Orality and Literacy*, 45–46, 147. See also, Genette, *Narrative Discourse*, 10.

more than a passing appearance.[116] While much scholarly attention may be applied to understanding the nature of these four and the horses upon which they ride,[117] all four play rather insignificant roles in the text.[118] This can be certain based on both their duration in the story but also by the way each of them are backgrounded through the use of the aorist verb to describe each of their actions. In short, they are presented in almost summary fashion, then brushed aside almost as quickly as they appeared. While it is the case that only the exit of the first horse is explicitly narrated (Rev 6:2), the fact that these participants do not reappear in the text indicates their low prominence. In contrast, two characters remain throughout each of the seven seals: John himself and the lamb who opens each of the seals.[119] Perhaps, then, the lamb and his authority should receive the weight of the attention through scene 3 (Rev 6:1–8) rather than the four horses and their riders.[120]

Other participants, however, rank higher in prominence in the present section under review (Rev 6:1—8:1). The souls of those under the altar introduced in scene 4 (Rev 6:9–17) are marked for a higher prominence than the riders, demonstrated by a number of grammatical features evident in the text itself. First, as noted above, the introductory formula changes as the lamb opens the fifth seal. Second, the setting is moved from the center of the throne (where the lamb took and began opening the seals on the scroll) to under a newly introduced altar.[121] Third, these faithful martyrs are described using the perfect participle τῶν ἐσφαγμένων, bringing them to the front of the audience's attention.[122] Fourth, these participants cry out in a loud voice and their cry is recorded for the ancient listener (Rev 6:10). Fifth, not only is their cry heard, but they receive a response, which is also reported (Rev 6:11). Finally, these characters enjoy nineteen cola worth of material dedicated to their part

---

116. The same is true of the angels who signal the trumpet judgments as well as six of the seven angels who deliver the bowl judgments. One of the bowl-angels is restaged in the episodes that follow.

117. For a summary, see Beale, *Book of Revelation*, 370–89.

118. Barr, *Tales of the End*, 119–20.

119. The lamb is introduced in scene 2 (Rev 5:1–14) and is explicitly carried into this scene in Rev 6:1, but the lamb is not explicitly mentioned again except by way of the continual third-person aorist ἤνοιξεν verb (Rev 6:1, 3, 5, 7).

120. Beale, *Book of Revelation*, 370–371.

121. Smalley, *Revelation to John*, 158–59.

122. Mathewson, "Verbal Aspect in the Apocalypse," 68.

of the narrative, marking their prominence as elevated in comparison with the four that came before.

The faithful martyrs are contrasted with another set of participants (Rev 6:15),[123] thus heightening both sets in order to produce a clever rhetorical effect on the audience. This second group is depicted with similar markers for prominence as the martyrs: the pattern from the first four seals is again altered (Rev 6:12), the setting is changed to the destruction on the earth, they cry out and their cry is recorded (Rev 6:16), and they receive seventeen cola worth of material. This group's introduction, however, is demonstrably different than any of the previously introduced actors in Rev 6 in that their welcome follows a barrage of violent events experienced on the earth (Rev 6:12–14). These images are sourced from a stock of apocalyptic images,[124] which enable the ancient performer to retrieve them in recall and the public composition of the text.[125] These events are presented in rapid-fire succession, using the backgrounded aorist verb to move them along in swift fashion.[126] The group also shares a repeated formulaic device used in its description: seven-fold repetition (Rev 6:15).[127]

The contrast between these two sets of participants, then, creates a dramatic narrative tension. In John's vision, both sets of participants introduced in this scene—the martyrs and the peoples of the earth—cry out for mercy. The first, however, do not experience the violent events that plague the earth as the sixth seal is opened. That plight is reserved for the second group.[128] The question posed by the first group receives an answer, while the question posed by the second group hangs in the air with no recorded reply. This clever design in the way these two seals are opened, and the action that follows, creates a contrast for the audience,

123. Beale, *Book of Revelation*, 395–96.

124. These violent events form a barrage of Old Testament metaphors regarding cosmic judgment. It is beyond the scope of this book to investigate the use of the Old Testament in the book of Revelation. However, it is important here simply to note that these events and the participants that John welcomes in connection with them are uniquely introduced, particularly in comparison with the four horsemen in the previous scene. See Beale, *Revelation of John*, 396; Smalley, *Revelation to John*, 166.

125. Vansina, *Oral Tradition as History*, 12, 21–22.

126. Mathewson, "Verbal Aspect in the Apocalypse," 61, 68.

127. Bauckham, *Climax of Prophecy*, 22–37; Smalley, *Revelation to John*, 169.

128. Scholars note that the violence that ushers in the second group is a result of the desperate cry of the martyrs for vengeance. See Smalley, *Revelation to John*, 166; Beale, *Book of Revelation*, 395–96.

and this contrast would have rhetorical effect. Put simply, the audience must choose between the two groups, and the choices made by John in developing the story this way highlight this choice.[129]

Lastly, in scenes 5 and 6 (Rev 7:1–8; 7:9—8:1), two groups take center stage. As the question posed by the peoples of the earth hangs in the air, John welcomes angels onto the stage. As noted above, the introductory formula Μετὰ τοῦτο εἶδον begins scene 5, marking this scene as a distinct literary unit.[130] This is compounded with John's repetition of Καὶ εἶδον to introduce the strong angel in Rev 7:2. Yet another participant cries out—this time the angel from the east—and again, the content of the cry is reported for the audience. These actions of the angels is largely presented summarily, with four aorist indicative verbs used in only three verses. Given their place in the story and that they are introduced following a structuring formula (Μετὰ τοῦτο), this functions to signal transition, which occurs elsewhere in the Apocalypse.[131]

Indeed, the prominence of these angels is overshadowed[132] by the participants that John highlights next: the 144,000 sealed from all the tribes of Israel.[133] Several techniques must be explored here, as John's intentional use of verbal aspect, recorded speech, and structuring devices all come together to prominently mark the great multitude from all the tribes on the earth. First, the event-line grinds to a crawl in this section.[134] Period 5 (Rev 7:4–8) contains fifteen highly repetitive cola with only one aorist verb in cola one.

1. Καὶ ἤκουσα τὸν ἀριθμὸν τῶν ἐσφραγισμένων,[135]
2. ἑκατὸν τεσσεράκοντα τέσσαρες χιλιάδες,
3. ἐσφραγισμένοι ἐκ πάσης φυλῆς υἱῶν Ἰσραήλ·
4. ἐκ φυλῆς Ἰούδα δώδεκα χιλιάδες ἐσφραγισμένοι,
5. ἐκ φυλῆς Ῥουβὴν δώδεκα χιλιάδες,

129. Resseguie, *Revelation of John*, 166.
130. Aune, *Revelation*, 450; Smalley, *Revelation to John*, 178.
131. Fanning, *Revelation*, 258.
132. It is the prominence of this group that enables the present writer to suggest that the role played by the angels is transitional at best.
133. It is beyond the scope of this book to explore the nature of this group as it relates to the continuity of Old Testament Israel and the church. For a detailed analysis, see Beale, *Revelation of John*, 416–24.
134. Fanning, *Revelation*, 258.
135. The aorist verb is in the first colon, and the repeated elements are underlined.

6. <u>ἐκ φυλῆς</u> Γὰδ <u>δώδεκα χιλιάδες</u>,
7. <u>ἐκ φυλῆς</u> Ἀσὴρ <u>δώδεκα χιλιάδες</u>,
8. <u>ἐκ φυλῆς</u> Νεφθαλὶμ <u>δώδεκα χιλιάδες</u>,
9. <u>ἐκ φυλῆς</u> Μανασσῆ <u>δώδεκα χιλιάδες</u>,
10. <u>ἐκ φυλῆς</u> Συμεὼν <u>δώδεκα χιλιάδες</u>,
11. <u>ἐκ φυλῆς</u> Λευὶ <u>δώδεκα χιλιάδες</u>,
12. <u>ἐκ φυλῆς</u> Ἰσσαχὰρ <u>δώδεκα χιλιάδες</u>,
13. <u>ἐκ φυλῆς</u> Ζαβουλὼν <u>δώδεκα χιλιάδες</u>,
14. <u>ἐκ φυλῆς</u> Ἰωσὴφ <u>δώδεκα χιλιάδες</u>,
15. <u>ἐκ φυλῆς</u> Βενιαμὶν <u>δώδεκα χιλιάδες</u> ἐσφραγισμένοι.

Second, the pedantic and redundant listing of the twelve tribes of Israel slows the pace even more.[136] Third, the four-fold repetition of the perfect participle ἐσφραγισμένοι brings these participants to the front of the mental stage. Fourth, John invites the audience to pay special attention to this group by the use of the command ἰδοὺ (behold/look).[137] Fifth, and most significantly, John simply records that he heard (ἤκουσα) the number of those who were sealed from among the tribes of Israel. He does not report any event or action, and he does not introduce any characters. In other words, John does not report an additional piece of the vision. Rather, by way of audition, he records what he heard.[138]

This literary technique of reported speech enables John to employ a rhetorical trick, as he did in scene 2 above (Rev 5:1–14). In both examples, John reports what he *heard*, but then *sees* something surprising and unexpected.[139] Here, John hears the number sealed from among the tribes of Israel but sees a ὄχλος πολύς (great multitude) from among the nations. As noted above, this multitude is marked for prominence by the repeated perfect participles that describe them (ἑστῶτες—standing; περιβεβλημένους—clothed), the four-fold formula depicting their constituents (ἐκ παντὸς ἔθνους καὶ φυλῶν καὶ λαῶν καὶ γλωσσῶν, out of every nation and tribe and people and language), and the recorded speech-act

---

136. In reading the book of Revelation out loud as well as the listening to the text read out loud, it was almost difficult to not want to skip forward or hit the fifteen second fast-forward button on the audio player. Resseguie, *Revelation of John*, 137–38.

137. Pattemore, "Revelation," 737.

138. Smalley, *Revelation to John*, 184.

139. Resseguie, *Revelation of John*, 136–37; Smalley, *Revelation to John*, 184.

that they shout in a loud voice. Their prominence is brought to the highest degree when all the previously introduced characters from scenes 1 and 2 analyzed above (Rev 4–5) join them in praising the one on the throne and the lamb. This unexpected reversal elicits excitement and heightens the drama of the narrative. Smalley notes that this prominence is further marked by the use of the historical present tense verb (κράζουσιν, they cry out). This ongoing effusion of praise would rise to the highest pitch on the lips of the performer.[140] As will be explored in chapter 5 of this book, the audience in the ancient world was expected to participate[141] in the story's recitation.[142]

Pace, Event, and Nonevent

Analysis has already been given in the above sections concerning the role verbal aspect plays in the book of Revelation. Following Mathewson's proposals, in these scenes, it remains demonstrable that the choice of verbal aspect enables the narrator to highlight certain actors and actions in the story as well as develop the background event-line of the narrative upon which the events occur. Therefore, it is sufficient here simply to summarize this material as it pertains to the pacing of the story itself.

The pace of the story of Revelation varies significantly throughout the book, but perhaps nowhere is this variation more significant than the section under investigation presently.[143] Scene 3 (Rev 6:1–8), for example, moves at a frenetic pace, with a flurry of aorist verbs and several characters both introduced and then brushed aside in rapid order. As seen in the table above labeled "Aorist verbs per one thousand words per chapter in the book of Revelation," chapter 6 contains one of the highest concentrations of aorist verbs in the entirety of the Apocalypse. This swift pace continues, albeit slowed slightly,[144] into the next scene (Rev 6:9–17) as the aorist verb continues in many of the cola that make up each of the periods in this scene. Scene 4, period 4 (Rev 6:12–14) contains nine lines with eight aorist indicatives alone. The action in this period is cosmic and violent, yet presented in such a way that the audience hardly has time to

140. Vansina, *Oral Tradition as History*, 34–35.

141. Smalley, *Revelation to John*, 192.

142. Vansina, *Oral Tradition as History*, 34–35. See also Rhoads, "Performance Criticism, Pt. II," 173–80.

143. Fanning, *Revelation*, 255.

144. Resseguie, *Revelation of John*, 129.

consider any of the events without being first ushered into the next event in succession.

Given the pacing established in Rev 6, it is then crucial for the analyst of Revelation to observe the variation that takes place in Rev 7. As seen in the aforementioned table, this chapter has one of the lowest concentrations of aorist verbs, and the pace slows dramatically.[145] With the redundant recording of the twelve tribes of Israel, the pace of the narrative is at a standstill. Even though the unveiling of the great multitude was grammatically marked for prominence, the pace of the story remains slow. Indeed, ten cola are reserved simply for describing this great multitude (S6:P1–2; Rev 7:9–10a), with another four lines simply noting the content of their speech. In fact, within the first five periods of scene 6 (Rev 7:9–17), John only employed two indicative aorist verbs. This intentional shift in the pace of the narrative is often overlooked in scholarship.[146] What is more, the way in which these shifts would be expressed in oral performance is not appropriately recognized.[147] The purpose of this book is to analyze the book of Revelation as a text intended for performance. The rhetorical effect of these features must be properly appreciated when studying this book.[148]

Additionally, it is again worth noting the way in which nonevents occur within the telling of the Apocalypse. Nonevents enable the author to orient the audience's attention, describe elements of setting, explain or evaluate characters' actions, and report speech or dialogue within the story.[149] In these scenes, the use of nonevent mirrors the pacing choice articulated above. In scene 3 (Rev 6:1–8), each rider receives only a brief depiction and then moves off the stage in quick succession. However, the amount of material given to both groups introduced in scene 4 (Rev 6:9–17)—the martyrs and the peoples of the earth—are more robust and detailed. Both groups produce speech-acts in the form of questions, and both groups' speech-acts are recorded (Rev 6:10; 16–17). The decision to depict the response to the first group, the martyrs, while leaving the

---

145. Resseguie, *Revelation of John*, 135.

146. Many scholars note that the action is interrupted, or that the pace is retarded, by the "interlude" but fail to note how this is accomplished by the analysis of the verbs and their aspect. Furthermore, these features would be particularly relevant for oral performance. See Resseguie, *Revelation of John*, 135–36; Koester, *Revelation*, 356.

147. Vansina, *Oral Tradition as History*, 34–35.

148. Koester, *Revelation*, 356.

149. Dooley, *Analyzing Discourse*, 82.

second group's question unanswered betrays a skillful rhetorical intentionality on the part of the author. The question posed by the second group—the peoples of the earth—seems to linger in the air. This second question, καὶ τίς δύναται σταθῆναι (and who is able to stand?), of both the exalted and the humbled functions as a key rhetorical question in the Apocalypse.[150] It is the combination of these features and how they work together to create an emotional impact on the audience that is often underdeveloped and forms the purpose of this book.[151]

Finally, John's ability to both retain the slowed pace as well as explain the nature of the prominent participants previously introduced is worth noting. By placing the dialogue between himself and one of the elders (Rev 7:13–17) immediately following the unexpected element of the vision (Rev 7:9), John provides clarity for the listening audience. Since dialogue occurs rarely in the book of Revelation,[152] the placement here implies a deliberate choice on the part of the author.[153] Thus, attention to John's use of dialogue (a nonevent) for explanatory purposes, in addition to variation in the pacing of the narrative, provides valuable insight in recognizing elements of prominence in the text. In this example, the elder is restaged from an earlier scene, which adds further prominence in the scene, forming a dramatic conclusion to this pericope.[154] Just like a modern film,[155] frenetic action on a cosmic scale gives way to a single conversation between two participants, with clear aim on the audience's experiential reception.[156]

BIBLICAL PERFORMANCE CRITICISM OF REV 6:1—8:1

Mnemonic Devices

In Revelation, John guides the participant through large sections of the story with the help of numbered sequencing. This observation is hardly

---

150. Resseguie, *Revelation of John*, 133. See also Fanning, *Revelation*, 252; Bauckham, *Climax of Prophecy*, 11.

151. Barr, *Tales of the End*, 148.

152. Smalley, *Revelation to John*, 195.

153. Longacre, *Holistic Discourse Analysis*, 15.

154. Smalley, *Revelation to John*, 195.

155. This technique is employed often in dramatic war movies, as massive battle scenes are interlaced with poignant dialogue between two principal characters.

156. Vansina, *Oral Tradition as History*, 34–35.

novel, and scholars consistently structure the book around these repeated sequences, with some even suggesting additional series of unnumbered sequences.[157] There are four explicit seven-fold numbered sequences in the book of Revelation: Rev 2–3; 6:1—8:1; 8:7—11:18; 16:2–21. As stated previously, these repeated sequences form the structural scaffolding for much of the material within the book. Even if the story was read from the written manuscript, authors in oral cultures guided their listeners through the narrative with emphatic and obvious structural markers.[158] Moreover, these clear structuring techniques may also serve as memory-aids for one reciting the text from memory, as techniques such as this were regularly employed in oral cultures.[159] Again, the goal of the present study is to provide a methodology for analyzing the text for aural performance features, as many scholars acknowledge that the book of Revelation was likely read aloud but fail to explore the way in which the text itself demonstrates such a proposal. The numbered sequencing serves as a prime example, with almost none of the commentators, reviewed and summarized in chapter 2 above, articulating the way in which this technique functions for both the listening audience[160] as well as the potential performer working from memory.[161] Since nine of the twenty-two chapters in the book of Revelation are guided by these numbered sequences, their value within an oral performance event cannot be overlooked.

Additional mnemonic aids surface within these scenes as well. The repetition noted above in opening of the first four seals enables the performer to call to mind each horse and rider with ease. The formula remains consistent for each of the first four seals: Καὶ ὅτε ἤνοιξεν τὴν σφραγῖδα τὴν δευτέραν (and whenever he opened the second seal). Each rider is announced by one of the four living creatures, attention is directed to three of the four by the imperative ἰδού, and three of the four are given something. As seen in the preceding section concerning

---

157. Aune, *Revelation*, xcvi–xcvii; Bauckham, *Climax of Prophecy*, 7–15. See also Fiorenza, *Book of Revelation*, 167.

158. Bauckham, *Climax of Prophecy*, 7. See also Ong, *Orality and Literacy*, i.

159. Barr, "Apocalypse as Oral Enactment," 244–47. See also Vansina, *Oral Tradition as History*, 39–47; Ong, *Orality and Literacy*, 145–46; Botha, *Orality and Literacy in Early Christianity*, 116; Rhoads, "Performance Criticism, Pt. II," 167; Barr, "Apocalypse as Oral Enactment," 246–47; Harvey, *Listening to the Text*, 41.

160. Indeed, Bauckham mentions that the structuring devices would have to be emphatic and obvious, but this is only stated in passing. Bauckham, *Climax of Prophecy*, 7. See Botha, *Orality and Literacy*, 116; Vansina, *Oral Tradition as History*, 21–22.

161. Vansina, *Oral Tradition as History*, 34–35.

structural repetition, however, it is the slight variation in this scene (Rev 6:1–8) that demonstrates Botha's assertion that composition was done out loud from memory[162] and likely not on the written page. Such slight variation is a hallmark of a culture adjusted to oral composition and reception of texts, as this variation is often edited out of printed text.[163]

Episodic Storytelling

Modern audiences are familiar with episodic storytelling. Many television shows, from crime dramas to sitcoms, follow this style of storytelling, cycling through the same elements again and again. The audience need not recall with exact precision an episode released months earlier, as each repeats similar themes and features. Ong notes that until the rise of the literate culture, episodic storytelling was a hallmark of ancient oral cultures, adjusted to tell and hear stories aloud. While the repetitive numbered sequencing in the book of Revelation noted in the previous section may be recognized as a mnemonic aid for ancient performers, these sequences also work to create redundant scenes that cycle through similar themes and elements again and again. In fact, scholars have observed this similarity, suggesting that many of the episodes recapitulate the same content.[164] Still others refute this suggestion, positing instead that the content of each numbered sequence occurs in succession.[165] It is beyond the scope of the present inquiry to wade into this multifaceted debate.[166] However, this paper aims to validate that the book of Revelation was written for oral performance and to analyze the text as such. In so doing, the nature of episodic storytelling in the ancient oral culture must be rightly recognized when investigating these numbered sequences. The literate culture, prepared for reading texts on the page with all the advantages that go with such a process,[167] may very well be able to follow a lengthy, climactic, linear plot.[168] In a world where most people were functionally

---

162. Botha, *Orality and Literacy*, 116.
163. Ong, *Orality and Literacy*, 78–115.
164. See Barr, who notes that the action of the main storyline is repeated again and again. Barr, *Tales of the End*, 15–25, 135–37. Also, Aune, *Revelation*, xci–xcvii.
165. See Fanning, *Revelation*, 61–63; Resseguie, *Revelation of John*, 56–60.
166. Again, for summary, see Bandy, "Layers of the Apocalypse," 469–99.
167. Ong, *Orality and Literacy*, 36, 139–51.
168. Ong, *Orality and Literacy*, 143.

illiterate,[169] where even written texts were read out loud,[170] themes were developed through episodic repetition. This aided the performer's public recitation of the story, enabling him to memorize patterns and elements that cycle over and over again.[171] This also aided the audience's ability to follow the story, with themes returning again and again.[172]

To the present author, this feature of ancient oral culture may indeed prove to be one of the strongest arguments in favor of the recapitulation theory (or some version of it).[173] To put it simply, the ancient hearer could join the performance of John's Apocalypse during any of the seven numbered judgments (seals, trumpets, bowls) and ascertain the same themes without having heard the previous scenes read aloud. It is possible that each of these numbered judgment series have the ability to be performed on their own without the inclusion of the additional episodes.[174] Each contributes many of the same themes and elements individually without the need of repetition. Certainly, the combination of all three elicits a rhetorical effect on the audience, in effect, hitting the audience over the head again and again in order that they do not miss the point.[175] This is a hallmark of an episodic style, thus enabling the performer to recycle similar elements again and again, and it is this recognition that further establishes the thesis of this book.[176]

Prosody Features in Rev 6:1—8:1

It is worth restating again that skill in public speaking was prized in the ancient world. This included the theater, public orations, and public storytelling. The way in which this skill was prized within the early church is impossible to measure. However, given that the book begins with a blessing to the one reading it aloud, it is not unreasonable to assume that the public reading/performing of the book also included techniques that

169. See the "Review of Literature" in chapter 2 above, pages 39–43.
170. Harvey, *Listening to the Text*, 40–42.
171. Harvey, *Listening to the Text*, 41.
172. Ong, *Orality and Literacy*, 33–36, 57–68, 139–51. See also Barr, "Apocalypse as Oral Enactment," 244–47.
173. Barr, *Tales of the End*, 15–25, 135–37.
174. Barr, *Tales of the End*, 15–25, 135–37. See also Bauckham, *Climax of Prophecy*, 7–15.
175. Resseguie, *Revelation of John*, 55.
176. Vansina, *Oral Tradition as History*, 43.

benefited the audience's reception of the narrative. Moreover, the book is full of sounds. Speech, noise, and praise pervade the Apocalypse.[177] Not only does the text depict this sound throughout, but cues are evident in the text as to the way the sound was meant to be experienced, with regular adjectives describing the volume or magnitude of the sound itself.[178] As noted in the above section regarding pace, events, and nonevents, recorded speech-acts are recorded from nearly every character. This speech takes the form of acts of praise, declarations, and even the prices of goods on the earth.

While scholars disagree regarding the normative function of the public reader in the Roman world, it is certainly possible if not likely that these reported speech-acts provided opportunities for prosody for the ancient reader/performer. Monotone recitation would not be sufficient for such a moment, and ancient performers were prepared for these announcements, moving their vocal cadence up and down as was necessitated by the occasion.[179] John includes the command ἰδού (behold/look) four times in these three chapters, with three occurring alongside the opening of the first four seals (Rev 6:2, 5, 8), and the last reserved for the unveiling of the great multitude in Rev 7:9. Such cues for direction alert the speaker and hearer alike, signaling what comes next. Ancient performers would raise their voices for dramatic effect, as well as act out the story with gestures.[180] The repetition of ἰδού cues such vocal variation.[181]

Additionally, it must be seen that the text not only notes that a participant speaks but also the manner in which the participant speaks. In scene 3, the living creature speaks with a voice ὡς φωνῇ βροντῆς (as the sound of thunder [Rev 6:1]). The souls under the altar cry out φωνῇ μεγάλῃ λέγοντες (with a great sound saying [Rev 6:10]) and the peoples of the earth cry out to the mountains and the rocks (Rev 6:16). In chapter 7, both an angel and the great multitude are presented crying out φωνῇ μεγάλῃ (Rev 7:2, 10). Each of these loud cries would be occasioned with

---

177. Resseguie, *Revelation of John*, 21.

178. Barr, *Tales of the End*, 25. This occurs so regularly throughout almost every section of the book of Revelation that it is not worth listing the individual examples here, as the list would be too long.

179. Vansina, *Oral Tradition as History*, 34–35. Also, Rhoads, "Performance Criticism, Pt. II," 167.

180. Vansina, *Oral Tradition as History*, 34–35.

181. Barr, *Tales of the End*, 9–12.

PERFORMANCE ANALYSIS OF A NUMBERED SEQUENCE SCENE 179

a change in the vocal pitch of the performer.[182] Dialogue forms the latter half of scene 6, with John and one of the elders discussing the nature of the great multitude, and this gives further place for prosody in the performance.[183]

Two moments preserved in the text of Revelation were likely crucial in generating prosody for the ancient performer. To conclude the opening of the first six seals, John records a question posed by the peoples of the earth that goes unanswered. This question is followed by a regularly used transitional marker in the Apocalypse (Μετὰ τοῦτο εἶδον; after this I saw [Rev 7:1]) that begins a new scene.[184] This combination—the unanswered question and the abrupt transition—likely cued the speaker to pause between the two, allowing the question generated by the peoples of the earth to linger in the air: καὶ τίς δύναται σταθῆναι (and who is able to stand? [Rev 6:17]). This question, while not answered directly by one of the participants, is nevertheless answered in the two scenes that follow, as the great multitude takes center stage.[185]

Finally, the numbered sequence of the "opening of the seals" episode concludes with the opening of the seventh seal to begin chapter 8. The pattern that began with the opening of the first four seals is repeated nearly identically, but the outcome of this seventh seal differs from all the rest. John simply notes that ἐγένετο σιγὴ ἐν τῷ οὐρανῷ ὡς ἡμιώριον (there became silence in heaven as half an hour [Rev 8:1]). Given the sheer volume of noise in the book of Revelation, both amount of noise as well as literal sound-level generated by the performer's prosody, this silence provides a welcome intermission before the action develops further.[186] It is beyond the scope of this book to discuss the ways that this silence has been interpreted,[187] but for the present aims, it may simply be acknowledged that this silence may very well have generated a pause in the performance itself, allowing both the speaker and the audience to reflect on material previously presented. Put simply, the audience is given a moment to catch their breath before the story continues.[188]

---

182. Vansina, *Oral Tradition as History*, 34–35.
183. Vansina, *Oral Tradition as History*, 34–35.
184. Beale, *Book of Revelation*, 152–70; Fanning, *Revelation*, 196.
185. Resseguie, *Book of Revelation*, 135–36.
186. Aune, *Revelation*, 507.
187. Beale, *Revelation of John*, 446–61.
188. Aune, *Revelation*, 507.

SUMMARY FOR THE ANALYSIS OF REV 6:1—8:1

The four scenes that comprise this section under review depict a flurry of actions and events that the audience must carefully follow in rapid succession. John's continuous style flows from cola to cola, with repeated structural formula guiding the way for both the performer and the audience. Formulas anchor the opening of the seven seals scene with a sevenfold numbered sequencing, again allowing both the speaker and hearer to follow the flow of the narrative. Careful attention to the way in which John employs verbal aspect to both encode a background storyline as well as bring certain participants and actions to the front of the stage sheds valuable light on the themes and elements that are highlighted grammatically in the text. The dynamic pacing of these scenes, while evident in the written text, are particularly pronounced when the text is read aloud as rapid-fire action slows to redundant recitation of the numbers of those sealed from the tribes of Israel. Each of these choices made by the author betray an awareness of the rhetorical effect they would have on the listening community. As seen in the first scenes analyzed (Rev 4–5), within these chapters it is the nonevents that provide the author the ability to describe and evaluate the events of the story. Dialogue brings clarity for the hearer, and the concluding silence gives the hearer a chance to ponder and reflect on what has transpired in the story.

Additionally, as demonstrated in the first scenes under review, written cues triggered prosody in ancient recitation. For the ancient storyteller reciting the story from memory, the combination of these elements work together to help bring the story to life in the gathered community. Many of the characteristics of orality are present in the sections of Revelation explored in this chapter, further verifying the thesis of this study that the book of Revelation was composed with oral delivery in mind. Cues to validate this claim remain in the written text, and this chapter has sought to unearth those cues.

5

Performance Analysis of the Epilogue

INTRODUCTION TO REV 22:6–21

THIS FINAL SECTION TO be analyzed will employ the same methodology as the previous two, but here the focus will narrow to the much debated[1] epilogue of the book of Revelation. The choice is not accidental, for the structure of the ending is both highly contested and enables comparison with the introduction of the book as well. Thus, it is hoped that a detailed performance analysis of the epilogue will also shed light on the prologue, with points of comparison noted in the footnotes within this chapter. While it is beyond the scope of this present book to adjudicate the various scholarly opinions concerning which verse begins the epilogue itself, for the purposes of analyzing the ending of the Apocalypse, the present study at least provides a suggestion. The final episode under examination begins at Rev 22:6, as John transitions the audience from the "taleworld" back to the "storyrealm" in order to provoke the audience to live differently in their "real world."[2] With much yet to be explored, the purpose of this chapter is to build on the previous two, applying the same methodological considerations, with the goal to further validate that the

---

1. The debate largely concerns the extent of the epilogue, with scholars offering differing opinions as to where the epilogue begins. For a thorough overview, see Aune, *Revelation*, 1141–50, 1200–1205. See also Pattemore, "Revelation," 721–26.

2. To be explored below, but this movement from taleworld to storyrealm is crucial in oral performance, especially in oral cultures. See Young, *Taleworlds and Storyrealms*, 1–68; Goffman, *Frame Analysis*, 506–11.

book of Revelation was composed for an aural reception. Additionally, this chapter suggests that the epilogue's complexity, which all scholars acknowledge, may be greatly reduced when the book of Revelation is read as a text composed for oral performance.³

THE SCIENCE OF SOUND IN REV 22:6–21

Sound Map of Rev 22:6–21 with Analysis

Episode 7 (Rev 22:6–22)

Period 1 (Rev 22:6a)

1. Καὶ εἶπέν μοι·
2. οὗτοι οἱ λόγοι πιστοὶ καὶ ἀληθινοί,

   Period 2 (Rev 22:6b)

1. καὶ ὁ κύριος
2. ὁ θεὸς τῶν πνευμάτων τῶν προφητῶν ἀπέστειλεν τὸν ἄγγελον αὐτοῦ
3. δεῖξαι τοῖς δούλοις αὐτοῦ
4. ἃ δεῖ γενέσθαι ἐν τάχει.

   Period 3 (Rev 22:7a)

1. καὶ ἰδοὺ ἔρχομαι ταχύ.

   Period 4 (Rev 22:7b)

1. μακάριος ὁ τηρῶν τοὺς λόγους τῆς προφητείας τοῦ βιβλίου τούτου.

Since these periods work together, they will be analyzed together. As the epilogue begins, the angel speaks to John with a preponderance of smooth and flowing consonant sounds combined with short o and ι sounds (this sound is also caused by the οἰ and ει diphthongs). Pleasant open αι vowels also feature prominently, making these periods euphonic in meter. The final colon of period 2 contains a voiceless aspirate (χ), which gives finality and closure to the period and is included again in the same word in period 3, linking these two periods. The voiceless stop (κ) serves a similar function in period 4, giving a snapping sense of urgency

---

3. Horsley, *Text and Tradition*, 223.

to the blessing to follow. More will be discussed below, but the speakers in these two periods are difficult to identify.

Period 5 (Rev 22:8)

1. Κἀγὼ Ἰωάννης ὁ ἀκούων καὶ βλέπων ταῦτα.
2. καὶ ὅτε ἤκουσα καὶ ἔβλεψα,
3. ἔπεσα προσκυνῆσαι ἔμπροσθεν τῶν ποδῶν τοῦ ἀγγέλου τοῦ δεικνύοντός μοι ταῦτα.

Period 6 (Rev 22:9)

1. καὶ λέγει μοι·
2. ὅρα μή·

Period 7 (Rev 22:10)

1. σύνδουλός σού εἰμι
2. καὶ τῶν ἀδελφῶν σου τῶν προφητῶν
3. καὶ τῶν τηρούντων τοὺς λόγους τοῦ βιβλίου τούτου·
4. τῷ θεῷ προσκύνησον.

Period 8 (Rev 22:10)

1. Καὶ λέγει μοι·
2. μὴ σφραγίσῃς τοὺς λόγους τῆς προφητείας τοῦ βιβλίου τούτου,
3. ὁ καιρὸς γὰρ ἐγγύς ἐστιν.

The interaction between John and the angel will be considered together. Period 5 is marked by hiatus, demarcating the alternation in speaker. Hiatus forces the speaker to slow the pace of the spoken word in order to properly pronounce each syllable.[4] The final colon of period 5 utilizes the technique of elongation splendidly, and the longer colon contains a repeated πρ- consonant cluster appropriate for the theme of worship. Additionally, the elongated colon has several other clusters of consonants, marking the importance of this theme for the audience. The repetition of the οὐ diphthong combined with long ῶ vowel sounds creates a solemn tone in period 7. The σφρ- blend resurfaces yet again here in the epilogue, but period 8 is otherwise entirely euphonic.

---

4. Lee, *Sound Mapping*, 176–79.

Period 9 (Rev 22:11)

1. ὁ ἀδικῶν ἀδικησάτω ἔτι
2. καὶ ὁ ῥυπαρὸς ῥυπανθήτω ἔτι,
3. καὶ ὁ δίκαιος δικαιοσύνην ποιησάτω ἔτι
4. καὶ ὁ ἅγιος ἁγιασθήτω ἔτι.

Repetition is the clear sound device in this period, as each colon ends with the same word, each contains a third-person imperative ending in τω, and the first three periods are dominated with δ and ῥ sounds. In fact, the rolling force contained within the second colon would be particularly pronounced in oral recitation, which matches the content of the ongoing nature of the command.

Period 10 (Rev 22:12)

1. Ἰδοὺ ἔρχομαι ταχύ,
2. καὶ ὁ μισθός μου μετ' ἐμοῦ
3. ἀποδοῦναι ἑκάστῳ ὡς τὸ ἔργον ἐστὶν αὐτοῦ.

Period 11 (Rev 22:13)

1. ἐγὼ τὸ ἄλφα
2. καὶ τὸ ὦ,
3. ὁ πρῶτος
4. καὶ ὁ ἔσχατος,
5. ἡ ἀρχὴ
6. καὶ τὸ τέλος.

Hiatus marks the switch in speaker that begins period 10. Given the clear repetition in the previous period, this hiatus may force the speaker to pause for a moment, aiding the audience's ability to notice the change of speaker. Both the open ἀ/αὶ and ἡ vowel sounds and the repetition of -ος at the end of several words provides a pleasing rhythm to period 11. Is it noteworthy that the meter and style of the spoken material attributed to Jesus is highly euphonic, particularly when announcing his identity and credentials. The repetition of the voiceless stop τ- consonant works to close the period.

Period 12 (Rev 22:14)

1. Μακάριοι οἱ πλύνοντες τὰς στολὰς αὐτῶν,
2. ἵνα ἔσται ἡ ἐξουσία αὐτῶν ἐπὶ τὸ ξύλον τῆς ζωῆς
3. καὶ τοῖς πυλῶσιν εἰσέλθωσιν εἰς τὴν πόλιν.

Period 13 (Rev 22:15)

1. ἔξω οἱ κύνες
2. καὶ οἱ φάρμακοι
3. καὶ οἱ πόρνοι
4. καὶ οἱ φονεῖς
5. καὶ οἱ εἰδωλολάτραι
6. καὶ πᾶς φιλῶν
7. καὶ ποιῶν ψεῦδος.

Again, determining the speaker for each period within the epilogue is arduous; more will be said in the pages that follow, and the above two periods will be explored in unison. Both the blessing formula in period 12 and the listing of those outside the gates of the city are marked by consistent hiatus. This is particularly pronounced in the second colon of period 12, forcing the speaker to carefully pronounce each word as the vowel sounds end and begin subsequent words. Hiatus joins with a combination of double consonants (ξ) and difficult voiced aspirates (ζ) to provide a sharply different meter to this colon. This suits the content, since the blessing formula also contains a bit of a warning, which is made explicit in the listing of the outsiders in period 13. Period 13 contains a high repetition of the οἱ and αἱ diphthongs and is also marked by hiatus, since καὶ οἱ opens the second colon and all that follow. The sharp consonants that make up the first colon, ἔξω οἱ κύνες (outside the dogs), arrest the attention of the audience, signaling the importance of the warning.

Period 14 (Rev 22:16a)

1. Ἐγὼ Ἰησοῦς ἔπεμψα τὸν ἄγγελόν μου
2. μαρτυρῆσαι ὑμῖν ταῦτα ἐπὶ ταῖς ἐκκλησίαις.

Period 15 (Rev 22:16b)

1. ἐγώ εἰμι ἡ ῥίζα
2. καὶ τὸ γένος Δαυίδ,
3. ὁ ἀστὴρ
4. ὁ λαμπρὸς
5. ὁ πρωϊνός.

The words of Jesus again reflect pure euphony, with pleasing vowels and liquid consonants creating a flowing and open meter appropriate for the speaker. Here, the contrast in sound with the previous two periods is most striking.

Period 16 (Rev 22:17)

1. Καὶ τὸ πνεῦμα καὶ ἡ νύμφη λέγουσιν·
2. ἔρχου.
3. καὶ ὁ ἀκούων εἰπάτω·
4. ἔρχου.
5. καὶ ὁ διψῶν
6. ἐρχέσθω,
7. ὁ θέλων λαβέτω ὕδωρ ζωῆς δωρεάν.

The liturgical antiphonal chant contains a repetition of the ου diphthong, combined with the third person imperative ending -τω. Elongation provides closure to the period.

Period 17 (Rev 22:18a)

1. Μαρτυρῶ ἐγὼ παντὶ τῷ ἀκούοντι τοὺς λόγους τῆς προφητείας τοῦ βιβλίου τούτου·

Period 18 (Rev 22:18b)

1. ἐάν τις ἐπιθῇ ἐπ' αὐτά,
2. ἐπιθήσει ὁ θεὸς ἐπ' αὐτὸν τὰς πληγὰς τὰς γεγραμμένας ἐν τῷ βιβλίῳ τούτῳ,

Period 19 (Rev 22:19)

1. καὶ ἐάν τις ἀφέλῃ ἀπὸ τῶν λόγων τοῦ βιβλίου τῆς προφητείας ταύτης,
2. ἀφελεῖ ὁ θεὸς τὸ μέρος αὐτοῦ ἀπὸ τοῦ ξύλου ἧς ζωῆς

3. καὶ ἐκ τῆς πόλεως τῆς ἁγίας

4. τῶν γεγραμμένων ἐν τῷ βιβλίῳ τούτῳ.

The warning contained in the above periods must be explored together. An array of the sibilant consonant marks period 17. These were to be avoided if possible due to the shrill nature of the sound.[5] This pattern continues in the other two periods under examination, marking a variation in sound pattern from the previous material, appropriate for the warning content. What is more, the amount of liquid consonants drops in these periods and is replaced with a higher concentration of π, κ, and τ consonants, giving them a slightly less euphonic quality.

Period 20 (Rev 22:20)

1. Λέγει ὁ μαρτυρῶν ταῦτα·

2. ναί,

3. ἔρχομαι ταχύ.

Period 21 (Rev 22:20b)

1. Ἀμήν,

2. ἔρχου κύριε Ἰησοῦ.

Period 22 (Rev 22:21)

1. Ἡ χάρις τοῦ κυρίου Ἰησοῦ μετὰ πάντων.

The final periods explored in this study return to a mostly euphonic meter. The exception is the again abruptness found in the request ἔρχομαι ταχύ. As the benediction is given, the matching harmony in style is warranted.

John's Grouping of Cola into Periods

The pattern established in the previous two sections, in which most of the cola begin with καί, no longer persists in the epilogue. Here, less than half of the cola begin with καί. Even more significant, however, is the καί + aorist construction that often begins periods elsewhere in the book is wholly absent from this pericope, with the exception of S7:P1/

---

5. Caragounis, *Development of Greek*, 409.

Rev 22:6a.[6] This is even more striking considering the fact that in the previous macro-section of the text (Rev 21:9—22:5), this construction occurs often, marking discourse units (Rev 21:9, 10, 16, 17, 22; 22:1, 6).[7] Beginning with the blessing announced in Rev 22:7b, though, the continuous style accomplished by the repetition of καί at the start of each period drops out completely. This surprising shift in pattern gives valuable insight as to the beginning of the end of the book. As noted above, scholars regularly debate where the epilogue begins but do not note this alteration in pattern. This same pattern begins the book, with the prologue containing few uses of the καί + aorist construction that pervades the rest of the book.

Not everything in John's style is changed, however, as the periods still evidence limited grammatical subordination. There are few dependent clauses, and even when John utilizes a dependent clause (such as the ἵνα clause in Rev 22:14) it is only an additional two lines. Much of the style established above persists, with most of the cola and periods providing simple independent clauses stacked paratactically one after another. It is worth stating again, however, that the greatest variation is that, in the previous sections analyzed in this investigation, John connected these regularly with καί. This creates a choppier style for the epilogue, contributing to the confusion among scholars regarding its structure.

Rounding and Elongation in Rev 22:6–21			
Rounding	Verse	Elongation	Verse
E7:P1 (repetition of οι sounds)	22:6a	E7:P1	22:6a
E7:P5 (repetition of ταῦτα)	22:8	E7:P5	22:8
E7:P9 (repetition of τω sounds and ἔτι)	22:11	E7:P16	22:17
E7:P11 (repetition of τό)	22:13	E7:P22	22:21
E7:P13 (repetition of οι sounds)	22:15		
E7:P20 (repetition of ιε sounds)	22:20		

In the ancient world, most people interacted with texts by hearing them read out loud. Even those reading from a written manuscript did so without the aid of punctuation and spelling markings, thus readers/hearers were aided in recognizing the beginning and ends of periods by

---

6. As will be seen in the structural markers section of the investigation below, this period serves as part of a transitional paragraph from the narrative to the epilogue.

7. Mathewson, "Verbal Aspect in the Apocalypse," 65. See also Pattemore, "Revelation," 730.

the use of techniques such as rounding, elongation, change of setting, change of speaker, or change of topic.[8] Within this pericope, many of the periods share these common techniques. Rounding occurs when a sound or word is repeated at the beginning and end of a period, signaling its close. Whereas a balanced period contains cola that are parallel in length and sound. Finally, elongation involves the lengthening of the final colon of a period or the use of multiple long vowel sounds in the final colon.[9] As seen in table 3, rounding occurs in six of the sixteen periods within the epilogue, with elongation occurring twice. These techniques signal period boundary markers and the grouping of cola together. Additionally, as seen in the sound map and tables above, many of the periods contain repeated sounds, words, and phrases, which also cluster cola into period units.[10] The final tool for period boundary marking is indeed the most salient in that periods typically function to bind units of discourse and are grammatically complete.[11] For example, in E7:P6 (Rev 22:9b), the angel speaks to John, and the six cola within this speech-act function as the content of that speech.[12] The discourse unit is complete. In E7:P7 (Rev 22:10), the angel speaks again. Both of these periods share identical first cola, which introduces each discourse unit: Καὶ λέγει μοι (and he said to me).

The Style of Sound in Rev 22:6–22

Period Style

The style of the epilogue exhibits both continuity and discontinuity with the previous two episodes already evaluated in this study. The material within this pericope contains many thematic parallels with material previously presented in the book, especially the prologue (Rev 1:1–8).[13] When comparing the prologue and the epilogue, a number of words and phrases repeat identically and in a similar order, forming a bracket around the entirety of the book itself. Additionally, characters previously

8. Lee, *Sound Mapping*, 108–11.
9. Lee, *Sound Mapping*, 171.
10. Lee, *Sound Mapping*, 108–9.
11. Lee, *Sound Mapping*, 109.
12. This is also the case in the prologue as the various speech-acts form discrete discourse units.
13. Aune, *Revelation*, 1201.

introduced within the narrative are restaged in the epilogue: John the narrator, one of the angels, and Jesus. These characters participate in a lively dialogue that provides both encouragement and warning for the attentive reader.[14] In short, the prologue and epilogue reveal a thematic continuity with the rest of the Apocalypse, even amidst the differences with the rest of the narrative.

However, there are striking stylistic elements of discontinuity in this final episode. As already noted, the redundant use of καί decreases significantly in this section, particularly at the beginning of periods. Many of the periods in the epilogue seem to stand on their own, creating a rather uneven or even disordered style.[15] Indeed, what baffles scholars across the board is the difficulty in arranging the material in this section. Statements, exhortations, warnings, and promises bombard the audience in a staccato-like manner.[16] Additionally, the very identification of the speakers in this section is difficult to ascertain. While it is beyond the scope of the present section to solve this difficulty (more to come below), it is worth noting the stylistic variation in the epilogue. Without the connecting καί to string periods together, the periods stand on their own. It is as if they are to be spoken independently of each other, with each receiving its proper attention, creating an urgency for the hearer.[17]

For a representative example, the angel speaks to John in Rev 22:10, instructing him not to seal the words of the prophecy followed by a supportive clause: ὁ καιρὸς γὰρ ἐγγύς ἐστιν (for the time is near). The angel's spoken word is followed by two poetic couplets likely derived from Dan 12:10.[18] Each cola is highly structured and strophic,[19] forming a clear discourse unit marked in the sound map above as period 9 (Rev 22:11). The style of the couplets differs significantly from the previous periods, causing many scholars to suggest that they are not spoken by the angel

---

14. Fanning, *Revelation*, 552.

15. Aune, *Revelation*, 1204. Aune notes that some suggest the epilogue is beyond repair and must be reworked in order to provide a coherent narrative arrangement. Still others see a novel liturgical back-and-forth behind the structuring of the text in its present form. For a representative view, see Vanni, "Liturgical Dialogue," 348–72. Additionally, Pattemore suggests that Relevance Theory provides helpful guidance for understanding the stylistic change that occurs here in the epilogue. See Pattemore, "Revelation," 724–25.

16. Pattemore, "Revelation," 724–25.

17. Fanning, *Revelation*, 557, 559.

18. Smalley, *Revelation to John*, 571.

19. Smalley, *Revelation to John*, 571. See also Aune, *Revelation*, 1217.

who speaks in the previous verse.[20] In fact, some scholars go even further, suggesting that this verse is a later addition.[21] The poetic pair is then followed by a speech-act most likely from Jesus himself, beginning with the urgent attention-arresting command Ἰδοὺ (Behold! Look!). What is one to make of the sheer variation in the style of these periods, seemingly flowing one after another? Pattemore acknowledges the "major problem"[22] in sorting this variation of voices. It is argued here that it is not simply the variety of voices but the variation in style that compounds the problem.

This same style occurs in the prologue as well. The book's first period makes a dramatic statement, indicating that the material revealed came from God himself. Next, the chain of the transmission of the message is reported, ending with John. The next statement, however, contains a blessing formula, commending both the reader and the hearer, noting the urgency of the moment (ὁ γὰρ καιρὸς ἐγγύς, the time is near). This statement stands paratactically, without grammatical connection to the previous material, thus Rev 1:1–2 and Rev 1:3 function as separate periods. This is made even more clear by the seven-fold repetition of blessing formulas in the rest of the Apocalypse. Next, John directly addresses the audience with a typical epistolary introduction.[23] In just four verses, three discrete discourse units introduce the audience to the oral performance event.

The variation in style of the prologue and epilogue of Revelation betrays intentionality on the part of the author.[24] What is more, these stylistic differences would be particularly effective in oral recitation,[25] enabling the performer to pause briefly between each period for dramatic effect. The continuous style evidenced in the previously explored material dissipates, with the more staccato style in view here in the epilogue. This creates a dizzying array of warnings, exhortations, promises, and blessings all singing from multiple voices at the same time. The epilogue is no longer simply an account of what John saw but rather a story that

20. Beale, *Book of Revelation*, 1131.
21. Charles, *Critical and Exegetical Commentary*, 221–22.
22. Pattemore, "Revelation," 724.
23. Barr, *Tales of the End*, 3–4.
24. Again, the unity of the text of Revelation is an assumption made by the present author in studying this text. It is beyond the scope of this book to wade into questions regarding the compositional process or redaction process of the text of Revelation.
25. More to be stated in defense of this claim.

invites the audience to join in themselves, considering the messages one at a time.[26] While scholars make differing proposals regarding the interpretation, structure, and background for much of this material, they often overlook the way in which the stylistic choice would be heard in the ears of the ancient audience. They fail to note the way in which this staccato style signals the performer for moments of dramatic effect.[27]

NARRATIVE DISCOURSE ANALYSIS OF REV 22:6–21

Markers of Orality

Structural Markers

Repeated Formula

Structurally, the epilogue has baffled scholars for ages, with scholars differing on the rightful transition from the story to the story's ending. Many scholars suggest that the epilogue begins at Rev 22:6,[28] while others favor Rev 22:10.[29] Others, however, recognize Rev 22:18 as the beginning of the end.[30] Still others posit that Rev 22:7 serves as the transition to the final section of the book.[31] While it is beyond the scope of the present investigation to adjudicate the matter in full, the structural markers must be analyzed carefully, and then the nature of discourse framing must be properly appreciated. It is the position of the present author that the difficulty in solving the structural conundrum of the epilogue may in fact be yet another clue to the oral performance event involved in the reception of the Apocalypse.

First, Aune rightly demonstrates that the material in Rev 21:9—22:10 parallels that which is depicted previously in Rev 17:1—19:10.[32] Both sections begin with John being transported in the Spirit[33] and end

---

26. Pattemore, "Revelation," 725.

27. Much more will be said in subsequent sections. Barr, *Tales of the End*, 258–61, 320–24. Also, Vanni, "Liturgical Dialogue," 348–72.

28. Mounce, *Book of Revelation*, 388–90; Osborne, *Revelation*, 777–78.

29. Aune, *Revelation*, 1200–1205; Fanning, *Revelation*, 549–52.

30. Smalley, *Revelation to John*, 582.

31. Aune, *Revelation*, 1205. See also Pattemore, "Revelation," 721–25.

32. Aune, *Revelation*, 1144–45. See also Mounce, *Book of Revelation*, 390.

33. For Bauckham (followed by Fanning), this is the primary structuring technique for the narrative as a whole. Thus, the book's macro-units are clustered by John's

with John being rebuked for worshiping an angel. Both share words, phrases, and themes.[34] Thus, it is crucial to recognize that, structurally, these two episodes parallel each other, and the repetition of these structural markers enables the audience to organize the material successfully.[35] For many, then, the material in Rev 21:9—22:10 clusters together structurally, prohibiting the epilogue to begin until after Rev 22:10.

The case may not be so open and shut, however. Scholars also regularly note the way in which Rev 22:6-9 parallels the prologue (Rev 1:1-3). Bauckham posits that the precise verbal agreement shared in Rev 1:1 and 22:6 (δεῖξαι τοῖς δούλοις αὐτοῦ ἃ δεῖ γενέσθαι ἐν τάχει, to show his servants what is necessary to happen soon) structurally marks the epilogue's beginning.[36] Aune goes as far as to suggest that, due to the striking parallels found in Rev 1:1-3 and 22:6-10, it is probable they were crafted together toward the end of the revision stage of John's composition of the Apocalypse.[37] In any case, it is important to recognize the way in which Rev 22:6-9 serves as a conclusion to the previous episode (Rev 21:9—22:9) as well as a return to the prologue.

Structurally, then, these verses serve to transition[38] the audience from the world of the story to the realm of the storytelling. Here, approaching the Apocalypse as a work intended to be received within an oral performance event provides crucial insight into the way these verses function within the book. Katharine Galloway Young, following the work of William Labov and Joshua Waletzky, posits that movement between the "real world" to the "taleworld" is vital in oral storytelling.[39] The taleworld is the realm inhabited by the characters within the story, upon which the events of the story unfold.[40] This is the imagined world into which the speaker must transport the hearer.[41] In order to accomplish

---

signaling that he is moved in the spirit to experience a new visionary location. See Bauckham, *Climax of Prophecy*, 3-7; Fanning, *Revelation*, 58-64.

34. Aune, *Revelation*, 1144-45.

35. Ong, *Orality and Literacy*, i. These parallels also serve as another example of the episodic nature of the book of Revelation, with each episode following similar patterns and themes.

36. Bauckham, *Climax of Prophecy*, 23.

37. Aune, *Revelation*, 1146. See also Mounce, *Book of Revelation*, 389-90.

38. Aune, *Revelation*, 1208; Pattemore, "Revelation," 721-25.

39. Young, *Taleworlds and Storyrealms*, 16-19.

40. Young, *Taleworlds and Storyrealms*, 15-16.

41. Barr, *Tales of the End*, 117-18.

this, the speaker cannot be too obvious or too opaque.[42] The telling of the story plays out in a mediating realm between the "real world," in which the audience inhabits,[43] and the taleworld inhabited by the imagined characters. Young refers to this mediating intersubjective world as the storyrealm, a social interaction between the performer and the audience.[44] The storyrealm establishes the portal between which the speaker can carefully lead the listener to the taleworld.[45]

For a modern comparison, a movie's director creates a taleworld into which the audience travels. This taleworld temporarily removes the audience from their "real world," particularly if the movie is especially engaging. The movie theater, filled with rows of seats faced toward a screen, thus becomes the storyrealm through which the audience is transported between the "real world" to the taleworld. This entire process must be navigated carefully. Typical theaters dim the lights, roll the movie-trailers and advertisements, widen the curtain of the screen, and turn up the volume in order to signal to the audience that the time has come to enter the taleworld. This storyrealm fades into the background, unless of course someone else interrupts it, either by opening up an exit door, allowing their phone to ring out loud, or talking loudly to their companion. Moreover, if the story is poorly executed or unengaging, the audience may become again aware of both the storyrealm as well as their own "real world." This same sort of comparison may be made by examining the way that this process is experienced while reading a modern novel on the printed page. Young notes that a written text clamps down on the thresholds between realms, "circumscribing its own horizons by separating storyteller from hearer, by withdrawing story from conversation, fixing its form, and enclosing it in a book."[46]

In an oral presentation, the speaker must also navigate this process successfully.[47] Since publicly recited stories play out amidst the continuities between realms,[48] the audience must be transported from their "real

---

42. Young, *Taleworlds and Storyrealms*, 19.

43. Indeed, all stories are ultimately anchored in the surroundings in which they are given. See Goffman, *Frame Analysis*, 500.

44. Barr, *Tales of the End*, 16.

45. Young, *Taleworlds and Storyrealms*, 17–19.

46. Young, *Taleworlds and Storyrealms*, 14.

47. For an interesting study of the way this often happens in the world, see Tannen, *Framing in Discourse*.

48. For an additional perspective, see Bauman, *Story, Performance, and Event*, 7–8.

world" social setting into the imagined world that the story plays out within and back again.⁴⁹ Without the benefit of lights to dim or bookcovers to open and close, the speaker must use clever techniques to move the group gathered to listen from "real world" to taleworld. Thus, the performer must carefully move the "real world" social setting into an oral performance event, so that the audience can experience something outside their "real world." This enables the hearers to share in the experience of the tale, and therefore return to their "real world" social setting with a different perspective.⁵⁰

For many oral cultures, the performance occurs when the community gathers around the storyteller.⁵¹ The storyrealm is established when the audience and performer mutually agree to the performance and begin the process of engaging the narrative as active participants. This may be through verbal invitation or through the formal sitting down to hear the story. In oral storytelling, both the speaker and audience are aware of each other's presence, their surroundings, and their experience of time and space.⁵² The task of the performer, then, is to transport the audience into the taleworld, leaving behind the "real world" as well as the storyrealm. For a successful performance, the hearers must be taken into a different set of surroundings with a different experience of time and space.⁵³ This occurs through a deliberate and oftentimes theatrical process.⁵⁴ The storyrealm often contains discourse frames that help transition the hearer from the realm of normal conversation to the taleworld.⁵⁵

Consider the following familiar prologue in modern storytelling: "Once upon a time . . . ." This simple statement begins the process of moving the audience from their ordinary realm through the storyrealm of their social setting and into the taleworld. Also consider the way in which a modern comedian may begin his set by addressing the audience directly, acknowledging some commonality between them. Many even point out a noteworthy feature of the city in which the performance occurs or the venue itself. These draw attention to the storyrealm, build

---

See also Fox, "Worlds with Words," 29–32; Goffman, *Frame Analysis*, 496–559.

49. Young, *Taleworlds and Storyrealms*, 14–20.
50. Barr, *Tales of the End*, 39, 316–24. See also Pattemore, "Revelation," 725.
51. Vansina, *Oral Tradition as History*, 34–35.
52. Goffman, *Frame Analysis*, 500.
53. Young, *Talewords and Storyrealms*, 16–17. See also Koester, *Revelation*, 223.
54. Goffman, *Frame Analysis*, 504.
55. Young, *Taleworlds and Storyrealms*, 19–25.

rapport with the audience, and then help to move both performer and listener to the prepared set material.

Consider, then, the way in which John carefully transitions his audience in and out of the taleworld.[56] In the prologue (Rev 1:1–3), John begins with a dramatic declaration: Ἀποκάλυψις Ἰησοῦ Χριστοῦ ἣν ἔδωκεν αὐτῷ ὁ θεός (the revelation of Jesus Christ that God gave him [Rev 1:1a]). The speaker is ambiguous at this point,[57] since John does not formally introduce himself until Rev 1:4.[58] While it was a regular feature of ancient writings to begin with such a titular statement,[59] this particular enigmatic statement alerts the hearer to the importance of what follows. It would have been too much to simply begin the story outright, and this mysterious and dramatic statement is necessary in order to begin the process of moving the audience into the taleworld.[60]

Barr refers to this anonymous voice that begins the Apocalypse as the Rhetor,[61] while Vanni calls this voice the Lector.[62] The enigmatic introduction provokes a sense of anticipation, calling the audience into the tale,[63] while also orienting them to background material.[64] Then the blessing formula (Rev 1:3) that follows commends both speaker and hearer.[65] This formal recognition of both the performer (ὁ ἀναγινώσκων, the *one* reading aloud) and the audience (οἱ ἀκούοντες, the *ones* hearing) establishes the storyrealm through which the listener must go and

---

56. It is impossible to be certain about the social setting in which the Apocalypse was intended to be delivered. Barr suggests an eucharistic liturgical setting, with the book of Revelation setting up the eucharist. See Barr, "Apocalypse as Oral Enactment," 249–56. Others see the influence of Greek drama on the Apocalypse, positing that perhaps a social gathering more in line with the Greek theater should be in view. See Janse van Rensburg, "All the Apocalypse" 1–8; Brewer, "Influence of Greek Drama," 74–92.

57. Barr refers to this voice as the "rhetor," whom he distinguishes from the narrator, John, to follow.

58. Seal, "Reception and Delivery," 3–4.

59. See also the beginning of the Gospel of Matthew and the Gospel of Mark. Barr, *Tales of the End*, 4.

60. Koester, *Revelation*, 220–21.

61. Barr, *Tales of the End*, 50.

62. Vanni, "Liturgical Dialogue," 348–49.

63. Tannen, *Framing in Discourse*, 22–26.

64. Beale notes that by beginning the book this way, John is likely not using a technical term for a type of genre called apocalyptic literature. Rather, he points his audience immediately to the book of Daniel, where this term is used repeatedly. Beale, *Book of Revelation*, 181.

65. Koester, *Revelation*, 221.

must go urgently, for the time is near (ὁ γὰρ καιρὸς ἐγγύς).⁶⁶ With that, John is then able to introduce himself and the visions that follow. Resseguie notes that these first verses serve to startle the audience out of the ordinary realm and awaken them to something new and fresh.⁶⁷

It is crucial at this point in the investigation to recognize that each of these steps is vitally important in forming a successful oral performance event. Too abrupt an entry into the taleworld and the audience is not ready. Too laborious an entry into the taleworld and the audience loses interest.⁶⁸ Scholars who acknowledge that Rev 1:1–3 likely indicates that the text was orally delivered in its original reception are certainly correct, but they do not go far enough. By closely examining this complex introduction through the lens of oral performance techniques, the functional necessity of these verses becomes even more clear, as well as the certainty of Revelation's orality. Again, since the ὁ ἀναγινώσκων (one reading aloud) is specifically commended by the blessing formula, it may be assumed that the role of the reader was significant for the communication of the message of John's Apocalypse. Thus, skillful public recitation may have been a necessary accompaniment to the experience of telling and hearing the book of Revelation.

After introducing himself (Rev 1:4),⁶⁹ John certifies the authority of the transmission of the message he received.⁷⁰ John then assumes the role of narrator for the remainder of the performance, with the rest of the book of Revelation playing out from his first-person account.⁷¹ Before turning to the visionary experiences themselves, he first acknowledges the social situational context, addressing his audience directly: Ἰωάννης ταῖς ἑπτὰ ἐκκλησίαις ταῖς ἐν τῇ Ἀσίᾳ· χάρις ὑμῖν καὶ εἰρήνη (John, to the seven churches in Asia. Grace to you and peace [Rev 1:4]). Again, it must be stated that moving into the formal taleworld requires careful guidance in public performance.⁷² The anonymous interruption in Rev 1:7 (ναί, ἀμήν, yes, amen), likely serves a dialogical purpose,⁷³ as the gathered as-

66. Osborne, *Revelation*, 785.
67. Resseguie, *Revelation of John*, 62.
68. Young, *Taleworlds and Storyrealms*, 17–20.
69. Barr, *Tales of the End*, 52–53.
70. Resseguie, *Revelation of John*, 62.
71. As noted, this participatory tone invites the audience into the story directly and is a hallmark of oral cultures. See Ong, *Orality and Literacy*, 45–46.
72. Young, *Taleworlds and Storyrealms*, 17–20.
73. Vanni, "Liturgical Dialogue," 349–55. See also Koester, *Revelation*, 229.

semblies of the early church regularly utilized a responsorial dialogue.[74] This again attunes the audience to their social context, inviting them to provide assent to the prophet's words.[75] Finally, just before John moves the audience officially into the taleworld in Rev 1:9, God[76] finally speaks: Ἐγώ εἰμι τὸ ἄλφα καὶ τὸ ὦ, λέγει κύριος ὁ θεός, ὁ ὢν καὶ ὁ ἦν καὶ ὁ ἐρχόμενος, ὁ παντοκράτωρ ("I am the alpha and the omega," says the Lord God, "who was, and who is, and who is coming, the almighty" [Rev 1:8]). This powerful declaration contains the final words heard before the transition into the taleworld.[77] In effect, they reverberate in the background of the rest of the performance.[78]

Attention to these structural devices at the beginning of the Apocalypse proves insightful in examination of the end of the Apocalypse. Again, as noted by Aune, Rev 22:6–10 serves as a transitional unit between the close of the previous episode (Rev 21:9—22:10) and the epilogue (22:11–21). What is underdeveloped by scholars of Revelation, however, is the way in which this transitional pericope returns to the storyrealm established at the start. Here, the performer must move his audience from the taleworld back to the social situational context of their "real world." As with the initial invitation, too abrupt or too opaque an ending would be noticed by the listeners.

Thus, the parallels between the Rev 1:1–3 and 22:6–10 reveal more than just a later redaction, rather they demonstrate the careful framing of the Apocalypse for a listening audience. The repetition is obvious: δεῖξαι τοῖς δούλοις αὐτοῦ (to show his servants), ἃ δεῖ γενέσθαι ἐν τάχει (what is necessary to happen soon), μακάριος (blessed), τοὺς λόγους τῆς προφητείας (the words of this prophecy), ὁ γὰρ καιρὸς ἐγγύς (for the time is near).[79] In Rev 1:4, John assumes the primary voice through which the taleworld plays out, specifically addressing the audience. In Rev 22:6–9, that pattern repeats, with John again directly addressing his audience. This deliberate statement calls attention to the storyrealm

74. Cabaniss, *Pattern*, 1–70; Vanni, "Liturgical Dialogue," 348–49.

75. Seal, "Reception and Delivery," 3–7.

76. There is intentional ambiguity between the voice of God here and the voice of Jesus later in the book of Revelation, as these very words are clearly on the lips of Jesus later in the story. This shows that the two must be seen together. See Koester, *Revelation*, 230.

77. Koester, *Revelation*, 222–23. See also Seal, "Reception and Delivery," 6.

78. Smalley, *Revelation to John*, 26; Resseguie, *Revelation of John*, 70–72. See also Koester, *Revelation*, 221.

79. Aune, *Revelation*, 1148–49.

established in the prologue, signaling to the audience that a return to the "real world" is approaching. It is worth noting as well that just as in Rev 1:1–3, in 22:6–9, the speaker is again ambiguous. It is as if the voice that initiated the storyrealm in Rev 1:1 and pronounced blessing over the recipients of the story in Rev 1:3 now returns to again call attention to the storyrealm. Perhaps the ambiguity in the speaker within the epilogue is not a result of poor redacting or later insertions within the text but rather a carefully crafted technique designed with the listening audience in mind.[80] The experience of telling and hearing the Apocalypse was meant to transform the hearer, stiffening them against the social pull of the Roman culture.[81]

Reported Speech

Much of the material contained in the epilogue of Revelation consists of reported speech-acts. Given the importance of the spoken word to understanding the epilogue itself, the present investigation will devote much of its analysis of the epilogue to the present section. The sheer volume of spoken material would be particularly effective in oral storytelling, enabling the performer to apply prosody to the dialogue and enact the spoken word.[82] As will be seen below, the variation in style and intonation of the material in the epilogue would have allowed the audience to recognize which participant said which utterance.[83] The printed text of Revelation exhibits ambiguity as to the speaker of much of the spoken material in this episode,[84] but such ambiguity would vanish in oral performance, as the performer could utilize prosody to provide clarity.[85]

Several features must be explored when analyzing the reported speech within the epilogue of the Apocalypse. This is particularly necessary given the aforementioned ambiguity that remains in the printed text. First, many of the speech-acts are introduced with an introductory formulae. These formulae signal the spoken word, but the grammatical form

---

80. Barr, *Tales of the End*, 15–20.
81. Barr, *Tales of the End*, 321.
82. Vansina, *Oral Tradition as History*, 34–35. See also Rhoads, "Performance Criticism, Pt. II," 173–80; Shiner, "Oral Performance," 49–63.
83. Vanni, "Liturgical Dialogue," 364.
84. Smalley, *Revelation to John*, 571.
85. Smalley, *Revelation to John*, 571.

alters, suggesting intentionality on the part of the author.⁸⁶ For instance, the formulas that introduce many of the spoken elements (often referred to as *verbum dicendi*) within the concluding dialogue demands attention, both for the similarities between them but also the peculiar differences⁸⁷ between them:

Καὶ εἶπέν μοι (22:6)

καὶ λέγει μοι (22:9)

Καὶ λέγει μοι (22:10)

καὶ τὸ πνεῦμα καὶ ἡ νύμφη λέγουσιν (22:17a)

καὶ ὁ ἀκούων εἰπάτω (22:17b)

Λέγει ὁ μαρτυρῶν ταῦτα (22:20)

Second, John dramatically shifts between first and third person, seemingly without warning (see the shift from S7:P2/Rev 22:6b to S7:P3/Rev 22:7a and S7:P11/Rev 22:13 to S7:P12/Rev 22:14).⁸⁸ Third, two of the seven blessing formulas within the book of Revelation occur in the epilogue.⁸⁹ These are spoken without formal introduction and paratactically with the preceding material. Fourth, much of the material is structured antiphonally (see Rev 22:20).

These features work together to fashion the narrative flow of the epilogue and must be approached carefully. It is important to first attempt to identify the speakers within this unit.⁹⁰ How do the above features signal changes in speaker within the final narrative scene? How would the audience recognize such signals? How would performers embody these signals in public storytelling? The transitional scene that moves the audience from the final visionary experience to the epilogue begins in Rev 22:6. Here, one of the angels introduced in Rev 17 and later restaged in Rev 21:9 addresses John directly in Rev 22:6.⁹¹ This appears to be the same angel who guided John's tour of the New Jerusalem. The angel's reported speech, however, shifts dramatically from third person to first person in S7:P3/Rev 22:7a,

---

86. Vanni, "Liturgical Dialogue," 356.
87. Vanni, "Liturgical Dialogue," 356.
88. Vanni, "Liturgical Dialogue," 357.
89. Vanni, "Liturgical Dialogue," 356–57.
90. Vanni, "Liturgical Dialogue," 361–63. See also Aune, *Revelation*, 1204–8.
91. Mounce, *Book of Revelation*, 390; Osborne, *Revelation*, 780.

likely indicating a new speaker.⁹² Given the repetition of these words on the lips of Jesus elsewhere in Revelation (Rev 2:16; 3:11), it is most likely that the reported utterances are spoken from the lips of Jesus himself. Here, the speaker/performer's variation of intonation and tone of voice would assist the hearer as to the change in speaker.

Next, one of the participants announces the sixth blessing formula in the book of Revelation. The first of these seven occurs in the prologue in Rev 1:3. In that first instance, the speaker, whose voice remains ambiguous, addresses both the performer (ὁ ἀναγινώσκων, the one reading aloud) as well as the audience (καὶ οἱ ἀκούοντες, and the ones hearing). Since John himself does not receive formal introduction until the following verse (Rev 1:4), two speakers have been proposed. The speaker could be the angel sent to John, introduced in Rev 1:2. This may indicate that the speaker of the blessing formulae in Rev 22:7b as well as Rev 22:14 is this same angelic figure. On the other hand, as noted above, Rev 1:1–3 serves to establish a mediating intersubjective storyrealm through which the audience may enter the taleworld. With this in mind, it is possible that the ambiguous voice of the rhetor⁹³ that invites the audience to the table in Rev 1:1–3 speaks again in the epilogue. Perhaps the answer is more elegant in that the voice of the angel and the voice inviting the audience into the storyrealm is one and the same.

Next, John reports the next phase of his dialogue with the angel with a pair of speech-acts introduced with the same formula: καὶ λέγει μοι (Rev 22:9, 10). Given the parallels with the prologue (ὁ καιρὸς γὰρ ἐγγύς ἐστιν, for the time is near [Rev 1:3; 22:10]), it is again worth considering the angel as the anonymous speaker in Rev 1:3. The subsequent period (S7:9/Rev 22:11) contains a highly strophic, structured pair of couplets,⁹⁴ likely influenced by Dan 12:10.⁹⁵ Two factors suggest that the angel continues to speak. First, John does not indicate a change in speaker from the previous material or change from first to third person. Second, it is an angel who speaks to Daniel in Dan 12:10.

---

92. Osborne, *Revelation*, 780; Vanni, "Liturgical Dialogue," 357. Smalley notes that it may still be the angel's voice but speaking in the first person on behalf of Jesus. See Smalley, *Revelation to John*, 567.

93. Again, Barr refers to this as the "Rhetor," while others refer to the voice as the "Lector." Barr, *Tales of the End*, 51. See also Vanni, "Liturgical Dialogue," 349.

94. Smalley, *Revelation to John*, 571.

95. Smalley, *Revelation to John*, 571.

John does signal the change in speaker in the subsequent line, however, shifting from third person to first person. As noted above, the repetition of these words from the mouth of Jesus likely indicate that Jesus is the speaker here as well. This is further confirmed by the subsequent parallel with the words of Jesus from the prologue in Rev 1:8 (ἐγὼ τὸ Ἄλφα καὶ τὸ Ὦ, I am the alpha and the omega) as well as additional parallels with Rev 1:17 (ὁ πρῶτος καὶ ὁ ἔσχατος, the first and the last). This is again followed (as above in Rev 22:6–7) with a blessing formula, spoken in the third person. Here, the subject of the blessing shifts from singular to plural (μακάριος to Μακάριοι) and also contains an attached ἵνα (in order that) clause, indicating result. Presumably, the speaker here is the same as the one who pronounced the blessing in Rev 22:7a.[96] The speech-act includes a seven-fold grouping of those unable to enter the city.[97]

John signals the subsequent change in speaker by both adjusting from third person to first person as well as naming the person directly. In Rev 22:16, Jesus speaks, but again, it is worth noting that the words of Jesus are not introduced with a *verbum dicendi* formula. John simply changes the speaker without narrative interruption. Again, voice intonation would be appropriate in guiding the audience through these changes in speaker.[98] The written text again betrays intentionality on the part of the composer to enable the audience to move from the taleworld back to the "real world." This is accomplished by the variation in pronoun use in Rev 22:16. Here, Jesus states that He sent His messenger-angel to a corporate entity μαρτυρῆσαι ὑμῖν ταῦτα ἐπὶ ταῖς ἐκκλησίαις (to testify to *y'all* these things for the churches). That the ὑμῖν in view in the passage refers to the collective members of the church itself, the seven churches in particular, or representatives who receive the message on behalf of the churches does not matter.[99]

What is significant here is the way in which the spoken material would move the hearer between storyrealm and taleworld, regardless of which particular audience was there for the occasion. The very Jesus who occupied such significance in the taleworld now breaks through the taleworld into the storyrealm in order to address the listening community

---

96. Vanni, "Liturgical Dialogue," 359.

97. Mounce, *Book of Revelation*, 394.

98. Vansina, *Oral Tradition as History*, 34–35. See also Rhoads, "Performance Criticism, Pt. II," 173–80; Shiner, "Oral Performance," 49–63.

99. See Aune for a summary of the different proposals in Aune, *Revelation*, 1125–1226. See also Beale, *Book of Revelation*, 1143–46; Fanning, *Revelation*, 562.

directly.[100] Barr notes that to hear the performer declare this publicly in front of the listening congregation "must surely have made a dramatic impression."[101] Vanni goes as far as to suggest that after addressing the audience directly, it would be customary for the listeners to react verbally.[102]

Reported speech is introduced in the next period (S7:16/Rev 22:17) by the narrator in the third person. The spirit (τὸ πνεῦμα)[103] and the bride (ἡ νύμφη) make their request in response to the words of Jesus. The bride is restaged from an earlier episode (Rev 19:7–9), likely indicating the church.[104] The church, however, must take an active role and John provides the invitation to join the chorus.[105] While this remains evident in the written text of the Apocalypse, the effect of this chorus on the audience would be particularly striking. The referent and extent of this this entreaty is debated.[106] Yet all acknowledge the antiphonal back-and-forth, with many recognizing that the hearer is expected to respond.[107]

What is consistently overlooked, however, is the way that this request moves between the taleworld to the storyrealm. If, as many suggest, the gathered community of the churches are addressed and expected to respond, they would now again become aware of their social setting as a listening community.[108] As Young suggests, this sort of technique is not required when reading silently from a written text,[109] yet it is crucial in

---

100. Vanni, "Liturgical Dialogue," 359.

101. Barr, "Apocalypse as Oral Enactment," 252.

102. Barr, "Apocalypse as Oral Enactment," 252.

103. The identification of the Spirit is most likely put in conjunction with Jesus' words intentionally, indicating the importance in the Spirit's role in the revelation of Jesus' words to the church. Aune, *Revelation*, 1227–28.

104. Beale, *Revelation of John*, 1148.

105. Vanni, "Liturgical Dialogue," 360; Aune, *Revelation*, 1228.

106. Aune, *Revelation*, 1228–29; Beale, *Revelation of John*, 1148–49.

107. Janse van Rensburg, "All the Apocalypse," 3–7; Smalley, *Revelation to John*, 582, 584–85. Barr suggests a eucharistic liturgical setting behind the social context of Revelation's delivery in the early church, noting similarities between the Apocalypse and the Didache. See Barr, "Apocalypse as Oral Enactment," 254. See also Shiner, "Oral Performance," 59–61.

108. Beale notes that the issues in identifying the speaker and the referent in each of the four imperatives in Rev 22:17 is solved if the Apocalypse was first given to a group of representatives sent on behalf of the seven churches who would then go back and report the message to the churches themselves. Beale, *Revelation of John*, 1149. See also Bauman, *Story, Performance, and Event*, 1–10.

109. Young, *Taleworlds and Storyrealms*, 14–17. See also Barr, "Apocalypse as Oral Enactment," 249.

oral storytelling. Thus, it is better to recognize this antiphonal call and response as further evidence of the performance setting of the Apocalypse. This back-and-forth creates a liturgical dialogue that John expects his audience to join, which is characteristic of oral performance.[110] This provides the audience with a new perspective on their "real world" social context, giving them a new lens through which to see their experiences.[111] The provision of a heavenly perspective on earthly events is a hallmark of apocalyptic literature in the ancient Jewish and early Christian world,[112] and John follows this tradition well.

John's invitation to join the chorus is followed by a warning (Rev 22:18b–19). This warning is addressed to the entire listening community: παντὶ τῷ ἀκούοντι τοὺς λόγους τῆς προφητείας· (all the ones hearing the words of this prophecy [Rev 22:18]).[113] This public warning echoes Rev 1:3 and was expected to be heeded, as John cautions his audience directly.[114] Again, it must be stated that, as the epilogue draws to a close, elements from the taleworld and "real world" are addressed side-by-side. The storyrealm is fully in view as the speaker addresses the listening audience purposefully and directly. The speaker in Rev 22:18 is introduced in the first person (Μαρτυρῶ ἐγώ, I testify), most likely indicating that it is a different speaker than the one who testifies in Rev 22:20, as the latter is introduced in the third person (ὁ μαρτυρῶν ταῦτα, the one testifying to this). Since the speaker in Rev 22:20 is almost certainly Jesus, given the repetition of the speech reported, most scholars take the speaker in verses 18–19 to be John himself. Aune disagrees and suggests that the speaker in both is Jesus and that the warning comes with added drama, due to this identification of Jesus as its deliverer.[115]

Next, Jesus' speech is explicitly reported. Perhaps due to the fluidity between realms and the possible confusion it may produce, John here introduces Jesus' words with a *verbum dicendi* formula (Λέγει ὁ μαρτυρῶν ταῦτα·, the one testifying to these things says [Rev 22:20]). Jesus' previous

---

110. Vanni, "Liturgical Dialogue," 360; Barr, *Tales of the End*, 310–24.

111. Barr, *Tales of the End*, 316–21. See also Collins, *Crisis and Catharsis*, 141–61.

112. Collins, *Apocalyptic Imagination*, 5–11, 37–42. See also Rowland, *Open Heaven*, 73–155.

113. Vanni, "Liturgical Dialogue," 360.

114. Mounce, *Book of Revelation*, 395.

115. For the present purposes, it does not matter if the speaker here is John or Jesus. Scholars differ, but the liturgical setting is most important for the present purposes. For an overview regarding the identity of the speaker, see Aune, *Revelation*, 1229–30.

words in the epilogue did not receive such an introduction, but here it may be necessary for clarity. The now familiar words on the lips of Jesus resound yet again (Ναί· ἔρχομαι ταχύ., Yes I am coming quickly [Rev 22:20]), providing divine approval for the warning that preceded them.[116] In what follows, the audience is invited to speak, again drawing attention to the storyrealm.[117] This antiphonal call and response may indicate a liturgical aspect to the end of the book.[118] John concludes the book with a typical epistolary conclusion,[119] which again echoes the prologue (1:4). Having taken the audience through the visionary experience recorded in the Apocalypse,[120] John now collapses the storyrealm and the narrative is over.[121]

Reported speech plays a central role in the epilogue as well as the prologue, and the previous analysis enables the analyst to see the general flow of the dialogue and the participants. Recognition of the spoken material as well as the one delivering it is crucial for both the performer as well as the audience, yet scholars regularly disagree as to the identity of the speaker in each case. It is at this critical point that the thesis of this book proves most helpful. While the written text of the epilogue may be fraught with difficulty, recognition of the speaking voice would be relatively effortless, as prosody was expected in performance.[122] These storytelling techniques enable the public reader to signal the speaker's source to the hearers, acting out the words of each character through intonation and gesture.[123] More on this subject is forthcoming, yet with all the previous analysis in mind, a reconstruction[124] of the epilogue is possible:

John: Καὶ εἶπέν μοι· (22:6a)

---

116. Vanni, "Liturgical Dialogue," 363. Again, the previous words may in fact also be meant to be understood as coming from Jesus.

117. Koester, *Revelation*, 857.

118. Barr, "Apocalypse as Oral Enactment," 252–56. See also Aune, *Revelation*, 1230. Vanni, "Liturgical Dialogue," 363; Smalley, *Revelation to John*, 584–85.

119. Beale, *Revelation of Jesus*, 1156; Fanning, *Revelation*, 565.

120. Koester, *Revelation*, 858.

121. Barr, "Apocalypse as Oral Enactment," 248–49.

122. Vansina, *Oral Tradition as History*, 34–35. See also Rhoads, "Performance Criticism, Pt. II," 173–80. Also see Shiner, "Oral Performance," 49–63.

123. Vansina, *Oral Tradition as History*, 34. See also Barr, "Apocalypse as Oral Enactment," 252–54; Rhoads, "Performance Criticism, Pt. II," 173–80; Shiner, "Oral Performance," 49–63.

124. Vanni, "Liturgical Dialogue," 361–63.

Angel: Οὗτοι οἱ λόγοι πιστοὶ καὶ ἀληθινοί, καὶ ὁ κύριος, ὁ θεὸς τῶν πνευμάτων τῶν προφητῶν, ἀπέστειλεν τὸν ἄγγελον αὐτοῦ δεῖξαι τοῖς δούλοις αὐτοῦ ἃ δεῖ γενέσθαι ἐν τάχει· (22:6b)

Jesus: καὶ ἰδοὺ ἔρχομαι ταχύ· (22:7a)

Angel (or rhetor)[125]: μακάριος ὁ τηρῶν τοὺς λόγους τῆς προφητείας τοῦ βιβλίου τούτου. (22:7b)

John: Κἀγὼ Ἰωάννης ὁ ἀκούων καὶ βλέπων ταῦτα. καὶ ὅτε ἤκουσα καὶ ἔβλεψα, ἔπεσα προσκυνῆσαι ἔμπροσθεν τῶν ποδῶν τοῦ ἀγγέλου τοῦ δεικνύοντός μοι ταῦτα. καὶ λέγει μοι· (22:8-9a)

Angel: Ὅρα μή· σύνδουλός σού εἰμι καὶ τῶν ἀδελφῶν σου τῶν προφητῶν καὶ τῶν τηρούντων τοὺς λόγους τοῦ βιβλίου τούτου· τῷ θεῷ προσκύνησον. (22:9b)

John: Καὶ λέγει μοι· (22:10)

Angel: Μὴ σφραγίσῃς τοὺς λόγους τῆς προφητείας τοῦ βιβλίου τούτου, ὁ καιρὸς γὰρ ἐγγύς ἐστιν. ὁ ἀδικῶν ἀδικησάτω ἔτι, καὶ ὁ ῥυπαρὸς ῥυπαρευθήτω ἔτι, καὶ ὁ δίκαιος δικαιοσύνην ποιησάτω ἔτι, καὶ ὁ ἅγιος ἁγιασθήτω ἔτι. (22:10b-11)

Jesus: Ἰδοὺ ἔρχομαι ταχύ, καὶ ὁ μισθός μου μετ' ἐμοῦ, ἀποδοῦναι ἑκάστῳ ὡς τὸ ἔργον ἐστὶν αὐτοῦ. ἐγὼ τὸ Ἄλφα καὶ τὸ Ὦ, ὁ πρῶτος καὶ ὁ ἔσχατος, ἡ ἀρχὴ καὶ τὸ τέλος. (22:12-13

Angel (or Rhetor): Μακάριοι οἱ πλύνοντες τὰς στολὰς αὐτῶν, ἵνα ἔσται ἡ ἐξουσία αὐτῶν ἐπὶ τὸ ξύλον τῆς ζωῆς καὶ τοῖς πυλῶσιν εἰσέλθωσιν εἰς τὴν πόλιν. ἔξω οἱ κύνες καὶ οἱ φάρμακοι καὶ οἱ πόρνοι καὶ οἱ φονεῖς καὶ οἱ εἰδωλολάτραι καὶ πᾶς φιλῶν καὶ ποιῶν ψεῦδος. (22:14-15)

Jesus: Ἐγὼ Ἰησοῦς ἔπεμψα τὸν ἄγγελόν μου μαρτυρῆσαι ὑμῖν ταῦτα ἐπὶ ταῖς ἐκκλησίαις. ἐγώ εἰμι ἡ ῥίζα καὶ τὸ γένος Δαυίδ, ὁ ἀστὴρ ὁ λαμπρός, ὁ πρωϊνός. (22:16)

John: καὶ τὸ πνεῦμα καὶ ἡ νύμφη λέγουσιν· (22:17a)

Spirit and the Bride: Ἔρχου· (22:17b)

John: καὶ ὁ ἀκούων εἰπάτω· (22:17c)

Audience: Ἔρχου· (22:17d)

---

125. The "rhetor" is the term often used when describing the voice that precedes the introduction of John in Rev 1:1-3. This person's voice is distinguished from John's in the prologue and delivers the first blessing formula in the book. See Barr, *Tales of the End*, 15-20.

John: καὶ ὁ διψῶν ἐρχέσθω, ὁ θέλων λαβέτω ὕδωρ ζωῆς δωρεάν.

Μαρτυρῶ ἐγὼ παντὶ τῷ ἀκούοντι τοὺς λόγους τῆς προφητείας τοῦ βιβλίου τούτου· ἐάν τις ἐπιθῇ ἐπ᾽ αὐτά, ἐπιθήσει ὁ θεὸς ἐπ᾽ αὐτὸν τὰς πληγὰς τὰς γεγραμμένας ἐν τῷ βιβλίῳ τούτῳ· καὶ ἐάν τις ἀφέλῃ ἀπὸ τῶν λόγων τοῦ βιβλίου τῆς προφητείας ταύτης, ἀφελεῖ ὁ θεὸς τὸ μέρος αὐτοῦ ἀπὸ τοῦ ξύλου τῆς ζωῆς καὶ ἐκ τῆς πόλεως τῆς ἁγίας, τῶν γεγραμμένων ἐν τῷ βιβλίῳ τούτῳ. Λέγει ὁ μαρτυρῶν ταῦτα· (22:17e–20a)

Jesus: Ναί· ἔρχομαι ταχύ. (22:20b)

Audience: Ἀμήν· ἔρχου, κύριε Ἰησοῦ. (22:20c)

John: Ἡ χάρις τοῦ κυρίου Ἰησοῦ μετὰ πάντων. (22:21)

Since one of the purposes in choosing the epilogue for analysis was its benefit in also exploring the prologue (Rev 1:1–8), a reconstruction of the prologue is also warranted here.

Rhetor: Ἀποκάλυψις Ἰησοῦ Χριστοῦ, ἣν ἔδωκεν αὐτῷ ὁ θεὸς δεῖξαι τοῖς δούλοις αὐτοῦ, ἃ δεῖ γενέσθαι ἐν τάχει, καὶ ἐσήμανεν ἀποστείλας διὰ τοῦ ἀγγέλου αὐτοῦ τῷ δούλῳ αὐτοῦ Ἰωάννῃ, ὃς ἐμαρτύρησεν τὸν λόγον τοῦ θεοῦ καὶ τὴν μαρτυρίαν Ἰησοῦ Χριστοῦ, ὅσα εἶδεν. μακάριος ὁ ἀναγινώσκων καὶ οἱ ἀκούοντες τοὺς λόγους τῆς προφητείας καὶ τηροῦντες τὰ ἐν αὐτῇ γεγραμμένα, ὁ γὰρ καιρὸς ἐγγύς. (1:1–3)

John: Ἰωάννης ταῖς ἑπτὰ ἐκκλησίαις ταῖς ἐν τῇ Ἀσίᾳ· χάρις ὑμῖν καὶ εἰρήνη ἀπὸ ὁ ὢν καὶ ὁ ἦν καὶ ὁ ἐρχόμενος, καὶ ἀπὸ τῶν ἑπτὰ πνευμάτων ἃ ἐνώπιον τοῦ θρόνου αὐτοῦ, καὶ ἀπὸ Ἰησοῦ Χριστοῦ, ὁ μάρτυς ὁ πιστός, ὁ πρωτότοκος τῶν νεκρῶν καὶ ὁ ἄρχων τῶν βασιλέων τῆς γῆς. (1:4–5a)

Audience: Τῷ ἀγαπῶντι ἡμᾶς καὶ λύσαντι ἡμᾶς ἐκ τῶν ἁμαρτιῶν ἡμῶν ἐν τῷ αἵματι αὐτοῦ—καὶ ἐποίησεν ἡμᾶς βασιλείαν, ἱερεῖς τῷ θεῷ καὶ πατρὶ αὐτοῦ—αὐτῷ ἡ δόξα καὶ τὸ κράτος εἰς τοὺς αἰῶνας τῶν αἰώνων· ἀμήν. (1:5b–6)[126]

---

126. It is here that the assumption that the book of Revelation was composed from and for oral performance is so valuable. The repetitive ναί, ἀμήν (yes, amen) likely calls for a response on the part of the audience. Twice in the prologue, this call and response is used. Additionally, Vanni notes the way Rev 1:4–5a switches from second-person plural pronouns (ὑμῖν) to a collection of first-person plural pronouns in a doxological formula spoken to Jesus (Τῷ ἀγαπῶντι ἡμᾶς, the one loving us). Vanni, "Liturgical Dialogue," 349–51. See also Aune, *Revelation*, 29–30.

John: Ἰδοὺ ἔρχεται μετὰ τῶν νεφελῶν, καὶ ὄψεται αὐτὸν πᾶς ὀφθαλμὸς καὶ οἵτινες αὐτὸν ἐξεκέντησαν, καὶ κόψονται ἐπ' αὐτὸν πᾶσαι αἱ φυλαὶ τῆς γῆς. (1:7a)

Audience: ναί, ἀμήν. (1:7b)

Jesus: Ἐγώ εἰμι τὸ Ἄλφα καὶ τὸ Ὦ, (1:8a)

John: λέγει κύριος, ὁ θεός, (1:8b)

Jesus: ὁ ὢν καὶ ὁ ἦν καὶ ὁ ἐρχόμενος, ὁ παντοκράτωρ. (1:8c)

Style Markers

The features of oral storytelling that were present in the previous two sections are further demonstrated in the epilogue. The cola continue to demonstrate an additive rather than a subordinate style,[127] even though the use of the connector καί does occur less frequently than previously noted. John's regular reliance on formula and epithet typical of aggregative prose occurs frequently in the final episode. The unusual title καὶ ὁ κύριος ὁ θεὸς τῶν πνευμάτων τῶν προφητῶν (and the Lord, the God of the spirits of the prophets [Rev 22:6]) likely derives from a shared piece of background material,[128] and the weight of this lengthy title reveals a style more in keeping with an oral culture than written one.[129]

Several examples of reported speech illustrate this formulaic style. The repeated phrase καὶ ἰδοὺ ἔρχομαι ταχύ (and look, I am coming quickly [Rev 22:7, 12, 20]) or similar phrases repeat again and again. The blessing formula is employed seven times in the book of Revelation, including twice in the epilogue alone (Rev 22:7b, 14). Some form of the following phrases are collocated in redundant fashion: τοὺς λόγους τῆς προφητείας τοῦ βιβλίου τούτου (the words of the prophecy in this scroll [Rev 22:10, 18, 19]), likely indicating a formulaic nature to this word-grouping.[130] Again, the title ascribed to Jesus may suggest a formula indicative of the

---

127. Here it is helpful to consult John Miles Foley, as he recognizes that the communicative system in which a word or story is told is most fundamental to recognizing the verbal art that is employed. See Foley, *Singer of Tales*, 7.

128. Beale, *Revelation of John*, 1124–25. Beale notes that this title is bracketed by references to Dan. 2.

129. Ong, *Orality and Literacy*, 39.

130. Almost certainly, this formula alludes to Dan 8:26; 12:4, 9; and 4 Ezra 12:37. Beale, *Revelation of John*, 1150–51.

aggregative nature of orality: ἐγὼ τὸ ἄλφα καὶ τὸ ὦ, ὁ πρῶτος καὶ ὁ ἔσχατος, ἡ ἀρχὴ καὶ τὸ τέλος (I am the alpha and the omega, the first and the last, the beginning and the end [Rev 1:8; 22:13]).[131] These examples also show the redundant and repetitive style mentioned above in the previously analyzed sections.[132]

The agonistic tone prevalent in oral cultures is also readily apparent here at the story's conclusion. The epilogue advances the context of conflict that marks the rest of the book, with several elements noting the simple contrast between those on the right side and those on the wrong side.[133] There is no middle ground in the book of Revelation.[134] The virtuous receive blessing (Rev 22:7, 14), reward (Rev 22:12), and are welcomed into the city (Rev 22:14, 17). The villains are cursed (Rev 22:18–19) and ousted (Rev 22:15). This is most striking with the sevenfold listing of those deemed unpermitted to enter the city. The first in the list names those outside the city as οἱ κύνες (the dogs). Dogs were despised in the ancient world as beasts whose only concern was their own physical appetite and well-being and who senselessly navigate life without reason.[135] The term was also used in Deut 23:17–18 in reference to cultic sexual abominations as well as at Qumran to refer to those who persist in uncleanness.[136] Regardless of the precise meaning, it is clear that the term is meant as an insult.[137] When paired with the others in the list, the agonistic tone is clearly apparent.

Finally, the participatory tone of the story is again on display. As stated previously, the story is told through John's eyes. John records his own interaction with the characters in the story. Participants speak to John directly and John replies in kind. What is even more striking, however, is that in this section the audience is also brought in, invited to participate themselves in the effusion of praise directed toward Jesus. In short, not only is John's style participatory for the narrator, but it is also participatory for the audience. This stylistic technique of direct audience address[138] and invitation to join in the story both highlights the way in

---

131. Koester, *Revelation*, 854.
132. Ong, *Orality and Literacy*, 39–40.
133. Ong, *Orality and Literacy*, 45.
134. Osborne, *Revelation*, 785–86.
135. Beale, *Revelation of John*, 1141–42.
136. Aune, *Revelation*, 1222–23.
137. Aune, *Revelation*, 1222–23.
138. For the importance of recognizing audience address among ancient oral

which the storyrealm unites the "real world"¹³⁹ to the taleworld. Here, though, it is worth noting that in the book of Revelation, John employs the technique of direct audience address regularly. These enable the storyteller to maintain a close relationship with the audience as the performance ensues.¹⁴⁰ The analysis of the previous sections did not require a careful articulation of this feature, yet it occurs throughout the book of Revelation,¹⁴¹ betraying the very participatory tone expected in oral storytelling.

Narrative Discourse Features

Verbal Aspect and Storyline

Given the fact that much of the material contained in the epilogue is presented in the form of reported speech, the way in which verbal aspect is employed must be adjusted here. As was noted in previous chapters, the storyline of the book of Revelation is established by the *background* use of the aorist, with *foregrounded* and *frontgrounded*¹⁴² material marked for prominence by the choice of a different verb from the default verb.¹⁴³ However, in this final episode, nonevents, in the form of reported speech, drive the storyline forward.¹⁴⁴ Some units of reported speech are clearly marked with formulaic *verbum dicendi* and others reported without introduction. In fact, the now familiar καὶ + aorist construction that previously anchored the storyline vanishes almost entirely, with the only instance of it as a marker for a discourse thought (Rev 22:6). The speech that is formally introduced occurs as follows:

---

cultures, see Iverson, *From Text to Performance*, 88–92. See also Boomershine, *First-Century Gospel Storytellers*, 276–96; Seal, "Reception and Delivery," 7–8.

139. Horsley, *Text and Tradition*, 22.

140. Iverson, *From Text to Performance*, 88.

141. This audience address would be particularly effective in oral performance and is pervasive in the book of Revelation. As will be noted in the concluding chapter of this book, more detailed analysis of the way in which John signals and utilizes audience address would be a helpful contribution to the scholarship of Revelation. Audience address is likely present in the following passages: Rev 1:3–5a, 9; 2:1—3:22; 13:9–10; 14:12; 18; 21:17b, 25. Possible audience address may also be evidenced in Rev 9:12; 11:14.

142. Mathewson, "Verbal Aspect in the Apocalypse," 65.

143. Runge, *Discourse Grammar*, 11.

144. Dooley, *Analyzing Discourse*, 79–85.

Καὶ εἶπέν μοι (22:6)

καὶ λέγει μοι (22:9)

Καὶ λέγει μοι (22:10)

καὶ τὸ πνεῦμα καὶ ἡ νύμφη λέγουσιν (22:17a)

καὶ ὁ ἀκούων εἰπάτω (22:17b)

Λέγει ὁ μαρτυρῶν ταῦτα (22:20)

The καί + aorist construction that marks the first example serves as a transition from the previous episode (Rev 21:9—22:9), following the style within. Each of the subsequent examples, however, are presented in the present tense with the exception of the imperative εἰπάτω (say!). Following Mathewson, this use of the present aspect would indicate that the material is to be foregrounded against the background material.[145] This proposal would necessitate that the background storyline persists. Yet, for the epilogue, the backgrounded material subsides altogether, as John only uses the καί + aorist construction once.

Mathewson's suggestion retains validity, however. It could be argued that the nonevent material presented in this concluding scene is brought to the front of the mental stage against the backdrop of the entire narrative previously presented. John's affirmation that Οὗτοι οἱ λόγοι πιστοὶ καὶ ἀληθινοί, which echoes the same statement in Rev 19:9 and 21:5, may in fact speak regarding the entirety of the book of Revelation.[146] This coupled with the repetition of material, from the prologue, the restaged participants, the direct audience address, and the content itself (warnings and exhortations), may indicate that the foregrounded material here is set against the entirety of the Apocalypse. Indeed, this would serve the function of an epilogue in an oral culture well, for epilogues serve to reorient the audience to the storyrealm in order to motivate and inspire action in the real world.[147] Thus, the use of the present verbal aspect moves the material in the epilogue to the fore, inviting the audience to consider the story depicted and then respond accordingly.[148] This technique, coupled

---

145. Mathewson, "Verbal Aspect in the Apocalypse," 65.

146. Osborne, *Revelation*, 780; Fanning, *Revelation*, 557.

147. Barr, *Tales of the End*, 316–24. See also Rhoads, "Performance Criticism, Pt. I," 128–29.

148. For the way in which technique was used in the oral biblical culture, see Boomershine, *First-Century Gospel Storytellers*, 299–339.

with the participatory tone noted above, would have been especially effective for an oral performance setting.

In analyzing the verb choice within the final pericope, the use of verbal aspect is perhaps overshadowed by the author's choice of verbal mood. Here, in only sixteen verses, John employs the imperative mood twelve times (Rev 6, 9, 11, 12, 17, 20). There is an additional obligatory subjunctive as well.[149] Within the Apocalypse, the subjunctive mood is almost entirely used to depict the potentiality of the action described.[150] Of the 86 uses of the subjunctive in the book of Revelation, the force of a command or obligation is implied in only exceptional cases (Rev 6:6; 7:3; 10:4; 11:2; 19:7; 22:10), with one here in the epilogue. Thus, the 114 uses of the imperative mood carry volitional force throughout the Apocalypse.[151] As seen in this table, the use of the imperative mood increases dramatically in this final section.

---

149. Wallace, *Greek Grammar*, 463.

150. Wallace, *Greek Grammar*, 461–63. For representative examples, see Rev 2:5, 10, 25; 3:3, 11, 18; 6:2, 11; 9:15; 10:7; 11:7; 12:4, 6; 13:15–16; 14:4; 15:8; 17:10; 18:4, 21–23; 19:15; 20:3; 21:23, 25, 27; 22:14, 18, 19.

151. Wallace, *Greek Grammar*, 485–89.

PERFORMANCE ANALYSIS OF THE EPILOGUE 213

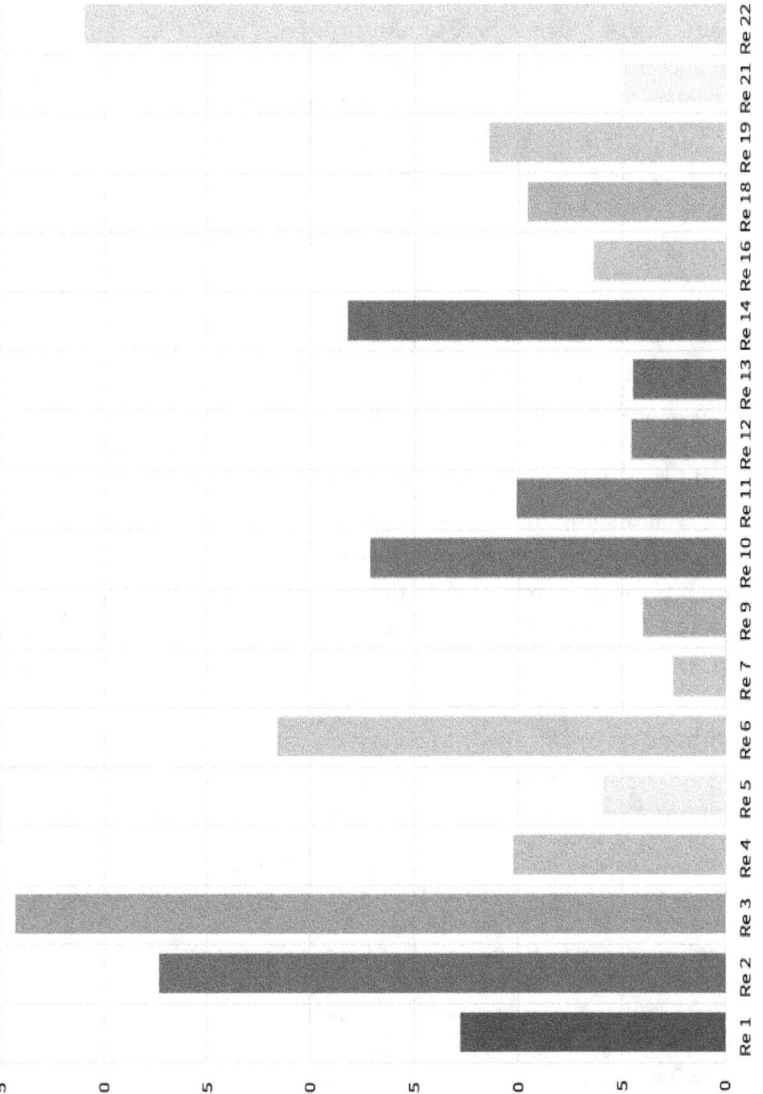

Use of the imperative mood per one thousand words in Revelation

This observation again corroborates the suggestion proposed above that the epilogue serves to reorient the audience to the storyrealm in order to go back into their "real world."[152] As John carefully guides his audience out of the taleworld, he does so with expectancy.[153] In other words, the story is not simply told for pleasure or entertainment, it also comes with a summons.[154] Thus, here at the end, John invites his audience to respond accordingly,[155] commanding them directly while acknowledging the storyrealm itself. Direct audience address returns the hearer to the social context of the performance,[156] and the prayer and response bring the event to a close.[157]

Participants and Rank

Since much of the content of the final episode involves speech, it must be stated that the spoken word is delivered by participants. Some are marked as more prominent than others.[158] John maintains his status as the most prominent participant in that the story is presented through his eyes. Indeed, John participates in every scene of the story, sometimes as a viewer and sometimes actively. The audience only hears what John presents to them. Thus, analysis of the participants in Revelation must acknowledge the primary place of the narrator in first-person storytelling.[159] John falls before the angel in an act of worship, only to be rebuked. He addresses the audience directly on separate occasions (Rev 22:18, 21). Other participants, however, also take the stage.

Without repeating the material in the above section labeled "Reported Speech," it is worth noting here that one of the angels from the episode presented in Rev 17 is restaged here in the final scene. This angel,

---

152. What is particularly striking is the way in which Rev 2–3 both directly addresses the audience in their "real world" setting while, at the same time, involves elements from the taleworld, introduced with the theophany scene in Rev 1:10–20. It is as if the narrative is suspended between the "real world" and taleworld as Jesus speaks directly to his churches.

153. Barr, *Tales of the End*, 321; Koester, *Revelation*, 848.

154. Fanning, *Revelation*, 558. See also Rhoads, "Performance Criticism, Pt. I," 130; Barr, *Tales of the End*, 3.

155. Mounce, *Book of Revelation*, 390.

156. Young, *Taleworlds and Storyrealms*, 17–22; Barr, *Tales of the End*, 320.

157. Aune, *Revelation*, 1241.

158. Runge, *Discourse Grammar*, 13–16.

159. Genette, *Narrative Discourse*, 10. See also Barr, *Tales of the End*, 15–20.

and the content that it shares, serves to transition the Apocalypse to its conclusion. The angel's speech is introduced by a *verbum dicendi* formula three times (Rev 22:6, 9, 10). Other material may also be attributed to the angel, as there are no grammatical indicators that the beatitude spoken in Rev 22:7b or the structured couplets in Rev 22:11 are spoken by a new participant. Thus, that the angel serves such an important role in communication, both here in the epilogue and also in the prologue (Rev 1:1),[160] the angel's prominence is clearly demonstrable.

Jesus also speaks several times in the epilogue, ranking him with more prominence than other participants in the story. Jesus speaks twice without an introductory *verbum dicendi* (Rev 22:12, 16), and once with an introductory formula (Rev 22:20). This follows a similar pattern as the prologue, which also depicts the words of Jesus without a *verbum dicendi* formula (Rev 1:8). Not only is Jesus restaged at the beginning and end of the Apocalypse, but his very words are restated, highlighting the importance of the participant. No other participants appear except the spirit and the restaged bride (first introduced in the previous episode) in Rev 22:17. These join the chorus, but their appearance and reported speech is brief.

BIBLICAL PERFORMANCE CRITICISM OF REV 22:6–21

Mnemonic Devices

There are several repeated phrases indicating that these may have been regularly used, again making recall easier for one wishing to read the text from memory. This sort of repetition served the speaker and, as noted above, produced an aggregative style that is typical in oral cultures. The refrain Ἰδοὺ ἔρχομαι ταχύ (behold I am coming soon) occurs twice within the epilogue (Rev 22:7, 12), and once more without Ἰδοὺ (Rev 22:20). Similar constructions of this same formula also appear in Rev 2:16 and 3:11. Additionally, in Rev 22:13, Jesus again speaks in the first person, identifying his power and presence (ἐγὼ τὸ ἄλφα καὶ τὸ ὦ, ὁ πρῶτος καὶ ὁ ἔσχατος, ἡ ἀρχὴ καὶ τὸ τέλος, I am the alpha and the omega, the first and the last, the beginning and the end).[161] This three-fold grouping of oppos-

---

160. It is quite possible that the angel in the prologue thus serves as one of the seven who deliver the bowls of judgment on the earth in Rev 17, as well as John's tour guide of the heavenly city in Rev 21–22.

161. Beale, *Revelation of John*, 1138.

ing pairs combines elements previously recorded in the Apocalypse but now placed together.¹⁶² The first bipolar pair was introduced on the lips of Jesus in Rev 1:8 and 21:6. The second appears in Rev 1:17 and 2:8, with the third also occurring in Rev 21:6 collocated with τὸ ἄλφα καὶ τὸ ὦ.¹⁶³ While the meaning of such titles receives due attention, it is the nature of their use in Revelation that demonstrates the oral performance setting explored in this study. The three-fold grouping was a memorized formula that was able to be utilized in the oral performance, easily recalled as a triple set of bipolar pairs.

Prosody Features in Rev 22:6–21

The most significant contribution of the application of the assumptions and methodology utilized in this inquiry surfaces here in this final section of analysis. Since much of the material in the epilogue contains reported speech, and since this material is not always clearly introduced with a *verbum dicendi* formula, identifying each speaker is fraught with difficulty. To put it crassly: who is saying what and to whom in this section? While this sort of issue remains for those reading the book of Revelation silently from the printed page, this difficulty dissolves in public performance.¹⁶⁴

Scholars working with primarily oral cultures suggest that it would be most typical for a skilled performer to act out the narrative.¹⁶⁵ Vansina's work among oral cultures is particularly helpful, as he states,

> A performer sits, often in the evening, surrounded by listeners and spins a tale. It is never just a recitation. The voice is raised or lowered, used as a means of dramatization. Nor does the storyteller just sit there. The tale is acted out with bodily gestures, even when the storyteller is sitting. Sometimes he or she may stand up, move around, and mime parts of the action narrated.¹⁶⁶

---

162. Bauckham suggests that John is deliberate with the identity of the speaker of each of the instances of this formula in the book of Revelation, with two being spoken by God and two by Jesus. Thus, he sees this formula as significant for John's Christology. Bauckham, *Climax of Prophecy*, 33–34.

163. Osborne, *Revelation*, 788–89.

164. Rhoads, "Performance Criticism, Pt. I," 128.

165. Vansina, *Oral Tradition as History*, 34. See also Barr, "Apocalypse as Oral Enactment," 252–54; Rhoads, "Performance Criticism, Pt. II," 173–80; Shiner, "Oral Performance," 49–63.

166. Vansina, *Oral Tradition as History*, 34.

While it is impossible to precisely reconstruct the way in which these ancient performers would embody their stories, whether inside or outside the community of the church, it is the contention of this investigation that the epilogue's nuances and difficulties are overstated and would be easily sidestepped if the text was performed out loud.[167] Put simply, the speaker's prosody would enable the audience to recognize the speaker without trouble. Each participant in the narrative would likely receive a different inflection and tone,[168] signaling to the audience at every turn. Here, then, to approach the book of Revelation as a text composed for oral performance[169] sheds valuable light on the complexity of the ending of the book. The many scholars who acknowledge that the book was likely read aloud to the gathered community would do well to apply this principle to their subsequent analysis of the book.

Additionally, the audience was no mere active spectator simply seeking entertainment. Audience members were expected to participate themselves.[170] Vansina continues, "The public is not just watching. The public is active. It interacts with the teller, and the teller provokes this interaction by asking questions, welcoming exclamations, and turning to a song sung by all at the appropriate points in the action."[171] In short, the speaker invites his audience to experience the story, and this experience involves the audience directly. With this in mind, the scholars suggesting a liturgical antiphonal setting for the epilogue may be proved correct.[172] Perhaps the switch to third-person imperatives in Rev 22:17 serves to trigger the audience to join in the act.[173]

---

167. For a rebuttal, see Parker, "Books and Reading Latin," 187–88; Hurtado, "Oral Fixation," 321–40. For a response to Hurtado, see Iverson, "Oral Fixation," 183–200.

168. Shiner, "Oral Performance," 54–57; Rhoads, "Performance Criticism, Pt. II," 173–80.

169. Which nearly every scholar acknowledges in principle. Again, see Horsley, *Text and Tradition*, 223.

170. Shiner, "Oral Performance," 59–61; Rhoads, "Performance Criticism, Pt. I,"

171. Vansina, *Oral Tradition as History*, 34.

172. Vanni, "Liturgical Dialogue," 348–72; Barr, "Apocalypse as Oral Enactment," 243–56; Aune, *Revelation*, 1206–8.

173. Again, this is where Barr's contention that the Didache serves as a helpful comparison is useful. Barr, "Apocalypse as Oral Enactment," 252–54.

SUMMARY FOR THE ANALYSIS OF REV 22:6–21

The epilogue of Revelation, with all of its difficulty and complexity, transitions the audience from the taleworld through the storyrealm in order to reorient the hearer's perspective on their "real world." This transition is accomplished through the concluding remarks of the angelic tour guide, immediately followed by the repeated refrain from Jesus himself (καὶ ἰδοὺ ἔρχομαι ταχύ, look I am coming quickly [Rev 22:7b]) and the subsequent seventh beatitude in the book. This flurry of spoken material returns the audience to the beginning of the performance, echoing many of the themes and concepts from the prologue. The Apocalypse, in effect, comes full circle. By the end, however, the listeners are invited to join in the chorus, affirming their allegiance to Jesus by declaring together Ἀμήν, ἔρχου κύριε Ἰησοῦ (Amen, come Lord Jesus! [Rev 22:20]).

The elements within the final episode have consistently puzzled commentators, with many noting its difficulties. These difficulties, however, fall by the wayside with right recognition of the situational oral performance context of John's Apocalypse. While the episode certainly contains features of discontinuity with the previous sections under investigation, many of the features that validate the central thesis of the present investigation maintain continuity with the material previously analyzed. Again, John's sound quality and style, repeated formula, and use of spoken material suggest that the book of Revelation was composed from performance and for performance. In fact, it is this stubborn recognition of the performance context of the Apocalypse that provides crucial insight into the way in which the epilogue is structured and arranged. The performer's vocal variation and bodily gestures would rightly guide the hearers through the final episode, as well as invite them to participate themselves.

6

Summary and Conclusion

INTRODUCTION

THE PURPOSE OF THIS book has been to analyze the text of selected representative episodes from the book of Revelation in order to propose and establish that John's Apocalypse was composed from oral performance and for oral performance.[1] Scholars frequently note that the book of Revelation was most likely originally delivered out loud before a listening audience.[2] However, most simply acknowledge this likelihood and move on, barely mentioning the premise again except in passing. No implications on the actual text are noted, no methodology for exploring performance features is suggested, and development of the idea remains noticeably limited.[3] This investigation has sought to explore this premise thoroughly, with the aim of "filling in the gap" on scholarship on John's literary masterpiece.

In the first chapter, an eclectic methodology was proposed, combining tools from various fields designed not only to validate the thesis of this study but also to aid further research on the book of Revelation. This working "toolbox" included investigating the science of the sound and syllables used in each section as well as stylistic choices designed with the listening ear in mind. Additionally, discourse analysis features were

---

1. See Horsley, *Text and Tradition*, 233.
2. Bauckham, *Climax of Prophecy*, 1–2, 7. See the literature review in chapter 2.
3. For an exception, see de Waal, *Aural-Performance Analysis*.

explored, noting in particular the way that ancient compositions were structured for oral storytelling. Mnemonic devices and other elements aiding in memory and recall were also revealed, as well as a detailed recording of the various characteristics present within the book that are typical in oral cultures. Chapter 2 interacted with relevant literature regarding literacy in the ancient Roman world as well as the way in which literature was experienced in a mostly illiterate culture. In addition, chapter 2 noted how various scholars approach the book of Revelation, with many recognizing that the book was intended to be heard out loud. However, as stated above, most do this in passing, with only a few scholars approaching the text of the Apocalypse with a methodology for exploring its oral characteristics.

The methodology proposed in chapter 1 was then applied to three sections of the book, chosen intentionally in order to certify that the methodology was not only profitable for specific passages but the book as a whole. These episodes included a theophany scene that many scholars note as the centralizing vision of the whole book.[4] Next, one of the four numbered sequences received due attention. Since this episode mirrors several others in the book, it was chosen as a representative in order to lay out a pathway for subsequent research on the other numbered sequences. Finally, the epilogue of the book was analyzed. This smaller unit was chosen strategically, for it enabled comparison with the prologue as well as the way in which John carefully moves his audience in and out of the taleworld and storyrealm. Since this is such a regular feature of the book of Revelation, and since the epilogue is so hotly debated among scholars,[5] it warranted thorough examination.

SUMMARY OF FINDINGS

Given the methodology proposed in the first chapter and its subsequent application to three episodes within the book, what has been said and what has been found? In chapter 3, the theophany scene evidenced many of the features common in orality. At the level of sound and syllable, Rev 4–5 were mapped with the many redundant sounds, words, and phrases marked

---

4. Gorman, *Reading Revelation Responsibly*, 102–15. See also Bauckham, *Theology of the Book*, 54–65.

5. The debate largely concerns the extent of the epilogue, with scholars offering differing opinions as to where the epilogue begins. For a thorough overview, see Aune, *Revelation*, 1141–50, 1200–1205. See also Pattemore, "Revelation," 721–26.

for further analysis. The cola and periods were identified, grouped, and investigated, noting the style and structuring features therein. Structural markers were identified, particularly the introductory formula that began the episode, enabling the audience to organize the material during the aural-listening experience.[6] Reported speech and style markers were also listed, with the characteristics of a text composed for performance given thorough attention. Following the methodology proposed by Walter Ong and Albert Lord, these characteristics include additive and aggregative prose, redundancy and repetition, an agonistic and participatory tone, and auditory features, as well as a lack of sequential parallelism.[7] These characteristics are prominent in Rev 4–5 and were noted accordingly.

Additionally, the methodology proposed a way to identify the backgrounded storyline of the narrative, as well as the participants and events marked for prominence in the narrative. With this in mind, chapter 3 proposed the way in which certain events were moved to the front of the audience's mental stage, which would be particularly relevant in oral storytelling.[8] Next biblical performance elements were marked, such as mnemonic devices as well as the episodic nature of the Apocalypse. Finally, elements that trigger prosody for ancient performers were noted, with a carefully constructed recreation of the performance event in mind.[9]

This same methodology was utilized in examining Rev 6:1—8:1 in chapter 4 above. Again, a sound map was developed, grouping literary units into cola and then periods, with these analyzed for stylistic and structural patterns. Chapter 4 may be particularly relevant for future study on the book of Revelation for two reasons: First, it examined one of the four numbered sequences in the book. Such structuring devices were common among oral cultures,[10] and thus, they were explored thoroughly here with the introductory and repetitive formula identified and considered for oral storytelling. Second, following Mathewson's proposal, the way in which verbal aspect and the variation in the repetition of the καὶ + aorist formula affects the pace of the narrative proved especially insightful.[11] To put it simply, by adjusting verbal aspect and style, John

6. Ong, *Orality and Literacy*, i.

7. Ong, *Orality and Literacy*, 34–56; Lord, "Characteristics of Orality," 54–72.

8. Vansina, *Oral Tradition as History*, 34–41.

9. Rhoads, "Performance Criticism, Pt. II," 173–80. Also see Shiner, "Oral Performance," 49–63.

10. Ong, *Orality and Literacy*, 139–46; Bauckham, *Climax of Prophecy*, 3–15.

11. Mathewson, "Verbal Aspect in the Apocalypse," 65. See also Pattemore, "Revelation," 737.

is able to shift the pace of this episode (Rev 6:1—8:1) dramatically.[12] This alteration in pace and style must be recognized as intentional,[13] and chapter 4 sought not only to recognize this feature but also the way in which it would have been utilized in oral performance. The analysis in this section of chapter 4 may guide future researchers to do the same in other episodes of the book. Lastly, the characteristics of the style of orality were noted, as well as the mnemonic devices[14] and features of prosody in performance.

Chapter 5 investigated a smaller pericope, but one with no less significance than the previous two, as the epilogue contains some of the most debated material in the Apocalypse. Much of this debate concerns the way in which the material is structured, leading to confusion as to the identification of the voice of the speaker throughout. Since much of this final section contains reported speech-acts, it was also necessary to analyze this unit for the way in which the spoken word was employed in oral cultures. Much of the same methodology was again applied here, but one additional feature was introduced: the interaction in oral cultures between "real world" and taleworld.[15] Following Young and Goffman (among others), these features were marked. Chapter 5 proposed that, while much of the material in the epilogue remains confounded for those reading the text silently from the printed page,[16] the confusion largely dissipates if one approaches the text with oral performance in mind. Prosody and variation in tone of voice would render such complications impotent, as well as move the listening community back and forth through the storyrealm.[17]

Each chapter of this book sought to provide evidence in order to validate a proposal: that the Apocalypse was composed to be read out loud and experienced aurally. Again, with this proposal most scholars of Revelation already agree. The aim of this book, however, was to do more than simply assume such a proposal, but rather to suggest a working methodology to certify that this proposal is not only valid but overlooked in most analysis of

12. Mathewson, *Verbal Aspect*, 120–81.

13. Runge, *Discourse Grammar*, 5. See also the helpful introduction to a manual of sorts for discourse analysis of the New Testament: Scacewater, *Discourse Analysis*, 1–30.

14. Barr, "Apocalypse as Oral Enactment," 249–56.

15. Young, *Taleworlds and Storyrealms*, 14–20.

16. Young, *Taleworlds and Storyrealms*, 14.

17. Vansina, *Oral Tradition as History*, 34–36. See also Shiner, "Oral Performance," 49–63.

the book of Revelation. If the thesis of this book can be validated, then this must be appreciated and recognized when studying the book of Revelation. Put simply, if scholars analyze the Apocalypse with an overemphasis on the written text, they may start their examination with wrong assumptions and wrong methodology. It is the rigorous commitment to analyzing the book of Revelation as a text composed from performance and for performance that is lacking among Revelation scholarship. This lack is ironic, indeed, as most scholars acknowledge the out-loud oral performance as the most likely situational context for the original hearers.

This book proposed a working methodology (chapter 1) for the task, invited relevant literature related to the investigation (chapter 2), and applied this methodology to representative sections (chapters 3 through 5). While it is impossible to be certain about the intentions of an ancient author, this book sought evidence that would indicate it is more probable that the text of Revelation was composed for oral performance. Additionally, exploring the book of Revelation accordingly provides important interpretive insight. What, then, are the findings?

Each of the sections explored in this investigation revealed several characteristics consistent with an oral culture. From the smallest level of sound and syllable repetition to the largest level of macro-structuring devices and narrative style, the evidence points again and again to these characteristics of orality. Triggers for prosody and alteration in sound occur frequently—again, common in oral performance. With the evidence amassed in chapters 3 through 5 collected, the thesis of this book may be demonstrated: the book of Revelation was most likely composed with the intention of being heard aurally in public performance.

EXEGETICAL VALUE

What is more, acceptance and recognition of the thesis of this book provides valuable interpretive insight. For example, when reading from the written text, the use of sound and syllable go largely ignored. However, sound, syllable, and breath-units were the foundational pieces of the audience's experience of the text.[18] These cola may follow modern versification encoded in printed Bibles, but they may not. The methodology proposed in this study, following that of Margaret Dean and Margaret Lee and Bernard Scott, offers a valuable starting point in studying the book of Revelation. Working from the cola outward, scholars may analyze

18. Lee and Scott, *Sound Mapping*, 168.

the way in which cola combine to form periods, enclosing a discourse thought. The techniques that signal the opening and closing of the various periods within a discourse offer insight into the structure of the text.

While certainly there are limitations in crafting sound maps of sections of Revelation, these sound maps may also provide interpretive value. The way that sound and syllables, harmony and dissonance work together offers yet another exegetical tool for students. Alliteration, repetition, cacophonous sounds, euphonic sounds, balance, and elongation all provide insight into choices made by an author. This is not simply a matter of style, but the reasons why an author employs certain stylistic elements in certain places requires interpretive evaluation.[19]

The ongoing conversation regarding verb use in ancient Greek remains animated, and this book did not seek to adjudicate the matter. However, Mathewson's proposal may provide functional insight into the way prominence was semantically marked in the choice of verb tense. While Mathewson's suggestion is not agreed upon universally, in application within the present investigation, his contribution certainly proved helpful. Since this study began with an acknowledged emphasis on analyzing the text of Revelation for its features of orality, the exegetical benefit rendered from following Mathewson's lead may serve subsequent scholars as well. This pertains not only to the verbs themselves but also the way in which they produce the pace and rhythm of the narrative as a whole, as well as indicate prominent events within the story.

Stylistic elements characteristic of orality must also be appreciated, providing data for analysis of the way they are used in the Apocalypse, but also as points of comparison with other ancient texts, especially among Jewish and Christian apocalyptic literature. The methodology proposed here aims to provide the framework for investigating such data. As noted in the analysis of the epilogue, some structural confusion may be lessened if scholars recognize the way in which prosody would affect the audience's ability to follow the story. Indeed, as noted by Walter Ong, "thought and expression in oral cultures is often highly organized but calls for an organization of a sort unfamiliar to and often uncongenial to the literate mind."[20] The scholars suggesting various and sometimes exotic proposals regarding the structure of the book of Revelation would do well to remember that episodic storytelling is a hallmark of orality.

19. Levinsohn, *Discourse Features*, viii.
20. Ong, *Orality and Literacy*, i.

These scholars may benefit from beginning their examination with this oral culture in mind before proceeding forward.

Finally, and perhaps too obvious to articulate, it is the thesis of this book that the book of Revelation was composed to be read out loud. This aural performance may have involved dramatic pause, facial expression, change of voice, and bodily gestures. As such, it is important for modern exegetes, from the academy to the pulpit, to read the text of Revelation out loud. The story is vivid, the characters are larger-than-life, and the scenes are wonderfully told. Too often, modern students of the Bible never hear the stories told out loud. Even in translation, the public telling of John's Apocalypse to a listening audience would be a valuable exegetical tool. Revelation scholars, therefore, must reposition themselves in order rehear the text as a text composed for oral performance.[21]

RECOMMENDATIONS FOR FURTHER RESEARCH

The methodology was robust and eclectic, borrowing tools and techniques from many fields, with the aim of revealing important evidence to validate the thesis of this study. This robust exploration, however, left several stones still unturned and provided a variety of pathways for future research. First, it is impossible to reconstruct the oral performance event as it happened nearly two thousand years ago. There were no tape-recorders or video cameras present when John's story was read. The printed text is all that remains of this past oral event. While agreement on the correct pronunciation of Koine Greek is not universally accepted, significant strides have been made in order to rightly reproduce this ancient oral event.[22] Therefore, while exact precision may be impossible, general accuracy as to the way in which the book of Revelation was heard centuries ago is possible. This recreation of the sounds and syllables of the text, noting the choices made between harmony and dissonance of the entirety of the Apocalypse, would make an excellent future study. Additionally, careful attention to the rhythm created by the metrical foot of each period would enhance the quality of any sound map.[23]

---

21. de Waal, *Aural-Performance Analysis*, 132.

22. See Caragounis, *Development of Greek*, 339–565; Kantor, *Short Guide to Pronunciation*, 1–112. For a summary, see Campbell, *Advances*, 192–208.

23. Caragounis, *Development of Greek*, 409–10.

Secondly, the characteristics typical of orality, put forward by Ong and Lord,[24] featured prominently in the passages analyzed in this paper, but continued application for scholarship of Revelation and other New Testament texts may prove valuable. This would be of particular relevance in looking at other Jewish apocalyptic texts. Do they contain the same characteristics or not? If so, how should that be interpreted by scholars within the field of apocalyptic literature?

Third, complex linear progression was uncommon in oral cultures;[25] stories were often told in an episodic fashion. With this in mind, analyzing the book of Revelation as such may provide crucial insight regarding the complex theories of the book's macro-structure (more below). As noted in the "Exegetical Benefits" above, it is crucial for those analyzing Revelation's macro-structure to begin with an oral cultural context in mind. Subsequent scholarship may reexamine the text's macro-structure with this episodic feature in mind, noting redundancy between episodes as well as the way in which they advance one to the next.

IMPLICATIONS ON SCHOLARSHIP

The first implication of this book is rather obvious: the text must be reheard. Any student or church community wanting to interpret and understand the book of Revelation should start by hearing it out loud. While doing so in translation would certainly obscure the style of the sound, this simple practice would at least enable the modern scholar to recreate the situational context of the original audience. Second, perhaps modern researchers would be better served analyzing the text not by chapter and verse but by cola and periods. Again, cola enclose literary thought-units around a typical speaker's breath-length.[26] Thus, in studying texts composed for performance, it is advisable to organize the text into a working sound map as done above.

Third, as previously stated, given that oral cultures organize stories in an episodic manner, the complex and intricate proposals concerning the structuring of the book of Revelation may be unnecessary. Indeed, these proposals betray a failure on the part of the modern scholar to

---

24. Ong, *Orality and Literacy*, 34–57; Lord, "Characteristics of Orality," 54–72.
25. Ong, *Orality and Literacy*, 147.
26. Lee, *Sound Mapping*, 9–10.

appreciate the way in which oral cultures structure thought and expression.²⁷ If Revelation is arranged as episodes, this creates a potentially significant implication: perhaps Revelation contains repetitive episodes that were able to be told on a variety of occasions that were later compiled together as the text in its present form.

Many scholars note the cyclical nature of the book, with features occurring again and again. The Apocalypse contains several events that would make for a fitting conclusion, yet frequently the story starts again.²⁸ Thus, it may be that John's narrative contains a collection of redundant episodes,²⁹ told and retold among communities of Jesus-followers, and later brought together as a single literary work.³⁰ Many scholars posit various ways in which the text was likely compiled and edited together,³¹ and the recognition of this characteristic of orality may provide useful insight.

Finally, and on a personal note, the prologue of John's Apocalypse contains a blessing formula: μακάριος ὁ ἀναγινώσκων καὶ οἱ ἀκούοντες τοὺς λόγους τῆς προφητείας καὶ τηροῦντες τὰ ἐν αὐτῇ γεγραμμένα, ὁ γὰρ καιρὸς ἐγγύς (Blessed is the one reading aloud the words of this prophecy and the ones keeping what is written in them, for the time is near [Rev 1:3]). The book of Revelation is noisy,³² a constant barrage of spoken words, shouts, trumpet blasts, admonitions, blessing, cursing, rumblings, thunderclaps, etc. Yet, it is the songs of praise that must be heard again here at last. Effusive praise, typical of the agonistic and participatory tone common in orality,³³ was meant to invite the audience into the story.³⁴ Here, the implication is clear:

> Τῷ καθημένῳ ἐπὶ τῷ θρόνῳ καὶ τῷ ἀρνίῳ
> ἡ εὐλογία καὶ ἡ τιμὴ καὶ ἡ δόξα καὶ τὸ κράτος
> εἰς τοὺς αἰῶνας τῶν αἰώνων. (Rev 5:13)

27. Ong, *Orality and Literacy*, i.
28. Barr, *Tales of the End*, 257.
29. Barr, *Tales of the End*, 20–25. See also Beale, *Book of Revelation*, 108–16. For an overview of the various proposals regarding the structure of the book of Revelation, see Bandy, "Layers of the Apocalypse," 469–99.
30. Indeed, Barr suggests as such. See Barr, *Tales of the End*, 33–34.
31. Charles, *Revelation of St. John*, l–lxi; Aune, *Revelation*, cv–cxxxv.
32. Resseguie, *Revelation of John*, 21.
33. Lord, *Singer of Tales*, 33.
34. Vansina, *Oral Tradition as History*, 34; Rhoads, "Performance Criticism, Pt. I," 130; Barr, *Tales of the End*, 3; Shiner, "Oral Performance," 49–63; Gorman, *Reading Revelation Responsibly*, 103.

Bibliography

Abbott, E. A. *Johannine Grammar*. London: A. & C. Black, 1906.
Achtemeier, Paul J. "*Omne Verbum Sonat*: The New Testament and the Oral Environment of Late Western Antiquity." *Journal of Biblical Literature* 109 (1990) 3–27.
Aland, Kurt, et al, eds. *Novum Testamentum Graece*. 28th ed. Stuttgart, DE: Deutsche Bibelgesellschaft, 2012.
Allen, W. Sidney. *Vox Graeca: The Pronunciation of Classical Greek*. Cambridge: Cambridge University Press, 1968.
Aristotle. *Art of Rhetoric*. Translated by J. H. Freese. Cambridge: Harvard University Press, 2020.
Arndt, W., et al. *A Greek-English Lexicon of the New Testament and Other Early Christian Literature*. Chicago: University of Chicago Press, 2000.
Aune, David E. *Revelation*. Word Biblical Commentary 52A–52C. Grand Rapids: Zondervan Academic, 1997.
Bailey, Kenneth E. "Informal Controlled Oral Tradition and the Synoptic Gospels." *Themelios* 20 (1995) 4–11.
Bandy, Alan S. "The Layers of the Apocalypse: An Integrative Approach to Revelation's Macrostructure." *Journal for the Study of the New Testament* 31.4 (2009) 469–99.
Barnett, Paul. *Jesus and the Rise of Early Christianity: A History of New Testament Times*. Downers Grove, IL: IVP Academic, 1999.
Barr, David L. "The Apocalypse as a Symbolic Transformation of the World: A Literary Analysis." *Interpretation* 38 (1984) 39–50.
———. "The Apocalypse of John as Oral Enactment." *Interpretation* 40.3 (1986) 243–56. *Tales of the End*. Salem, OR: Polebridge, 2012.
———. *Tales of the End*. Salem, OR: Polebridge, 2012.
Barr, James. *The Semantics of Biblical Language*. Eugene, OR: Wipf & Stock, 1961.
Bauckham, Richard. *The Climax of Prophecy*. New York: T&T Clark, 1993.
———. *Jesus and the Eyewitnesses*. Grand Rapids: Eerdmans, 2017.
———. *Jesus and the God of Israel: God Crucified and Other Studies on the New Testament's Christology of Divine Identity*. Grand Rapids: Eerdmans, 2008.
———. *The Theology of the Book of Revelation*. Cambridge: Cambridge University Press, 1993.
———. *Verbal Art as Performance*. Long Grove, IL: Waveland, 1977.

Bauman, Richard. *Story, Performance, and Event*. Cambridge: Cambridge University Press, 1986.
Beale, G. K. *The Book of Revelation: A Commentary on the Greek Text*. Grand Rapids: Eerdmans, 1999.
———. *Handbook on the New Testament Use of the Old Testament: Exegesis and Interpretation*. Grand Rapids: Baker Academic, 2012.
———. *Revelation: A Shorter Commentary*. Grand Rapids: Eerdmans, 2015.
Bergel, Łukasz. "God's Victory and Salvation: A Soteriological Approach to the Subject in Apocalyptic Literature." *HTS Theological Studies* 75.3 (2019) 1–6.
Blackwell, Ben C., et al. *Reading Revelation in Context*. Grand Rapids: Zondervan, 2019.
Boomershine, Thomas E. *First-Century Gospel Storytellers and Audiences: The Gospels as Performance Literature, Biblical Performance Criticism*. Eugene, OR: Cascade, 2022.
Botha, Pieter J. J. *Orality and Literacy in Early Christianity*. Biblical Performance Criticism. Eugene, OR: Cascade, 2012.
Boxall, Ian. *The Revelation of Saint John*. London: Continuum, 2006.
Bratcher, Robert G., and Howard A. Hatton. *A Handbook on the Revelation to John*. New York: United Bible Societies, 1993.
Brewer, Raymond R. "The Influence of Greek Drama on the Apocalypse of John." *Anglican Theological Review* 18 (1936) 74–92.
Brueggemann, Walter. *The Prophetic Imagination*. Minneapolis: Fortress, 2001.
Burton, Henry Fairfield. "The Worship of the Roman Emperors." *The Biblical World* 40 (1912) 80–91.
Cabaniss, Allen. *Pattern in Early Christian Worship*. Macon, GA: Mercery University Press, 1989.
Campbell, Constantine R. *Advances in the Study of Greek*. Grand Rapids: Zondervan, 2015.
———. *Basics of Verbal Aspect in Biblical Greek*. Grand Rapids: HarperCollins, 2008.
Campbell, David, and G. K. Beale. *Revelation: A Shorter Commentary*. Grand Rapids: Eerdmans, 2015.
Caragounis, Chrys C. *The Development of Greek and the New Testament: Morphology, Syntax, Phonology, and Textual Transmission*. Grand Rapids: Baker Academic, 2004.
Carcopino, Jérôme. *Daily Life in Ancient Rome*. New Haven: Yale University Press, 1940.
Carr, David M. "Literacy and Reading." In *The Eerdmans Dictionary of Early Judaism*, edited by John J. Collins and Daniel C. Harlow, 888–89. Chicago: Eerdmans, 2010.
Carruthers, Mary J. *The Book of Memory*. Cambridge: Cambridge University Press, 1990.
Carson, D. A., and Douglas J. Moo. *An Introduction to the New Testament*. Grand Rapids: Zondervan, 2005.
Chafe, Wallace, and Deborah Tannen. "The Relation Between Written and Spoken Language." *Annual Review of Anthropology* 16 (1987) 383–407.
Charles, R. H. *A Critical and Exegetical Commentary on the Revelation of St. John: With Introduction, Notes, and Indices, Also the Greek Text and English Translation*. Edinburgh: T&T Clark, 1920.
Charlesworth, James H. *The Old Testament Pseudepigrapha*. Peabody, MA: Hendrickson, 1983.

Chilton, Bruce D., and Werner H. Kelber. *Forgotten Compass: Marcel Jousse and the Exploration of the Oral World*. Eugene, OR: Cascade, 2022.

Clifford, Richard J. *The Cosmic Mountain in Canaan and the Old Testament*. Eugene, OR: Wipf & Stock, 1972.

Collins, Adela Yarbro. *The Combat Myth in the Book of Revelation*. Eugene, OR: Wipf & Stock, 1976.

———. *Crisis and Catharsis*. Philadelphia: Westminster, 1984.

Collins, C. John. *Reading Genesis Well: Navigating History, Poetry, Science, and Truth in Genesis 1–11*. Grand Rapids: Zondervan, 2018.

Collins, John J. *The Apocalyptic Imagination*. Grand Rapids: Eerdmans, 1998.

Collins, John J., and Adela Yarbro Collins. *Daniel: A Commentary on the Book of Daniel*. Hermeneia: A Critical & Historical Commentary on the Bible. Minneapolis: Fortress, 1993.

Collins, John J., and Daniel C. Harlow, eds. *The Eerdmans Dictionary of Early Judaism*. Chicago: Eerdmans, 2010.

Cotterell, Peter, and Max M. Turner. *Linguistics and Biblical Interpretation*. Downers Grove, IL: InterVarsity, 1989.

de Waal, Kayle B. *An Aural-Performance Analysis of Revelation 1 and 11*. New York: Peter Lang, 2015.

———. "Mimicry and Hybridity in the Book of Revelation." *Colloquium* 53 (2021) 7–28.

———. *Socio-Rhetorical Interpretation of the Seven Trumpets of Revelation*. New York: Edwin Mellen, 2011.

Dean, Margaret E. "The Grammar of Sound in Greek Texts: Toward a Method for Mapping Echoes of Speech in Writing." *Australian Biblical Review* 44 (1996) 53–70.

Dewey, Joanna. "Mark as Aural Narrative: Structures as Clues to Understanding." *Sewanee Theological Review* 36 (1992) 45–56.

DeSilva, David A. *Discovering Revelation: Content, Interpretation, Reception*. Chicago: Eerdmans, 2021.

———. *Honor, Patronage, Kinship, and Purity: Unlocking New Testament Culture*. Downers Grove, IL: IVP Academic, 2000.

———. "What Has Athens to Do with Patmos? A Rhetorical Criticism of the Revelation of John." *Currents in Biblical Research* 6 (2008) 256–89.

———. "X Marks the Spot? A Critique of the Use of Chiasmus in Macro-Structural Analyses of Revelation." *Journal for the Study of the New Testament* 30 (2008) 343–71.

Dionysus of Halicarnassus. *On Literary Composition*. Translated by Stephen Usher. Loeb Classical Library 466. Cambridge: Harvard University Press, 1985.

Dooley, Robert A., and Stephen H. Levinsohn. *Analyzing Discourse: A Manual of Basic Concepts*. Dallas: SIL International, 2001.

Dunn, James D. G. *Jesus Remembered*. Grand Rapids: Eerdmans, 2003.

Duvall, J. Scott. *A Theology of Revelation*. Grand Rapids: Zondervan Academic, 2025.

Ehrman, Bart D. *Jesus Before the Gospels*. New York: HarperCollins, 2016.

Elder, Nicholas A. "Between Reading and Performance: The Presence and Absence of Physical Texts." *Religions* 14 (2023) 1–13.

Ermatinger, James W. *The World of Ancient Rome*. Santa Barbara: Greenwood, 2015.

Evans, Craig A. *Ancient Texts for New Testament Studies: A Guide to the Background Literature*. Grand Rapids: Baker Academic, 2005.
Fanning, Buist M. *Revelation*. Zondervan Exegetical Commentary on the New Testament. Grand Rapids: Zondervan Academic, 2020.
———. *Verbal Aspect in the New Testament Greek*. Oxford: Oxford University Press, 1990.
Fiorenza, Elisabeth Schüssler. *The Book of Revelation: Justice and Judgment*. Minneapolis: Fortress, 1998.
———. "Composition and Structure of the Book of Revelation." *The Catholic Biblical Quarterly* 39 (1977) 344–66.
———. *Revelation: Vision of a Just World*. Minneapolis: Fortress, 1991.
Firth, David G., and Brittany N. Melton. *Reading the Book of the Twelve Minor Prophets*. Bellingham, WA: Lexham Academic, 2022.
Foley, John M. *Immanent Art: From Structure to Meaning in Traditional Oral Epic*. Bloomington: Indiana University Press, 1991.
———. *The Singer of Tales in Performance*. Bloomington: Indiana University Press, 1995.
Freedman, David Noel, ed. *The Anchor Yale Bible Dictionary*. New York: Doubleday, 1992.
———, ed. *Eerdmans Dictionary of the Bible*. Grand Rapids: Eerdmans, 2000.
Fox, Chelise. "Worlds with Words: Discourse and Frame Analysis of Performance Storytelling." MA thesis, East Tennessee State University, 2018.
Gamble, Harry Y. *Books and Readers in the Early Church: A History of Early Christian Texts*. New Haven: Yale University Press, 1995.
Geljon, Albert C., and Nienke M. Vos. *Rituals in Early Christianity: New Perspectives on Tradition and Transformation*. Boston: Leiden, 2021.
Genette, Gérard. *Narrative Discourse: An Essay in Method*. Ithaca, NY: Cornell University Press, 1980.
Gerhardsson, Birger. *Memory and Manuscript: Oral Tradition and Written Transmission in Rabbinic Judaism and Early Christianity*. Grand Rapids: Eerdmans, 1998.
Gignac, Francis T. A. *A Grammar of the Greek Papyri of the Roman and Byzantine Periods: Phonology*. Milano: Istituto Editoriale Cisalpino, 1976.
Green, Joel B., and Lee Martin McDonald. *The World of the New Testament: Cultural, Social, and Historical Contexts*. Grand Rapids: Baker Academic, 2013.
Goffman, Erving. *Frame Analysis*. Boston: Northeastern University Press, 1974.
Gorman, Michael J. *Reading Revelation Responsibly*. Eugene, OR: Wipf & Stock, 2011.
Haigh, Rebekah. "Oral Aspects: A Performative Approach to 1QM." *Dead Sea Discoveries* 26 (2019) 189–219.
Harris, William V. *Ancient Literacy*. Cambridge: Harvard University Press, 1989.
Harvey, John D. *Listening to the Text: Oral Patterning in Paul's Letters*. Grand Rapids: Baker, 1998.
———. "Orality and Its Implications for Biblical Studies: Recapturing an Ancient Paradigm." *Journal of the Evangelical Theological Society* 45.1 (2002) 99–109.
Hays, Richard B. *The Moral Vision of the New Testament: A Contemporary Introduction to New Testament Ethics*. New York: HarperOne, 1996.
Hearon, Holly E. "The Implications of Orality for Studies of the Biblical Text." Ch. 1 in *Performing the Gospel: Orality, Memory, and Mark*, edited by Jonathan A. Draper, et al. Minneapolis: Fortress, 2006.

Hearon, Holly E., and Philip Ruge-Jones. *The Bible in Ancient and Modern Media.* Eugene, OR: Cascade, 2009.

Heiser, Michael S. *The Unseen Realm: Recovering the Supernatural Worldview of the Bible.* Bellingham, WA: Lexham, 2015.

Henze, Matthias. "4 Ezra and 2 Baruch: Literary Composition and Oral Performance in First-Century Apocalyptic Literature." *Journal of Biblical Literature* 131 (2012) 181–200.

Heschel, Abraham J. *The Prophets.* New York: HarperCollins, 1962.

Holmes, Michael W. *The Greek New Testament: SBL Edition.* Atlanta: Society of Biblical Literature, 2010.

Homcy, Stephen L. "'To Him Who Overcomes': A Fresh Look at What 'Victory' Means for the Believer According to the Book of Revelation." *Journal of the Evangelical Theological Society* 38.2 (1995) 193–201.

Horsley, Richard A. *Text and Tradition in Performance and Writing.* Eugene, OR: Cascade, 2013.

Horsley, Richard A., et al. *Performing the Gospel: Orality, Memory, and Mark.* Minneapolis: Fortress, 2006.

Hurtado, Larry W. *Ancient Jewish Monotheism and Early Christian Jesus-Devotion.* Waco: Baylor University Press, 2017.

———. *Destroyer of the Gods: Early Christian Distinctiveness in the Roman World.* Waco: Baylor University Press, 2016.

———. *The Earliest Christian Artifacts: Manuscripts and Christian Origins.* Grand Rapids: Eerdmans, 2006.

———. *Lord Jesus Christ: Devotion to Jesus in Earliest Christianity.* Grand Rapids: Eerdmans, 2005.

———. "Oral Fixation and New Testament Studies? 'Orality', 'Performance' and Reading Texts in Early Christianity." *New Testament Studies* 60.3 (2014) 321–40.

Ito, Akio. "The Written Torah and the Oral Gospel: Romans 10:5–13 in the Dynamic Tension Between Orality and Literacy." *Novum Testamentum* 48 (2006) 234–60.

Iverson, Kelly R., ed. *From Text to Performance: Narrative and Performance Criticism in Dialogue and Debate.* Eugene, OR: Cascade, 2014.

———. "Oral Fixation or Oral Corrective? A Response to Larry Hurtado." *New Testament Studies* 62 (2016) 183–200.

Jang, Young. "Narrative Plot of the Apocalypse." *Scriptura* 84 (2003) 381–90.

Janse van Rensburg, Hanre. "All the Apocalypse a Stage: The Ritual Function of Apocalyptic Literature." *Hervormde Teologiese Studies* 75 (2019) 1–8.

Jersak, Bradley. *Her Gates Will Never Be Shut: Hope, Hell, and the New Jerusalem.* Eugene, OR: Wipf & Stock, 2009.

Johnson, William A., and Holt N. Parker, eds. *Ancient Literacies: The Culture of Reading in Greece and Rome.* New York: Oxford University Press, 2011.

Kantor, Benjamin. *A Short Guide to the Pronunciation of New Testament Greek.* Grand Rapids: Eerdmans, 2023.

Keener, Craig S. *The Gospel of John: A Commentary.* Grand Rapids: Baker Academic, 2003.

Kelber, Werner H. "Oral Tradition: New Testament." In *The Anchor Yale Bible Dictionary* 5, edited by David Noel Freedman, 30–37. New York: Doubleday, 1992.

———. *The Oral and the Written Gospel.* Philadelphia: Fortress, 1983.

Koester, Craig R. *Revelation: A New Translation with Introduction and Commentary.* New Haven: Yale University Press, 2014.

Koester, Helmut, ed. *Ephesos Metropolis of Asia: An Interdisciplinary Approach to Its Archaeology, Religion, and Culture*. Valley Forge, PA: Trinity Press International, 1995.

Korner, Ralph J. "'And I Saw . . .' An Apocalyptic Literary Convention Structural Identification in the Apocalypse." *Novum Testamentum* 42 (2000) 160–83.

Köstenberger, Andreas J., et al. *The Cradle, the Cross, and the Crown*. Nashville: B&H Academic, 2009.

Knox, Bernard M. W. "Silent Reading in Antiquity." *Greek, Roman, and Byzantine Studies* 9 (1968) 421–35.

Kuykendall, Michael. "The Twelve Visions of John: Another Attempt at Structuring the Book of Revelation." *Journal of the Evangelical Theological Society* 60 (2017) 533–55.

Labov, William, and Joshua Waletzky. "Narrative Analysis: Oral Versions of Personal Experience." *Journal of Narrative and Life History* 7 (Spring 1997) 3–38.

Lardinois, A. P. M. H., et al. *Sacred Words: Orality, Literacy and Religion*. Boston: Brill, 2011.

Lee, Margaret Ellen, and Bernard Brandon Scott. *Sound Mapping the New Testament*. Salem, OR: Polebridge, 2009.

Levinsohn, Stephen H. *Discourse Features of New Testament Greek: A Coursebook on the Information Structure of New Testament Greek*. Dallas: SIL International, 2000.

———. "The Relevance of Greek Discourse Studies to Exegesis." *Journal of Translation* 2 (2006) 11–21.

Longacre, Robert E. *The Grammar of Discourse*. New York: Plenum, 1996.

Longacre, Robert E., and Shin Ja Joo Hwang. *Holistic Discourse Analysis*. Dallas: SIL International, 2012.

Longenecker, Bruce W. "A Humorous Jesus? Orality, Structure, and Characterisation in Luke 14:15–24, and Beyond." *Biblical Interpretation* 16 (2008) 179–204.

———. *The Lost Letters of Pergamum*. Grand Rapids: Baker Academic, 2003.

Longman, Tremper, and David E. Garland. *Hebrews–Revelation*. The Expositor's Bible Commentary 13. Grand Rapids: Zondervan, 2006.

Lord, Albert B. "Characteristics of Orality." *Oral Tradition* 2 (1987) 54–72.

———. *The Singer of Tales*. Cambridge: Harvard University Press, 1960.

Louw, Johannes P., and Eugena A. Nida. *Greek-English Lexicon of the New Testament Based on Semantic Domains*. New York: United Bible Societies, 1996.

Mathews, Jeanette. "Scripture as Performance: Biblical Performance Criticism—What is It and How Do I Use It?" *St. Mark's Review* 249.3 (2019) 94–114.

Mathewson, David L. "Verbal Aspect in the Apocalypse of John: An Analysis of Revelation 5." *Novum Testamentum* 50 (2008) 58–77.

———. *Verbal Aspect in the Book of Revelation*. Boston: Brill, 2010.

———. *Voice and Mood, Essentials of Biblical Greek Grammar*. Grand Rapids: Baker Academic, 2021.

Maxey, James. "Performance Criticism and Its Implications for Bible Translation: Part One." *The Bible Translator* 60 (2009) 37–49.

Maxwell, Kathy. "From Performance to Text to Performance: The New Testament's Use of the Hebrew Bible in a Rhetorical Culture." In *From Text to Performance: Narrative and Performance Criticism in Dialogue and Debate*, edited by Kelly R. Iverson, 158–81. Eugene, OR: Cascade, 2014.

McKnight, Scot, and Grant R. Osborne. *The Face of New Testament Studies*. Grand Rapids: Baker Academic, 2004.

McLuhan, Marshall. *Understanding Media: The Extension of Man*. 5th ed. Cambridge: MIT Press, 1997.

Mellott, Matthew. "To the Victor: Understanding the Calls to Be Victorious in Rev. 2–3 in Light of Athletic and Gladiatorial Victory." PhD diss., Lutheran School of Theology at Chicago, 2019.

Metzger, Bruce M. *The Text of the New Testament: Its Transmission, Corruption, and Restoration*. Oxford: Oxford University Press, 1980.

Minchen, Elizabeth. *Orality, Literacy, and Performance in the Ancient World*. Boston: Brill, 2012.

Morales, Erwin T. "Discourse Analysis of the Book of Revelation." ThM thesis, Biola University, 2007.

Mounce, Robert H. *The Book of Revelation*. Grand Rapids: Eerdmans, 1977.

Naselli, Andrew David. *The Serpent and the Serpent Slayer*. Wheaton, IL: Crossway, 2020.

Naylor, Michael. "The Roman Imperial Cult and Revelation." *Currents in Biblical Research* 8 (2010) 207–39.

Niditch, Susan. *Oral World and Written Word: Ancient Israelite Literature*. Louisville, KY: Westminster John Knox, 1996.

O'Donnell, Matthew Brook. *Corpus Linguistics and the Greek New Testament*. Sheffield, UK: Sheffield Phoenix, 2005.

Ong, Walter J. *Orality and Literacy: The Technologizing of the Word*. New York: Routledge, 1982.

———. *The Presence of the Word*. Albany: SUNY Press, 1967.

Osborne, Grant R. *Revelation*. Ada, MI: Baker Academic, 2002.

Parker, Holt. "Books and Reading Latin Poetry." In *Ancient Literacies: The Culture of Reading in Greece and Rome*, edited by William A. Johnson and Parker N. Holt, 186–230. New York: Oxford University Press, 2011.

Pattemore, Stephen. "Revelation." Ch. 23 in *Discourse Analysis of the New Testament Writings*, edited by Todd A. Scacewater. Dallas: Fontes, 2020.

Patterson, Paige. *Revelation: The New American Commentary*. Nashville: B&H, 2012.

Paulien, Jon. "Recent Developments in the Study of the Book of Revelation." *Andrews University Seminary Studies* 26 (1988) 159–70.

Penner, K., and M. S. Heiser. *Old Testament Greek Pseudepigrapha with Morphology*. Bellingham, WA: Lexham, 2008.

Perry, Milman. *The Making of Homeric Verse*. Oxford: Oxford University Press, 1987.

Perry, Peter S. *The Rhetoric of Digressions: Revelation 7:1–17 and 10:1—11:13 and Ancient Communication*. Tübingen, DE: Mohr Siebeck, 2009.

Peterson, Eugene H. *Reversed Thunder: The Revelation of John and the Praying Imagination*. New York: HarperOne, 1988.

Porter, Stanley E. *Idioms of the Greek New Testament*. Sheffield, UK: Sheffield Academic Press, 1999.

———. "The Language of the Apocalypse in Recent Discussion." *New Testament Studies* 35 (1989) 582–603.

———. *Linguistic Analysis of the Greek New Testament: Studies in Tools, Methods, and Practice*. Grand Rapids: Baker Academic, 2015.

───. *Verbal Aspect in the Greek of the New Testament, with Reference to Tense and Mood.* New York: Peter Lang, 1989.

Porter, Stanley E., and D. A. Carson. *Linguistics and the New Testament: Critical Junctures.* Sheffield, UK: Sheffield Academic Press, 1999.

Porter, Stanley E., and Jason C. Robinson. *Hermeneutics: An Introduction to Interpretive Theory.* Grand Rapids: Eerdmans, 2011.

Quick, Laura Elizabeth. "Recent Research on Ancient Israelite Education: A Bibliographic Essay." *Currents in Biblical Research* 13 (2014) 9–33.

Quintilian. *Institutio Oratoria.* Translated by H. E. Butler. Loeb Classical Library. Cambridge: Harvard University Press, 1920–1922.

Reed, Jeffrey T., and Ruth A. Reese. "Verbal Aspect, Discourse Prominence, and the Letter of Jude." *Filologia* 18 (1996) 180–99.

Resseguie, James L. *The Revelation of John: A Narrative Commentary.* Grand Rapids: Baker Academic, 2009.

Rhoads, David. "Performance Criticism: An Emerging Methodology in Second Testament Studies—Part I." *Biblical Theology Bulletin* 36.3 (2006) 118–33.

───. "Performance Criticism: An Emerging Methodology in Second Testament Studies—Part II." *Biblical Theology Bulletin* 36.4 (2006) 164–84.

───. "What Is Performance Criticism?" In *The Bible in Ancient and Modern Media: Story and Performance*, by Holly E. Hearon and Philip Ruge-Jones, 83–99. Eugene, OR: Cascade, 2009.

Rhoads, David, et al. *Mark as Story: An Introduction to the Narrative of a Gospel.* Minneapolis: Fortress, 2012.

Richards, E. Randolph. *Paul and First-Century Letter Writing: Secretaries, Composition, and Collection.* Downers Grove, IL: IVP Academic, 2004.

Rowe, C. Kavin. *World Upside Down: Reading Acts in the Graeco-Roman Age.* Oxford: Oxford University Press, 2010.

Rowland, Christopher. *The Open Heaven: A Study of Apocalyptic in Judaism and Early Christianity.* New York: Crossroad, 1982.

Runge, Steven E. *Discourse Grammar of the Greek New Testament: A Practical Introduction for Teaching and Exegesis.* Bellingham, WA: Lexham, 2010.

Rutledge, Fleming. *The Crucifixion: Understanding the Death of Jesus Christ.* Grand Rapids: Eerdmans, 2015.

Scacewater, Todd A., ed. *Discourse Analysis of the New Testament Writings.* Dallas: Fontes, 2020.

Schniedewind, William M. "Orality and Literacy in Ancient Israel." *Religious Studies Review* 26 (2000) 327–32.

Seal, David. "The Reception and Delivery of the Oracle in Revelation 13:9–10." *Scriptura* 119 (2020) 1–13.

Shelton, Jo-Ann. *As the Romans Did: A Sourcebook in Roman Social History.* Oxford: Oxford University Press, 1998.

Shiner, Whitney. "Oral Performance in the New Testament World." In *The Bible in Ancient and Modern Media*, written by Holly E. Hearon and Philip Ruge-Jones, 49–62. Eugene, OR: Cascade, 2009.

Silberman, Lou H., ed. *Semeia 39: Orality, Aurality and Biblical Narrative.* Decatur, GA: Society of Biblical Literacy, 1987.

Silva, Moisés. *God, Language, and Scripture: Reading the Bible in Light of General Linguistics.* Grand Rapids: Zondervan, 1990.

Slater, Thomas B. *Revelation as Civil Disobedience: Witnesses Not Warriors in John's Apocalypse*. Nashville: Abingdon, 2019.
Smalley, Stephen S. *The Revelation to John: A Commentary on the Greek Text of the Apocalypse*. Downers Grove, IL: IVP, 2005.
Smith, Christopher R. "The Structure of the Book of Revelation in Light of Apocalyptic Literary Conventions." *Novum Testamentum* 36 (1994) 373–93.
Smith, James K. A. *Desiring the Kingdom: Worship, Worldview, and Cultural Formation*. Grand Rapids: Baker Academic, 2009.
———. *Imagining the Kingdom: How Worship Works*. Grand Rapids: Baker Academic, 2013.
Soukup, Paul A. "Contexts of Faith: The Religious Foundation of Walter Ong's Literacy and Orality." *Journal of Media and Religion* 5 (2006) 175–88.
Starling, David. "Dramatising the Gospel of the Kingdom: Colossians as Notes for Ecclesial Performance." *Colloquium* 53 (2021) 30–47.
Stein, Robert. "Is Our Reading the Bible the Same as the Original Audience's Hearing It? A Case Study in the Gospel of Mark." *Journal of the Evangelical Theological Society* 46 (2003) 63–78.
Tannen, Deborah. *Framing in Discourse*. New York: Oxford University Press, 1993.
Taylor, Richard A. *Interpreting Apocalyptic Literature: An Exegetical Handbook*. Grand Rapids: Kregel Academic, 2016.
Tolkien, J. R. R. *The Fellowship of the Ring*. Boston: Houghton Mifflin, 1982.
Tschen-Emmons, James B. *Artifacts from Ancient Rome*. Santa Barbara: Greenwood, 2014.
Uro, Risto. "Ritual, Memory, and Writing in Early Christianity." *Temenos* 47 (2011) 159–82.
Van Dijk, T. A. *Macrostructures: An Interdisciplinary Study of Global Structures in Discourse, Interaction, and Cognition*. Hillsdale, NJ: Lawrence Erlbaum Associates, 1980.
Vanni, Ugo. "Liturgical Dialogue as a Literary Form in the Book of Revelation." *New Testament Studies* 37.3 (1993) 348–72.
Vansina, Jans. *Oral Tradition as History*. Madison: University of Wisconsin Press, 1985.
Wallace, Daniel B. *Greek Grammar Beyond the Basics*. Grand Rapids: Zondervan, 1996.
Wendland, Ernst R. "The Hermeneutical Significance of Literary Structure in Revelation." *Neotestamentica* 48 (2014) 447–76.
Wright, Brian J. "Ancient Literacy in New Testament Research: Incorporating a Few More Lines of Enquiry." *Trinity Journal* 36.2 (2015) 161–89.
Wright, N. T. *Jesus and the Victory of God*. Minneapolis: Fortress, 1996.
———. *The New Testament and the People of God*. Minneapolis: Fortress, 1992.
———. *The Resurrection of the Son of God*. Minneapolis: Fortress, 2003.
Wright, N. T., and Michael Bird. *The New Testament in Its World*. London: SPCK, 2019.
Young, Ian. "Israelite Literacy: Interpreting the Evidence." *Vetus Testamentum* 48 (1998) 239–53.
Young, Katharine Galloway. *Taleworlds and Storyrealms*. Dordrecht, NL: Martinus Nijhoff, 1987.

www.ingramcontent.com/pod-product-compliance
Lightning Source LLC
Chambersburg PA
CBHW051637230426
43669CB00013B/2340